LANGUAGE AND DEMEANOR IN POLICE-CITIZEN ENCOUNTERS

Phillip Chong Ho Shon

University Press of America,® Inc.
Lanham · Boulder · New York · Toronto · Plymouth, UK

Copyright © 2008 by
University Press of America,® Inc.
4501 Forbes Boulevard
Suite 200
Lanham, Maryland 20706
UPA Acquisitions Department (301) 459-3366

Estover Road
Plymouth PL6 7PY
United Kingdom

Library of Congress Control Number: 2008925443
ISBN-13: 978-0-7618-4084-8 (paperback : alk. paper)
ISBN-10: 0-7618-4084-2 (paperback : alk. paper)

⊖™The paper used in this publication meets the minimum
requirements of American National Standard for Information
Sciences—Permanence of Paper for Printed Library Materials,
ANSI Z39.48—1984

Dedication

For shp: a nine year, self-made promise fulfilled—finally.

Table of Contents

Foreword

In the conclusion to this book, the author states that what he has written is not a "radical departure" from but "merely a logical extension" of other work on police-citizen encounters. I would argue that Phillip Shon is being unduly modest, admirable traits for the author of a text, but not required for the author of the foreword. *Language and Demeanor in Police-Citizen Encounters* represents a radical departure from prior works on the topic, breaking new ground by situating such encounters in the dynamic details of communicative practices. One wonders why, given the extensive nature of research on the topic and its applied significance, such a study has been so long in coming.

Even though police-citizen encounters consist of mundane talk, research has consistently focused on outcome variables, abstract theorizing, conceptual models and pre-specified coding schemes that consistently bleach the interaction order from view. Shon, on the other hand, takes the P-C encounter as a topic in its own right rather than as an unexplicated and taken-for-granted resource, that is to say, as a topic prior to the interaction being domesticated into the aims of the researcher's analytic project. In so doing, we gain a rare glimpse into the co-constructed and interactive processes of police-citizen encounters that provide the infrastructure of policing as a socio-legal institution.

Given the focus on the micro-discursive order, one might expect that more classic concerns in the literature of policing would be given short shrift in the analysis. However, this isn't the case here. Shon is well versed not only in the study of language use but policing as well, integrating both realms in a sophisticated analysis. For example, the reader is given a rare treat in Chapter 5 on the discourse of domestic violence as the dispute unfolds in the mediating presence of the officer. Shon's analysis reveals how the Minneapolis study and subsequent replications ignore a crucial aspect of domestic cases: how the parties frame the argument, evaluate their own and each other's claims, and provide evidence for those claims as the attending officer attempts to steer the talk towards a less emotional trajectory to determine the facts of the case (of course, this type of balanced analysis should be expected as Shon took his Ph.D. in criminal justice and did early graduate work in linguistics).

One final feature of the book is worth mentioning. Most of the data Shon uses comes from the *COPS* television program and, as Shon notes, some researchers claim that media mediated participation structures fail to portray policing in accurate light. Rather than engage in an epistemological and ontological debate or invidious comparisons between TV police work and "real" police work, Shon builds the distinction into his analysis by showing how multiple frames of police activity are contextualized and recontextualized from the police-citizen exchange to the narrated exchange for the viewing audience (and vice versa), enriching the analysis in a thoroughly interactive Goffmanian and conversation analytic study. I let the author take the stage from here.

Gregory M. Matoesian

Preface

Encounters between the police and the public that go awry, and result in the shooting of unarmed civilians periodically fill the airwaves and television sets across the U.S.; and just when the footage of the last notorious encounter is ready to be archived into storage rooms, another such occurrence reopens the wounds that might have begun to heal, and keeps the dust from ever settling on those old boxes. In my own time, I grew up watching the events of the Rodney King incident and its devastating aftermaths; in my own hometown, the Haggerty shooting received just as much press coverage, with the late Johnny Cochran serving as counsel for the victim's family. New York City has also experienced its share of police-citizen encounters that have served as catalyst for mass demonstrations and protests against police misconduct.

These cases not only reveal the tenuous link between peace and social disorder, but also the one between the police and the public, especially in minority communities where the historical baggage of bad policing and white supremacy still weigh heavily in the consciousness of residents. But before we can even undertake the task of explicating such problems and proposing remedies, we must first understand why those types of routine police-citizen encounters go wrong; and even before that, we must first give an accounting of how such encounters are socially organized and unfold in its own right. That is to say that to understand the spectacular, the routine and the mundane must first be explained. And that is what this book attempts to do. It begins with an examination of how the police and the public behave during their encounters by analyzing the way they talk to one another.

The office of the police represents one of the most symbolically visible inconsistencies of a democratic state. Police officers represent the public face of coercion, and the unadulterated powers of the state; yet, how such power is exercised, besides the intermittent voyeuristic glimpses of its wrongful exercise, is a question that has largely been unaddressed. It is my contention that the social and interactional order of police-citizen encounters is (re)produced, reified, and contested during moments of communication; that meaning, ideology, and demeanor come alive during such banal conversational moments. Hence, police power operationalized as the number of tickets written, vehicles summoned, and shots fired is rather uninteresting; how that office is embodied and transformed from an abstract and amorphous inkblot into a palpable and roaring entity through discourse is a much more theoretically titillating and empirically enticing way of approaching the study of police and society.

Phillip C. Shon
Terre Haute, Indiana

Acknowledgements

As Michael Walzer states acknowledgements and citations are the currency in which intellectual debts are paid. I consider this section a long overdue first down payment. I don't think I will ever be able to fully repay my intellectual debt to my dissertation chair and teacher, Gregory M. Matoesian. He taught me how to "take the analysis where others wouldn't even think of going," that is how to "talk to" and "listen to" the data. Yet despite such a firm grounding, I fear that my analysis will not go to the distant places he would like it to see it go; the fault is my own. Prof. Matoesian has also taught me that being clinically dysfunctional, stressed out, insecure, unhappy, constantly worried, and foolishly perfectionist (a rather tragic condition), is a highly generative resource to have for people in the academy, and that these feelings never go away. I hope they don't go away either, for when they do, I'll know it will be time for me to try my luck as a real architect.

I have been blessed to be the recipient of much needed support, encouragement, and unconditional friendship at various stages of my academic life. My teachers at the University of Illinois at Chicago, especially Lisa Frohmann and Joe Peterson, gave me the intellectual freedom to experiment with new ideas and always encouraged my creative endeavors as a graduate student. Other good people like Jim Thomas and Bruce Arrigo took it upon themselves to offer much needed support and advice. I am particularly indebted to Mindie Lazarus-Black, for I have constantly bombarded her with papers for comments, criticisms, and suggestions. I am certain that, at times, reading my papers must have seemed like a second full-time job. And now as a faculty member at Indiana State University, I find myself surrounded by and indebted to another group of highly supportive and talented colleagues and friends, especially Shannon Barton, Devere Woods, and Mark Hamm. I am particularly grateful to David Skelton for his moral and structural support to pursue my creative interests; I also thank the College of Arts & Sciences and the Office of Sponsored Programs at Indiana State University for providing me with the necessary material support to pursue this project.

A "spotter" is not only there to rescue the lifter in case a barbell crashes on his head, but he is also there to shout words of encouragement. I cannot find a more felicitous metaphor to express my indebtedness to Dragan Milovanovic. He has not only watched me grow in musculature, but has been the one who planted the seeds of criminological muscle. I was barefoot as I swaggered about the weight-room, quoting Nietzsche in between sets of squats, when Dr. Milovanovic led me to see the relevance of the "father" of postmodernism to criminology. But in addition to scholarly tutelage, he has demonstrated the more difficult task of teaching me how to serve as a mentor to future scholars. This, I fear, will be a task I will be unable to measure up to. This time, the fault is not my own. I would also like to thank "*COPS*, ©2007 Twentieth Television. All Rights Reserved" for granting me permission to use the transcripts of the encounters.

Life in Albany Park—and graduate school in particular—would have been lonely indeed were it not for the friendship and camaraderie of my fellow lifters in Chicago (the Coze, Liquor Sto' Andy, Two Gun Tony, Big D, Shoot em' up Henry, and Decline Kaz) and my "K-town" friends (Young Nam, Henry, Jason, Jong Guk, and Han). The indebtedness I feel toward my mother (Grace) and sister (Nancy) would be murdered were I to put it into words; they deserve a far greater honor for putting up with me. That is a task language can never accomplish.

Finally, as much as we desire to be without encumbrances and attachments, I have discovered (at least theoretically) that we do not, or, at least, should not, live that way. That is, we don't live on bread and weights alone. I have learned that there is a Being, for, in, and through whom we all live and move and have our being. I owe this highest honor to *Him*, for arranging events in my life and bringing me to ivy pastures I had never envisioned.

INTRODUCTION

This book provides a practical and situated glimpse of the way police officers verbally exercise their coercive power during their routinely occurring interactions with the public. Police-Citizen (henceforth, P-C) encounters are, by definition, asymmetrical since the police possess the brute and raw capacity to threaten, harm, and coerce the clients of their service into compliance. At the same time, the encounters are tinged with a veneer of sociality in that the bulk of police work involves a fundamentally interactive process—talking. That is, the essence of police work entails explaining, requesting, directing, and counseling citizens, victims, witnesses, and suspects to get them to do something. This leads to a major empirical question that I address in this book: how do the police and citizens talk to one another? How is the talk between the police and the public socially organized?

As the principal agents of social control, the police are the most visible, accessible, and available representatives of the criminal law, but face a nearly impossible task: they are ordained by the public as one of the most visible representatives of the criminal law, and act as its agents, thus fighting crime, apprehending criminals, and making arrests. This is their legal mandate (Manning, 1978). To that end, they are conferred a power that is unimaginably raw and brute: "the police are nothing else than a mechanism for the distribution of situationally justified force in society" (Bittner, 1978: 34). As William Muir (1977) notes, however, there is an inherent paradox in the nature of police work: the recipients of that coercive power are the very ones who bestow that right in the first place. And it is precisely that capacity to legally take a life—exercise coercive force—in the line of duty that fundamentally differentiates the police from the general public (see Dunham and Alpert, 2001; Reiss, 1971).

There is, however, a wide rift between the legal and ideological mandate of the police and the reality of routine police work: the police are officially and theoretically conceptualized as crime-fighters; but in actuality, they act as public servants: settling disputes, giving advice, getting teenage kids off corners, and other order maintenance activities—preventing calls rather than preventing crimes (Meehan, 1992; see also Bittner, 1967a, b; Cumming, Cumming, and Edell, 1965). It is this dissonance between their official mandate and their actual work practices that is a recurring source of cynicism and alienation (Manning, 1997).

The police have the capacity to exercise a significant amount of discretion in their decision to apply formal and informal sanctions—tickets, arrests— against citizens (Bayley, 1994, 1974; Manning, 1997; Rubinstein, 1973). As Black (1980: 97) puts it, "people who disrespect the police gamble with their freedom." Simply put, when the police come into contact with citizens, they do not necessarily have to write a ticket or make an arrest[1]; that is significantly determined by the citizens' behavior toward the police. In other words, the likelihood of receiving tickets, being arrested, and having other official—and unofficial—sanctions applied is contingent upon citizens' attitude and comportment toward the police.

The role of citizens' demeanor on arrest and other formal sanctions during P-C encounters and other legal settings has been the topic of research for quite some time. The central question prior scholars have asked is: does a citizen's disrespectful behavior toward the police lead to tickets, arrests, and other official sanctions? Police scholars have observed P-C encounters—traffic stops, DUI stops, domestic disturbance calls, suspicious person stops—to capture the diverse array of citizens' behaviors toward the police and their effect on the likelihood of official sanctions. That citizens' disrespect toward the police leads to arrest is considered to be a criminological axiom (Lundman, 1994). The dominant method of studying P-C encounters—quantitative—demonstrates an impressive body of research to support its axiomatic claims that disrespect toward a cop leads to a ticket (Black, 1971; Black and Reiss 1970; Bogomolny, 1976; Galliher, 1971; Lundman, 1974, 1979, 1994; Lundman, Sykes, and Clark, 1978; Pastor, 1978; Piliavin and Briar, 1964; Riksheim and Chermak, 1993; Sherman, 1980; Sykes and Clark, 1975; Worden and Pollitz, 1984). The validity of those findings, however, have been challenged and debated fruitfully during the past several years (see Fyfe, 1996; Klinger, 1994, 1996a, b; Lundman, 1994, 1996a, b; Worden and Shepard, 1996; Worden, Shepard, and Mastrofski, 1996).

The debate began with Klinger (1994) who challenged the criminological axiom by claiming that previous operationalization of hostility had included criminal behavior. He hypothesized that if crime were to be controlled for, the demeanor/arrest link would diminish. He concluded that hostile suspects were arrested because they committed illegal acts in the presence of the police, not because they failed to show proper deference.

In nearly all or most of the quantitative P-C encounter research scholars have been interested in discovering the relationship between citizens' demeanor and arrest. The "cues" that citizens display are then coded and tabulated for statistical analysis. For example, William Westley (1953: 38) was interested in examining when patrol officers used illegal violence against citizens: "when do you think a patrolman is justified in roughing a man up?" Westley found that thirty-seven percent of cops felt justified in using force if the citizen showed disrespect for the police—"the guy who talks back or any individual who acts or talks in a disrespectful way" (p. 39). Although Westley never systematically catalogued the details of what being disrespectful entails, except talking back, subsequent researchers have become increasingly sophisticated about the behavioral, situational, and linguistic cues of being disrespectful.

But even after Westley (1953) researchers such as Piliavin and Briar (1964), Black and Reiss (1970), Lundman, Sykes, and Clark (1978), Pastor (1978), Lundman (1979, 1974), Sherman (1980), Smith and Klein (1984) Smith and Visher (1981), Worden and Pollitz, (1984), Mastrofski, Snipes, and Supina (1996), Mastrofski, Worden, and Snipes (1995), Klinger (1996a), Worden and Shepard (1996), have not been able to systematically unpack the interactional details of demeanor. They have merely captured its occurrence and classified citizens' demeanor into categories such as *friendly, respectful, polite, cooperative, hostile, impolite, business-like,* and *cool* and *detached.*

Demeanor is important in P-C encounters because the attribution of a person's demeanor, as badly or well demeaned, shapes the treatment s/he receives from the police. More importantly, demeanor is fundamentally social, interactive, and reflexive: it is a communicative process in that through "deportment, dress, and bearing" an individual "serves to express to those in his [her] immediate presence that he [she] is a person of certain desirable or undesirable qualities" (Goffman, 1967:77). Simply put, demeanor is a self-presentation strategy rather than a self-professed state (Goffman, 1959).[2] For example, Emerson (1969) notes that conveying deference through demeanor is an important "ceremonial" aspect of courtroom interaction between judges and juvenile delinquents:

> Court staff directly sanction such denials of the overriding importance of the proceeding, including laughing, grinning, and even guarded smiling, as well as exaggerated gum chewing and whispering. By sanctioning such expressions of alienation from or limited commitment to the proceeding, the court exerts systematic pressure on the delinquent to show involvement in the ceremony and in the determination of his own guilt (Emerson, 1969: 194).

As Emerson (1969) notes, there are numerous ways that juvenile delinquents convey a disrespectful attitude. They can neglect to use honorary address terms when speaking to the judge, whisper and laugh while the court is in session, use incomplete sentences and other brief and curt phrases when responding to the judge's questions, and through their tone of voice. These types of linguistic and paralinguistic cues, Emerson (1969: 194) observes, "reduce" the delinquents' involvement with the court; but more importantly, it demonstrates that the delinquent is not "committed to the situation." There is an expectation that those who appear before the court will present a deferential self, that is show proper respect; and a delinquent's demeanor ought to be commensurate with the "solemn and serious" nature of the occasioned interaction. Those who violate such normative expectations, Emerson writes, evoke strong rebuke and sanction from the court authorities.

In prior police studies, the words spoken by citizens and suspects to the police have been consistently used to represent demeanor. A well-known example of this type of police classification of citizens is John van Maanen's "The Asshole," one who challenges police authority and openly displays his/her contempt for the police. But using language as a mere representation (reflection) of demeanor leads to a key analytical dilemma: some citizens are communicatively "sophisticated," meaning that they guise their hatred and contempt for the police under a cloak of deference. In the dominant method of P-C encounter research this category of citizens poses a significant problem since there is no principled or methodical way to represent and analyze cases of communicative subversion (see Black, 1980).

In the existing paradigms, the analytic aim is biased toward tabulating the outcomes of P-C encounters rather than expounding on the interactional processes. The social facticity of bureaucratic sanctions, however, is neither a fruitful nor theoretically titillating endeavor, for its exegesis entails nothing more than a statistical summation. Currently, there is little controversy about the validity of the demeanor/official sanction link; there is, however, a relative lack of consensus as to what constitutes disrespectful behavior. This condition leaves two noticeable gaps in the present literature on police behavior and demeanor: constitutive elements of disrespectful demeanor and its methods of representation. In quantitative police studies in particular, a citizen's demeanor toward the police is impressionistically inserted into preexisting coding schemes, while the interactional practices of the participants—the real data—are abstractly glossed over for the anecdotal impressions of the coder and the analyst. It is at this juncture that the existing paradigms face an impasse, their methods constrained by their methodological and analytical vision.

In quantitative studies, the prespecified categories—coding schemes—define and delimit the meaning of a social act, and treat the analytical concept under study in a reductionistic manner. That is, coding schemes treat "categories rather than particular data, as problematic" (Schegloff, 1984a: 30). In such cases, the meaning of a social act is already presupposed by the analyst rather than examined in use by the subjects themselves (Schegloff, 1996). If primacy is given to the mere occurrence of a word, clause, or sentence rather than its interactional effects, then its placement within a stretch of talk becomes secondary to what the actual language users are doing; with this formalistic move, the intentions and meanings of subjects become lost in the theoretical imperialism of the analyst (see Schegloff, 1997). For example, *sir/ma'am* is generally and formally used to indicate deference; however, to merely note its presence in a spate of talk as a performance of deference would be grossly inaccurate because depending on the way those address terms are articulated, they can be used to convey sarcasm and disrespect, the antithesis of what they formally represent.

That prior researchers have had to code citizens' verbal behaviors into *a priori* and abstract categories of action misses all the rich details of being— doing—friendly, cooperative, hostile, polite, impolite, respectful, and disrespectful. In other words, when demeanor is exogenously imposed, it misses the complex ways that demeanor and language are performed *in situ*, and come alive in the speaking moments of the interaction. That researchers cannot agree on the constitutive elements of disrespectful behavior, much less explicate how it emerges from the encounter and talk itself, highlights one of the major limitations of existing police scholarship. By drawing on Goffman's work on deference/demeanor, presentation strategies, and frame, this book unpacks the nascence of disrespect from the interactional details of verbal action. I do so by examining the discursive practices of police officers and citizens, prior to their classification into prespecified coding schemes. This book offers a real time, line by line, turn by turn, fine-grained analysis of demeanor via talk-in-interaction.

Using coding schemes may also overlook important prosodic features of talk. Prosody includes paralinguistic features such as "a) intonation, i.e., pitch levels on individual syllables and their combination into contours; b) changes in loudness; c) stress, a perceptual feature generally comprising variations in pitch, loudness, and duration; d) other variations in vowel length; e) phrasing, including utterance chunking by pausing, accelerations and decelerations within and across utterance chunks; f) overall shifts in speech register" (Gumperz, 1982: 100). Perhaps these sociolinguistic features can be more poignantly illustrated by using an example from a commonly occurring police initiated encounter, the traffic stop:

Excerpt 1 (Southern City Traffic Stop #1)
48 → PO: you have a good day sir
49   D: you too

In excerpt 1, a police officer pulls over a motorist and issues the driver a citation for speeding; and as the encounter is brought to a close, the officer utters the phrase "you have a good day sir." Now, there is nothing in the phrase itself, syntactical or grammatical, that could be interpreted as a sign of hostility or antagonism; it would commonly be found in "closing" sequences of service encounters (see Schegloff and Sacks, 1973). Moreover, the officer uses a deferential address term when talking to the motorist.

If the demeanor of the motorist and the officer in this segment of the encounter were to be coded by a researcher, it would most likely be classified as "polite" (if demeanor is generously defined) or "non-hostile" (if demeanor is parsimoniously defined) since both participants do not say things that could be construed as being belligerent; it would be difficult to code this brief closing sequence as being "hostile" or "antagonistic" because, formally, both participants negotiate the delicate order of the P-C encounter under the thin mien of sociality. In form and content both participants collaboratively produce the social order of communicative interaction: one party bids the other farewell, signals closing, and that uptake is noted and promptly returned in the very next turn. By examining the content (farewells), its structural (end of the traffic stop) and sequential place (adjacency pairs), then, we can see how "civil" or "cooperative" demeanor emerges from the micro-linguistic detail of social action. However, I am sure that the readers can imagine a way to articulate the utterance in such a way that "have a good day" means something else entirely, and its next turn response, "you too," is of a flippant kind.[3] It is precisely these types of details of talk that coding schemes are apt to miss.

Interpretation of utterances such as "have a good day" cannot solely be based on its grammatical—formal, referential, decontextual—features. There are other "surface" features of talk, such as tone, loudness, syllabicity, pitch, and other sociolinguistic features of conversation such as interruptions, sequences, requests, commands, politeness, verbal resistance, and ridiculing that determine how a given utterance is meant and interpreted by speakers and listeners. Gumperz (1982) refers to these features of talk as "contextualization cues." He states that although these features are "habitually used and perceived," they are "rarely consciously noted and almost never talked about; therefore, they must be studied in process and in context rather than in abstract" (Gumperz, 1982: 131). Of course, attempting to impressionisticly code these complex features of speech ends up doing precisely that: abstraction. That the operationalization of demeanor in prior studies of P-C encounters centers on suprasegmental and prosodic features of talk would pave the way for future research in a sociolinguistic direction.

In a very obvious way, language is the vehicle through which knowledge, information, and meaning is transmitted, along with a speaker's intention; furthermore, that the police use language to persuade and dissuade citizens from certain courses of action points to its assumed, yet empirically unexplored, rhetorical function. There are other aspects of language that has been overlooked in police scholarship: (1) the performative capacity of language to create the very object it is attempting to represent (2) the poetic and indexical capacity of language to describe itself. From this standpoint, aside from the obvious capacity to exercise coercion, a theoretically warranted question it generates is how that awesome power is embodied in a much more mundane form of social action—talk.

Despite the communicative nature of police work, there has yet to be a principled and rigorous empirical expatiation of this fundamentally intersubjective process. This gap in the literature leads to a simple, yet, unasked empirical question: what do the police and citizens say to one another during their interactions? More interestingly, how is it said? If the contours of police ideology, authority, and identity are extended to the realm of discourse, how might they be enacted and sustained during moments of talk? Does the coercive power of the police manifest itself even in something as prosaic as talk? More fundamentally, how is that coercive authority embodied in the structures of talk itself?

Language and Demeanor situates the study of P-C interaction as a speech event; in doing so, it reconfigures Egon Bittner's theory of coercive power on a more social-interactional plane, and adds an empirical bite to William K. Muir's observation that possessing the linguistic capacity to teach, inspire, and motivate citizenry and fellow officers is the hallmark of police professionalism. Yet, despite its importance in routine police work, talk has been virtually abandoned as a justifiable topic in its own right. Thus, subsequent police scholars have merely presupposed the interactional properties of language use, and neglected to study its sociolinguistic components—the way encounters between police and the public actually unfold. This book attempts to remedy that gap in the existing literature. To date, there exists no such study that treats the talk in P-C encounters as the principal object of analysis.

It would also be tempting—and easy—to treat the talk between the police and citizens as an instance of organizational communication merely because one of the speakers occupies the role of an institutional representative (e.g., a police officer), and because the occasioned business is bureaucratically related (e.g., a traffic stop). This type of analysis would be easy because once the respective categories are applied it would free the analyst from doing the actual work of empirical expatiation. However, it is my contention that the talk between the police and the public has an interactional character and order of its own, aside from the respective roles of the speakers; and that the roles themselves (e.g., police officer, hostile citizens) are constituted in and through the language they use.

Since this book examines P-C encounters from an interactional perspective, they are treated not only as occasions for talk, but talk itself is the principal object of analysis. By examining the actual talk between the police and the public, I hope to show how it is different from the ones engaged in by ordinary citizens in social settings (e.g., dinner table). Moreover, I will describe what has been generally treated as a theoretical derivative (capacity of the police to exercise coercive power) as a practical embodiment—something that is constituted, accomplished, and negotiated in the mundane details of discursive action. This work views the talk between the police and citizens as an instance of *institutional talk*. Institutional talk describes the structural features of communication in organizational discourse, whose properties have been modified from the naturally occurring format to meet the contextual particulars of a particular organization's business. Drew and Heritage (1992: 3) define institutional talk as *"the principal means through which lay persons pursue various practical goals and the central medium through which the daily working activities of many professionals and organizational representatives are conducted."*

Consequently, this study is not concerned with outcomes but with processes—of talk-in-interaction. This book examines, in their own right, the actual verbal utterances of police officers and citizens during routine calls for service prior to their intercalation into preexisting categories. In order to show how police officers and citizens communicatively manage their business ("pursue various practical goals"), this book also makes a fundamentally different assumption about the nature of language and its usage from prior police studies: it examines P-C encounters interactionally and sociolinguistically. I am more concerned with examining what the utterances of officers and citizens accomplish, do, rather than trying to answer what they mean. I arrive at the latter incidentally, after I analyze what the participants are trying to accomplish with their words. Consequently, I do not assume a grammatical, formal, and referential view of language. Instead, I view language as something that is contextual, indexical, and pragmatic (Garfinkel, 1967; Green, 1996; Levinson, 1983).

To demonstrate the work that utterances do in their verbal encounters, I will examine how police officers and citizens take turns, select word choices and address terms, and design their turns (Heritage, 1998a). Furthermore, I will examine how P-C encounters are structurally and sequentially organized, in addition to the knowledge claims that are made in them. In this book, I am interested in power, coercion, truth, and deception that exist in police work, which numerous police scholars have noted, to the extent that they are embodied in talk, and empirically demonstrable in the micro-moments of actual, real time discursive action (Schegloff, 1992a, b). I want to avoid descriptions about acts—the impressionistic characterizations, anecdotal accounts, and "war stories" of police work—and focus on the acts (spoken words) themselves.

This book is organized in the following manner. Chapter 1 begins with an accessible theoretical overview of the key analytical terms that will be used throughout the book; using these terms, I demonstrate the "technical" character of talk. Chapter 2 presents the two sets of data that are used in this book: transcriptions of actual P-C encounters and mass-mediated P-C encounters. Along with a detailed description of the mass-mediated data, I provide a particularly emphasized rationale for its use as a source of data for police studies, and a resource in its own right. Chapter 3 provides an empirical rationale to the validity of using mass- mediated P-C encounters by comparing the internal order and social organization of talk in "real" P-C encounters and mass-mediated ones.

Chapter 4 examines the structural features of talk between the police and citizens as an embodiment of demeanor in routine P-C encounters. Aside from merely describing the contents of the talk between the police and the public, I demonstrate how its acontextual and mechanical features function as a form of coercion for those who wield it. This chapter is concerned with outlining some of the basic conversational features of talk, and how they contribute to the speakers' interactional aims. Using ordinary conversations as a reference point, I demonstrate how talk between the police and citizens differ from other institutional discourses and natural conversations. This chapter also provides an empirical bite to the primary theoretical question raised in the earlier chapters; that is how the police actually go about exercising their coercive authority. By examining the sequential organization of talk in P-C encounters, I illustrate the way police officers socialize citizens into the bureaucratic order of talk. This point, as it intersects with the study of citizens' demeanor, theory of coercive power, and its manifestation, demonstrates the sequential exercise of coercive power.

Chapter 5 begins with empirically titillating and theoretically relevant question: what does a domestic dispute look like if it is conversationally represented? This chapter examines the way domestic disputes are sequentially organized as conversational narratives, and the methods disputants use to attribute blame, put themselves forward, and discredit the moral character of their interactional foes. I demonstrate in detail some of the conversational tactics that disputants employ to discredit each other and portray themselves in a morally favorable light.

Chapter 6 integrates the empirical findings of previous chapters, and reconceptualizes the interactional order of P-C encounters as a collaboratively and mutually accomplished affair. While the capacity of the police to exercise coercion is absolute, its routine practice is not. As I show, that brute power is often mitigated and softened—cloaked under a guise of sociality. Thus, in addition to the physical capacity of the police to coerce, I uncover and expand on the verbal embodiment of their power. These insights are then critically discussed in the context of community policing. Finally, I discuss some of the limitations inherent in works such as this, and offer other scholars avenues for future research.

Notes

1. Mastrofski et al. (2000: 307) examine how the police deal with citizens' requests to control another citizen; and according to the authors, the police control citizens by "advising or persuading them, warning or threatening them." However, rather than explaining what those mean and how they work, the questions they ask and set out to answer are already constrained by the inherent methodological limitations that coding schemes entail. They conclude that legal consideration is the most significant (in a statistical sense) variable in granting the request. I have cause to doubt the question they posed (not their conclusion), for the way they have operationalized a request, and the assumptions it entails, displays the formalist assumptions of language that I have critiqued in this chapter.

Making a request, giving advice, persuading someone to do something, giving someone a stern warning, and making threats are all types of speech acts. And when Masfrofski et al. (2000: 307) write, "this study examines how patrol officers respond to citizen requests that officers control another citizen," they have essentially taken the verbal data of their subjects and made it their own. That is so because the actual data are chosen over the impressions of the coders and analysts. Moreover, they never clearly define what they mean by a "request" from the outset; they assume that the reader knows what a request would be. Thus, when an alleged victim tells the responding patrol officer on scene, "Officer, he hit me; please arrest that man," it is possible to understand that utterance as a request since there is a correspondence between the form of the utterance and meaning

Consider, however, cases when a request looks nothing like a request. When an alleged victim voices his or her "request," accompanied with stress, rising intonation, and increased volume ("ARREST THAT MAN!") there is nothing in the linguistic or prosodic features of the utterance what would lead one to believe that it is a request. There are no overt politeness markers such as 'please' nor are there any modal verbs (can, would, could) which give requests their structure and appearance. In fact the request that the police arrest the man looks more like an order, a command, despite the complainant's status as a victim. And by formulating all class of such utterances under the general rubric of "requests," the researchers have already given a hint as to the type of analysis they will provide: the scope of the answer is already delimited by the scope of the question since the question presupposes and prefers a particular type of answer. The question of 'how' is settled with a 'how many' instead.

2. As Goffman (1967: 78) notes, a person cannot create demeanor by "verbally avowing that he possesses them."

3. In my informal interviews with the police, several officers mentioned a colleague who had a rather extensive complaint file. They related to me that most of those complaints came from motorists who had been angered at the ticketing officer's condescending de-

meanor as he was issuing the ticket; they said that the officer would say the phrase with a smirk and in a belittling manner, and that was what the motorists found so indignant. Of course, when supervisors would look into the officer's file, what they'd find is that the officer had merely said, "have a nice [good] day" to the citizens, a charge that is hardly sanctionable.

CHAPTER 1
INTRODUCTION TO THE
TECHNOLOGY OF TALK

There has been much interest in language—discourse—throughout various academic disciplines (Jaworski and Coupland, 1999; Raymond, 2000: 2-27). The most recent and widely known interest in language and systems of 'discourses' has been in a philosophical and socio-political context that describes the global power relations of various legal and medical institutions, and the control they exercise over individuals (Foucault, 1979, 1977). A more obscure contemporary of Foucault has used the same term to describe the structures of a subject's—*speaking being*—unconscious mind (Lacan, 1977, 1973). Linguists have used it to delineate morphological, lexical, clausal, and sentential level utterances in their analysis (see Schiffrin, 1994). The diverse array of meanings associated with discourse/language and its incumbent usage are principally attributed to an epistemological shift in the academic disciplines (Jaworski and Coupland, 1999; Lee, 1990; see also Conley and O'Barr, 1998).

This epistemological shift is reflected even in the criminal justice sciences with the development of postmodern criminology (see Schwartz and Friederichs, 1994) and constitutive criminology (Henry and Milovanovic, 1999, 1996, 1991). In this field, the main tenet of post-structuralism has been applied to show that the law and definitions of crime, much like signifiers in a communicative system, do not merely transmit knowledge in a purely referential way. Rather, constitutive theorists have argued that the very transmission of a message, along with its reception, *constitutes* the ideological system it represents (Henry and Milovanovic, 1996, 1991).

Linguists, most notably Noam Chomsky, have traditionally taken a formalistic stance toward language, hence, "focusing on prosody, good descriptions of the grammar, and pronunciation of utterances at the level of the sentence" (Jaworski and Coupland, 1999: 4; Levinson, 1981b). And it is from this descriptive and "universalizing" linguistic tradition that the next major analytical shift toward an action oriented one occurred.

The capacity of language to bring about change in external reality, rather than merely describe it, is best reflected in the work of John Austin (1962) in his speech act theory. The primary lesson of speech act theory is that language is used to perform a set of actions. Speech act theory provides a theoretical scaffolding with which to recognize the conditions and rules underlying the production and comprehension of utterances "as a particular linguistically realized action" (Schffrin, 1994: 61).

For Austin (1962) utterances can be classified as constatives and performatives. The former refers to declarative statements in which the truth and falsity conditions of statements can be evaluated. The latter refers to a class of statements that perform a set of actions. For example, "I sentence you to sixty years in prison," is a performative utterance; the performative verb "sentence" realizes—creates—a particular action. The preceding sentence, when uttered by a judge in a courtroom, is sensible and coherent because it meets all the felicity conditions of a particular linguistic action (sentencing): the speaker, judge, possesses the authority to issue such a statement; the setting of the speaking situation, courtroom, also meets the *felicity conditions* of such a speech act. A convicted felon who issues such a statement to a judge in a courtroom, however, is nothing more than a farceur, and the statement he issues makes no sense since the speaker (felon) does not meet the necessary felicity conditions of the very speech act he is engaging in.

Austin's emphasis—and later Searle (1969)—on the capacity of language to perform a set of actions highlights another important philosophical, linguistic, and sociological point, one which quantitatively oriented (police) researchers are apt to miss: that there is no necessary link between the form and function of an utterance (Heritage and Atkinson, 1984; Fish, 1989; Schegloff, 1984a). Simply put, the grammatical and syntactic form an utterances takes (what Austin calls locutionary acts) has no logical or necessary correspondence to the actual work (what Austin calls illocutionary acts) that it does. In other words, a speaker may intend to say one thing, but produce an entirely opposite effect—its perlocutionary force (Austin, 1962).

Searle's exposition on indirect speech acts shows how one speech act can do the work of another. For instance, if Frank, a retired accountant, yells, "It's cold in here" while watching television in his son's living room with Marie (his wife), Deborah (his daughter-in-law), and his son Ray, and only Marie gets up from her seat and closes the window that had been open, then we can state that Frank's utterance is or is not a mere description of the weather. What we can claim with a greater degree of certitude is that Marie has understood Frank's utterance ("It's cold in here") not only as a description of reality (weather, room temperature) but also as an indirect request to do something about that state of reality that is causing him discomfort—to close the window. In a similar way, an utterance such as "May I see your driver's license and registration please?" that a police officer utters in the context of a traffic stop need not necessarily be understood as a request although it fulfills all the formal—grammatical—requirements of a request. It can be intended and understood as a question, a command, and a threat, in addition to being a "request."

In speech act theory speakers' intentions and hearers' comprehension of those intentions, and an analyst's inference of those categories are all deemed important in the production of meaning; but that there is no way to do so in a principled and rigorous way points to a shortcoming of speech act theory, one which critics have already noted (see Drew and Heritage, 1992; Levinson, 1980, 1981a, b). Functional aspects of actual language use are conspicuously absent in speech act theory. That is, though Austin and Searle examine belief, meaning, and action in the context of language use, they do not examine actual statements of real life people who are situated in a concrete social context, in the context of a social interaction. Speech act theorists use hypothetical—made up—utterances spoken by fictitious speakers and hearers. The intentions and purposes of speakers are considered to be important in speech act theory, as Austin and Searle note, but how those concepts actually work, in sequence, and embody in real talk, as demonstrated by speakers and hearers themselves, is not something that speech act theory adequately addresses (Levinson, 1981a, b; Schegloff, 1988b).[1]

The primary theoretical and methodological difference between a philosophical view of language, represented in the works of Michel Foucault, John Austin, and John Searle, and sociology of conversation, best represented by figures such as Sacks (1992), Schegloff (1968), Sacks et al. (1974), Heritage and Atkinson (1984), and Drew and Heritage (1992), and sociolinguistics, best represented by figures such as Gumperz (1982), Brown and Levinson (1987) and Goffman (1981, 1967) is that the latter two traditions ground their analysis in interaction, between speakers and hearers. This is especially true for those who study politeness and conversation.

As Goffman (1967: 5) observes, we are all embedded in a "world of social encounters," either directly, through face to face contact, or through mediated contact (e.g., telephone). When we are caught in a social encounter, Goffman (1981) notes, we desire to be positively valued. And the self that is projected onto discourse is an interpersonal identity, or what Goffman (1967) defines as *face*. In the field of sociolinguistics, face is defined as "the negotiated public image, mutually granted each other by participants in a communicative event" (Wardaugh, 1984: 35). Goffman (1967) recognized the interactive nature of face, hence, called it *face-work*. Face-work then is not a solitary affair; it requires the cooperation of the other participant(s). This field of study within sociolinguistics is referred to as politeness theory (see Brown and Levinson, 1987).

The paradoxical nature of face is something all participants in a conversation or any communicative event must negotiate. As Scollon and Scollon (1995: 36-39) state, human interaction is marked by its necessity for remaining autonomous, hence independence, while displaying involvement to the other participant—positive politeness (Brown and Levinson, 1987). It is only logical to involve the other speaker and approve the other's values because if such involvement is not practiced, then there is no reason for the other speaker to acknowledge our values. Involving the other speaker in the conversation utilizes linguistic strategies that show involvement; this may manifest through linguistic forms of attendance, exaggeration, in-group membership, common perspectives, optimism, reciprocity, and the use of the others' language (Lakoff, 1973a). Achieving competence as a speaker and member of a speech community thus requires a delicate balancing and negotiation of independence and involvement.

Granting independence to the other speaker stresses his/her individuality. This entails not being dominated and overwhelmed by the imposing values of others, or what Brown and Levinson (1987) refer to as *negative face*; it entails being given a certain amount of autonomy and freedom. Scollon and Scollon (1995) state that discourse strategies that reflect the independence of the other speaker is to offer options and the use of formal names and titles. Some other linguistic strategies of independence include making minimal assumptions about other speaker's wants, giving option not to do the act, not imposing, minimizing threat, and using the other speaker's own language or dialect—restraint (Bailey, 1997).

Politeness strategies are contingent on the power differential between participants. In addition to power, Lakoff (1973b) mentions two other factors that bring a face/politeness system into existence: distance and weight of imposition. Power is the "vertical disparity between the participants in a hierarchical structure" (Scollon and Scollon, 1995: 42). The asymmetrical participation of institutional interaction would be an example of such power differentials. Hence, on the street, a police officer would be said to possess this power over the rest of the citizenry. The power to prevail in "explicit contests" is what Molotch and Boden (1985) call the first face of power.

Distance between participants refers to the level of intimacy between the participants, not power. Thus, two close friends would be characterized as having little distance while two strangers would be said to have a great distance between them. Applying this criterion to our example, the distance between police officers and citizens would be positive, meaning that there is little degree of familiarity or intimacy.

According to sociolinguists, there are three different types of politeness systems, deference, solidarity, and hierarchical; and two central factors compose them: power and distance (Scollon and Scollon, 1995; Brown and Levinson, 1987). The deference politeness system is characterized by an absence of power differential and a presence of distance. This entails a mutual exchange of respect since the two participants are equal or near equals. In the solidarity politeness system, there is an absence of both components. It is thoroughly egalitarian in character and expression of intimacy is possible. In the aforementioned systems of politeness, the relationship is symmetrical. No one participant possesses a greater social good (power) over the other.

In the hierarchical politeness system, there is a presence of power and presence or absence of distance. But the key point is that there is a clearly demarcated line of authority: one is dominant (i.e., police officer), the other subordinate (i.e., citizen). Since there exists a discrepancy in status, this relationship is said to be asymmetrical: the person occupying the "master position" uses involvement strategies while the subordinate uses independence strategies. In other words, one talks "down" while the other talks "up." Such asymmetrical relationships have been a significant feature of institutional settings where one participant holds the power to control topics, set agendas, and control turns.

The Sociology of Conversation

For those who study talk sociologically—Conversation Analysis (CA)—the analytical emphasis is sequential. That is, instead of accepting the validity of concepts such as class, race, gender, role, status, and power as pregiven entities, CA seeks to explicate how those concepts (i.e., social structure) are embodied in the context-free structures of talk itself, aside from the occasion for talk, in their sequential organization (Atkinson and Heritage, 1984; Schegloff, 1991). And unlike speech act theorists, researchers in the CA tradition use talk that occurs naturally, in banal settings and mundane circumstances—talk that is not fabricated. Furthermore, CA is religiously empirical. CA research begins with the "description and explication of the competences that ordinary speakers use and rely on in participating in intelligible, socially organized interaction" (Heritage and Atkinson, 1984: 1). A crucial assumption behind CA is that ordinary people exchange speech to produce and reproduce the social order that is meaningful for them; they make their intentions known to one another, and demonstrate their understanding of those intentions on a turn by turn and moment by moment basis.

And because conversation involves other speakers, it is conceptualized as a form of social action, to be more precise, social interaction—the "primordial site of sociality, where it is embodied and enacted" (Schegloff, 1999a: 141). Hence, one of the leading figures in CA, Emanuel Schegloff (1987), aptly characterized the field of study as "talk-in-interaction." CA is premised on the belief that social actions can be studied systematically, rigorously, and scientifically.

The empirical, rigorous, systematic, and scientific character of CA derives not from its "method" per se, but due to its technological origin. It is more appropriate to assert that CA is not a scientific "method" in that researchers in CA follow and adhere to no set procedures or rules that will yield valid reproducible findings. The analytical task is more intuitive, artistic, and unmotivated—unmotivated in that the researchers do not set out to examine a particular phenomenon per se (Silverman, 1998). Certain conversational phenomena (e.g., blaming, accusing, projecting a particular moral identity) emerge from the discursive activities—in structures, sequences—of the participants themselves. The goal of CA is to demonstrate first and foremost how activities, goals, and intentions of conversationalists are meaningful and orderly for those who are engaged in the talk (Maynard and Clayman, 1991; Schegloff, 1991).

The analysis of conversations did not exist until the advent of the tape recorder (Sacks, 1992). With this new technological advancement, one could, in essence, "freeze time," and make repeated observations on a chosen social activity (e.g., telephone calls). This technological advancement overcame two major limitations in observation based research: (1) memory (2) subjectivity.

First of all, it is impossible to recall every piece of detail that occurs in a spate of talk; a descriptive summary is possible, but a detailed accounting of pauses, its length, onset of interruptions, overlaps, and simultaneous starts and stops is just not humanly possible—the details that configure implicatively in the ascription of demeanor. Thus, the availability of data and the ability to make repeated observations overcomes one of the limitations of observation-based research.

The second limitation concerns the interpretive—subjective—process. When readers are treated to narrative descriptions of life in some exotic place, the impressions, descriptions, and selected excerpts from fieldnotes belong solely to the ethnographer; this process adds an additional filter between reality and its representation. Consequently, readers must, necessarily, read through the lived experience of natives through the "eyes" of the original ethnographer; readers cannot verify or confirm certain observational facts because those facts are not available to them (Atkinson and Drew, 1979). That is to say that the nature of observation is relentlessly historical and resembles the behavior of time.[2]

But once audio recordings (and now video recordings) are made and transcribed, history can be re-lived and re-experienced because the initial phenomenon under scrutiny is available for inspection. The key difference between ethnographic accounts and audio/video recordings is that the descriptive accounts do not remain as a privileged domain of the researcher: they are open and accessible to all readers. In this way, social experience is captured "raw," prior to interpretation, prior to preexisting classification and coding schemes, and allows access to other researchers for their description, transcription, and analytical interpretation (see Drew and Heritage, 1992; Duranti, 1997; Heath and Luff, 2000; Heritage and Atkinson, 1984; Gubrium and Holstein, 1997; Sacks, 1992; Schegloff, 1989; Silverman, 1998).

CA, as a scholarly discipline, then, owes its existence to technology. For Harvey Sacks, however, the pioneer in the field of CA, talk (language, discourse) is also *technical* in that it works *like* a machine: talk is rule driven, orderly, and its orderliness is found in structures within the talk itself, and (re) produced during moments of talk-in-interaction by the people who are situated in an occasion for the talk. The fundamental premises behind conversation analysis are (Psathas, 1995: 2):

1. Order is a produced phenomenon
2. Order is produced by the parties in situ; that is, it is situated and occasioned
3. The parties orient to that order themselves; that is, this order is not an analyst's conception, not the result of the use of some preformed or preformulated theoretical conceptions concerning what action should/must/ought to be, or based on generalizing or summarizing statements about what action generally/frequently/often is.
4. Order is repeatable and recurrent.

5. The discovery, description, and analysis of that produced orderliness is the task of the analyst.

6. Issues of how frequently, how widely, or how often particular phenomena occur are to be set aside in the interest of discovering, describing, and analyzing the structures, the machinery, the organized practices, the formal procedures, the ways in which order is produced.

7. Structures of social action, once so discerned, can be described and analyzed in formal, that is, structural, organizational, logical, atopically contentless, consistent, and abstract, terms.

Sacks originally "discovered" the machine-like character of talk in his work at the Suicide Prevention Center in Los Angeles. As he began to collect and analyze recordings of calls to the Center, he observed that certain sequences began to emerge in the conversations. As Schegloff (1989: 188) writes in a memoir about Sacks, "A great many of them [Sacks' intellectual preoccupation] had his involvement with the suicide prevention center as a point of departure, thereafter taking the often surprising directions which his distinctive mind imparted to them." For instance, the social workers at the Center would answer a call and experience trouble getting the caller to give a name:

Excerpt 1 (Psathas, 1995: 13)
Answerer: This is Mr. Smith may I help you
Caller: Yes, this is Mr. Brown

Excerpt 2 (Schegloff, 1989: 189)
Answerer: This is Mr. Smith may I help you
Caller: I can't hear you
Answerer: This is Mr. Smith
Caller: Smith

Sacks referred to instances in excerpts 1 and 2 as "asking for a name without asking"; he noted that this type of indirect request for a name is interactionally and morally valuable since it precluded the answerer from being held accountable for a motive. That is, if the caller asks why his/her name is required, the answerer must provide a satisfactory answer. However, by providing a place in the talk itself or a sequential slot for the other speaker to give a name, the answerer sidestepped that accountability. As can be readily observed, the caller in excerpt 2 does not give his name despite the fact that the answerer at the Center gives his name. Sacks noted that the name's absence did not necessarily mean it didn't exist, but that the opportunity to give a name had been missed, ignored, foreclosed, but never "opened" (Silverman, 1998).

Sacks observed that these types of exchanges occurred in units; he also noticed that other speech exchanges also occurred in a "class" of units, or in sequences (see Sacks et al., 1974: 716):

Excerpt 3 (Greeting-Return Greeting)
A: Hello

B: Hello

Excerpt 4 (*COPS* Data: Greeting-Return Greeting)
Police Officer: How you doin?
Motorist: Hi

Excerpt 5 (Closings)
A: Bye dear
B: Bye

Excerpt 6 (*COPS* Data: Question-Answer)
Police Officer: Where'd you get the car man?
Male Citizen: It's my car I just bought it

Excerpt 7 (Invitation-Acceptance of Invitation)
A: Wanna go out tonight?
B: Sure

Excerpt 8 (Invitation-Decline)
A: Wanna go out tonight?
B: Sorry, I'm busy

Excerpt 9 (Accusation-Denial)
Professor: Did you cheat on the last exam?
Student: No way

Excerpts 3-9 illustrate a fundamental analytical concept in conversation analysis: *sequential implicativeness*. This simply refers to the fact that what the second speaker does in his/her second turn has *conditional relevance* to what preceded in the prior turn: *"By the conditional relevance of one item on another we mean: given the first, the second is expectable: upon its occurrence it can be seen to be a second item to the first; upon its absence it can be seen to be officially absent—all this provided by the occurrence of the first item"* (Schegloff, 1968: 1083).

A colleague of Sacks, Emanuel Schegloff (1968) examined the opening sequences in 500 telephone calls as a part of his Ph.D. dissertation, and found that phone calls were interactionally ordered and sequentially organized. Schegloff (1968) noted that telephone openings are marked by several "core" sequences: the ringing of the telephone constitutes a summons, beckoning the called party to answer, thereby establishing a means of communication, thus forming a (1) summons/answer sequence. (2) The identification/recognition sequence is concerned with establishing the identity of the called party; and this is accomplished through the (3) greeting sequence where "each party asserts or claims recognition of the other" (Schegloff, 1968: 129). And it is after the (4) "how are you" sequence that the (5) reason for the call is introduced. That burden—introducing the first topic—Schegloff (1968) notes, "canonically," belongs to the caller.

The turn by turn and line by line organization of talk, in other words, is not isolated and chaotic, but socially organized and orderly—made orderly through the collaborative efforts of speakers. And in CA it is these types of "paired"—first and second—sequences that are the primary unit of analysis (see Heritage and Atkinson, 1984; Schegloff, 1968). For instance in excerpt 3, speaker A utters a greeting, and in the next turn, speaker B returns that greeting. In excerpt 4, a police officer greets a motorist who has been pulled over for speeding; the motorist "hears" the greeting as such and it is returned in the very next turn. The same type of implicativeness operates in the closing sequence in excerpt 5: speaker A bids farewell; speaker B returns that goodbye in the next turn (see Schegloff and Sacks, 1973).

These types of exchanges occur with such predictability and regularity that they are referred to as *adjacency pairs* (Sacks et al., 1974); that is, they occur in immediate turns and in sequence. Thus, if a first pair part is a greeting, the second pair part is also a greeting. This means that speakers face a definite constraint in their response to the first pair part: the "design and type of some actions can impose such strong constraints on the next turn at talk that only a limited narrow range of responses should follow" (Raymond, 2000: 10; Atkinson and Heritage, 1984). For example, when someone says hello, we are expected to return that hello; when we do not, we can be held accountable for its absence (Schegloff, 1968). That accountability is moral, meaning that the absence of a return greeting generates an inference about our moral character.

Matoesian (1993: 84) notes, however, that even though adjacency pairs are common structures in ordinary talk, "conversation is not a seamless stretch of these sharply constraining and tightly organized structures." Rather, it is based on the assumption that utterances are to be understood as occurrences which are a response to or in relation to what preceded before (sequential implicativeness). "This assumption provides a framework in which speakers can rely on the positioning of what they say to contribute to the sense of what they say as an action" (Heritage, 1984a: 261, in Matoesian, 1993: 84).

Notice how the first two turns in excerpt 6 exemplify the idea of sequential implicativeness. The first speaker (police officer) asks a question, the next speaker (motorist) provides an answer. This type of question-answer format is not only routine in talk between the police and citizens in traffic stops and other P-C interaction, where there is an institutionally normative expectation for its occurrence, but it is also pervasive in ordinary conversations (Button, 1987; Raymond 2000). That is, one speaker asks a question to another speaker and expects an answer. The notion of sequentiality operates not only in question/answer formats, but also in numerous other structures. For example, when invitations—to go to a party, to go on a date, to go out to dinner—are proffered, they are accepted outright, with little delay between the invitation and the acceptance. When they are rejected, they are not done bluntly but "softly"—mitigated with excuses, justifications, and rationales for why invitations had to be declined.

Excerpt 9 also works in a similar manner. In excerpt 9 a professor accuses a student of cheating and in the next very next turn the student denies the accusation. These types of adjacent pairs also illustrate another key idea in CA, that of *preference organization*. Preference organization does not mean "subjective or psychological desires or dispositions" (Heritage and Atkinson, 1984: 53). Preference organization refers to alternatives—linguistic options—that are available to speakers in the course of a conversation; it refers to a "range of phenomena associated with the fact that choices among nonequivalent courses are routinely implemented on ways that reflect an institutionalized ranking of alternatives" (Atkinson and Heritage, 1984: 53). In excerpt 9 a denial follows an accusation; furthermore that denial is direct, immediate, and swift. There is no pause between the turns, nor are there qualifications, excuses, and accounts. Researchers have found that denials are the "preferred" responses to accusations (Atkinson and Heritage, 1984; Garcia, 1991; Komter, 1994; Pomerantz, 1984; Sacks et al., 1974). In other words, accusations and denials are typically found in sequentially adjacent places, as the first and second pair parts in a unit.

In the excerpts discussed thus far, the speakers display little trouble with understanding one another. That is, no miscommunication takes place. In ordinary conversation, however, misunderstandings and other "troubles" in talk are fairly common (see Schegloff, 1987; 1984a):

Excerpt 10 (Sacks et al., 1974: 723)
M: Whad are you doin'
L: Me?

Excerpt 11 (*COPS* Data: Naked Man in a Garage)
Police Officer: Put your hands up
Male Citizen: Put my hands up?

Sacks et al. (1974) note that repair mechanisms exist for dealing with trouble in virtually all aspects of talk. For instance, if two or more speakers start to talk at the same time, one or more of the speakers may withhold the completion of their turn at talk. In excerpt 10, M (mother) asks her daughter (L) "whad are you doin?" but the daughter is not sure to whom the question is addressed since there are three "parties" on the bed (third being the family dog), where the talk is taking place. Consequently, the daughter attempts to clarify—repair—the proper recipient of her mother's question (see Sacks et al., 1974: 723-724).

In excerpt 11, police officers receive a call about a naked man in a garage who may be under the influence of narcotics. As one of the responding officers approaches the man, he observes a knife-like object in the man's hand. As a result, the officer commands the man to raise his hands vertically into the air, to which the male citizen repeats the officer's command, requesting a clarification. It is through such *repair sequences* that problems involving miscommunication, misunderstanding, and other interactional dilemmas that speakers in a conversation collaboratively come to a mutual understanding of one another and achieve intersubjective social relations (Schegloff, 1992a).

One elementary "device" that is used to repair trouble in talk is the *turn taking system* (Sacks et al., 1974). Sacks et al. (1974) write that the turn taking system and repair are "made for each other." However, the turn taking system is much more than a mere repair mechanism; it is a primordial form of social action. And sustaining that social order within the situated social action entails that the participants orient to the underlying rule to accomplish the conversational task at hand; that underlying rule can be found in the turn taking system. In a seminal paper on turn taking, Sacks et al. (1974: 700-701) noted gross but recurrent features of talk in general:

1.   Speaker-change recurs, or at least occurs
2.   Overwhelmingly, one party talks at a time
3.   Occurrences of more than one speaker at a time are common, but brief
4.   Transitions (from one turn to the next) with no gap and no overlap are common. Together with transitions characterized by slight gap or slight overlap, they make up the vast majority of transitions.
5.   Turn order is not fixed, but varies.
6.   Turn size is not fixed, but varies.
7.   Length of conversation is not specified in advance.
8.   What parties say is not specified in advance.
9.   Relative distribution of turns is not specified in advance
10.   Number of parties may vary
11.   Talk can be continuous or discontinuous
12.   Turn-allocation techniques are obviously used. A current speaker may select a next speaker (as when he addresses a question to another party); or parties may self-select in starting to talk.
13.   Various 'turn constructional units' are employed: e.g., turn can be projectedly 'one word' long, or they can be sentential in length.
14.   Repair mechanism exist for dealing with turn-taking errors and violations; e.g., if two parties find themselves talking at the same time, one of them will stop prematurely, thus repairing the trouble.

The general features of talk stipulated above indicate that conversation is locally organized: who gets to talk, what gets talked about, how much a topic gets talked about, and when a speaker gets to talk is not pre-specified; instead, those things are managed interactionally on a turn by turn basis at "transition relevant places," where there are gaps, pauses, and lulls in the conversation (Sacks et al., 1974). In this way, ordinary conversations that unfold over a dinner table or over coffee differ from speech exchange systems such as a debate, a courtroom cross examination, or a P-C encounter in that in the latter, turn order, turn size, and topic are pre-allocated as a function of institutionality (see Atkinson and Drew, 1979; Drew and Heritage, 1992; Matoesian, 1993; Schegloff, 1992b; Zimmerman, 1992).

If management of conversations is not decided in advance—local—it can be said to be context sensitive. That is, talk may follow a different contour depending on its setting, roles of the participants, and topic: talk is sensitive to its occasion. Talk, however, is also independent of its occasion— context free—in that the structural and formal properties of talk itself—its sequential character—operate across contextual particulars, such as setting, identities of speakers, topic of talk, and race, class, and gender of speakers (Sacks et al., 1974; see Schegloff, 1992b, 1991).

In an institutional setting, the procedures for allocating turns are different from those found in ordinary conversation. For example, it has commonly been found that the opportunity to participate in talk in institutionalized settings is asymmetrically distributed (Atkinson and Drew, 1979; Heritage, 1998a). Thus, the local management of turns is transformed into a prestructured allocation of opportunity for talk. Unequal access to the mechanisms of talk is embedded as an existing feature of institutional settings: speaker selection (who gets to talk), topic selection (what gets to be talked about), and turn size (how much a topic gets talked about) are already determined before the conversation even takes place (Drew and Heritage,1992; Matoesian, 1993). The ability to control such mechanics of speech exchange systems is contingent upon the possession of a scarce commodity: power.

One of the characteristics of institutional talk is the asymmetrical distribution of power across social formations such as race, class, age, gender and professional relations (Schegloff, 1992b). The social structural aspects of talk present in institutional settings has been referred to as *socially structured talk;* the power that the institutional agents possess as *sequential institutional power* (Matoesian, 1993: 101). In other words, by possessing this valued commodity, one can set agendas and topics in the flow of talk or in a more raw form, it can be used to "make one's account count."

The differential access to talk in institutional settings, as opposed to ordinary talk, can be most powerfully illustrated in citizen calls for emergency services such as police and fire.

Excerpt 12 (Zimmerman, 1992: 428)
```
1    CT: Nine one one what is you emerg-((cut off by
2          transmit static))
3          (.2)
4    C:  GO::D MY WIFE JUST SHOT HERSELF (.3) TWENTY
5          TWO SIXTY EIGHT (GRANT) AVENUE HURRY U:::::P
6          (.2)
7    CT: What happened?
8          (.2)
9    C:  (AR::)=SHE JUS SHOT HERSE::LF=
10   CT: =SHE (SHEL)?
11         (.2)
12   C:  SHE SHOT HERSELF WITH A SHOTGUN
```

Citizens who call the emergency services do so to request assistance for troubles they are experiencing or witnessing, and as excerpt 12 illustrates, sometimes, the occasion for the talk itself is quite harrowing. Yet, despite the fact that the occasion for the call is tragic and disturbing, the mechanisms—structures— of talk operate independent of, apart from, the exigent content of the talk.

Whalen and Zimmerman (1990, 1987) and Zimmerman (1992) examined opening sequences in emergency calls for service, and found that openings—and talk in general—in institutional settings differ from openings in ordinary conversations. That is, the properties and structures of talk found in institutional talk, such as the one found in calls for emergency, are different from ordinary conversations. We'll examine one particular aspect of talk, the opening sequence.

Openings in calls for emergency assistance are composed of a (1) prebeginning (2) opening/identification/acknowledgement (3) request (Zimmerman, 1992). Prebeginnings refer to the—unobservable—physical act of picking up a phone and dialing the other party's number (911), "thereby summoning another to interact" (Whalen and Zimmerman, 1987: 180). In emergency calls to 911, the callers generally remain anonymous: the task of self-identification falls to the institution, and it is "categorical." Asking what the emergency is immediately after the categorical self-identification, according to Zimmerman (1992: 419), initiates "interrogation prior to a request for assistance." When requests are made by callers, they are formulated as (1) descriptions (2) direct or indirect requests for assistance (3) ambient events (Whalen and Zimmerman, 1987: 178).

A key point of difference between openings in ordinary telephone conversations and emergency calls for assistance is reduction of opening sequences: "reduction plays an important role in achieving an institutionally constrained focus to the talk, for it routinely locates the first topic slot to the callers in their first turn, which is the second turn of the call" (Whalen and Zimmerman, 1987: 175). In ordinary talk the caller or the called party may introduce the topic through preemptive moves (Schegloff, 1968; 1986); however, Whalen and Zimmerman (1990) and Zimmerman (1992) find that in calls to emergency centers, the caller's first turn is the environment where topics are initiated.

Another reduction that is noteworthy is the absence of recognitionals and greetings in calls to emergency centers. Theoretically, that absence may be explained by the fact that an emergency call to the police is just that, a pressing and urgent matter. The reason for the call—problem, topic—to the institution is practically and bureaucratically foregrounded into the occasion itself, and to engage in socially lubricative talk such as greetings would delay the statement of the problem and the request for assistance (see Zimmerman, 1992).

The noteworthy point to be made thus far is that language is not only the vehicle of communicative action in the service of social action (e.g., to request assistance); it is a form of social action in itself (i.e., prebeginning, opening, identification, request), within the mechanisms of talk an already embedded social order (Maynard, 1988). The scholarly activity of conversation analysts, such as the ones I've discussed thus far, involves examining how participants in a conversation make sense out of talk, use language to organize such a social activity, and (re) produce the social order in it (Schegloff, 1992a). The principal question that is posed in this work is: how does the talk between the police and the public unfold? What sequences exist in the talk between the police and people? How is it similar to and different from ordinary conversation and other institutional talk? What features of talk between the police and the public give that bureaucratic flavor? What are the police and citizens trying to accomplish through their talk?

Extended Talk: Narratives

The *turn constructional component* noted by Sacks et al. (1974) refers to the fact that turns may be varied in length. For instance, some turns may be lexical or merely a single word:

Excerpt 12 (Sacks et al., 1974: 702)
     Guy: Is Rol down by any chance dju know?
→ Eddy: Huh?

Some turns may be a phrase or a clause:

Excerpt 13 (Sacks et al., 1974: 702)
     A: Oh I have the-I have the class in the evening
→   B: On Mondays?

Some turns are a bit lengthier and resemble a narrative or a story (see below, lines 43-59):

Excerpt 14 (*COPS* data: Jimmy Dean)
42 PO: What happened here today sir?
43 BM :   →I came back to move my stuff (though)
44   we talked about it last night
45   I told her I was moving [she
46 PO: [how long ya
47   been living together?
48 BM: →   Well I just moved in like probably about a week
49   two weeks maybe I told her "I'll need to move"
50   you know what I'm saying by the end of the
51   week I mean end of the month cuz I need to
52   get a place right? so she said "Okay" you know
53   "you could move in for awhile" I said "Okay no
54   problem" so last night we talked about it ( ) and I
55   was moving today she's mad because I took my
56   Jimmy Dean sausage that I bought you know I'm
57   taking my food with me and stuff like that right
58   so ( )bit me in the hand tore up my shoulders
59   scratched me up

Stories and narratives such as the one given above are found routinely in P-C encounters, especially in domestic disputes. When police officers ask an open-ended question such as "tell me what happened," the next turn is, more often than not, likely to be extended. A narrative, such as the one between a boyfriend/girlfriend in excerpt 14, is a real or fictional event/state that occurred in the past relative to the moment of speaking or narration (Polanyi, 1979). Simply put: "a story consists of events that took place in specific circumstances involving specific characters and gave rise to states of affairs that contrast in some important way with the situation obtaining in the story world at the beginning of the story" (Polyani, 1985:188). According to Polyani (1979) narratives contain three kinds of information: (1) narrative structure provides the temporal context (e.g., time-line). Narratives are also structured in a way that reflects the ordering of events: sequential placement of a story event within the story is to mirror how the event actually occurred. (2) Descriptive structure provides environmental and character centered information, or things that have significance to the story being told that cannot be omitted. (3) Evaluative structure provides "contextualizing information" which informs the hearer of the "crucial information" in the story being told.

A competently told narrative synchronizes the events of the reporting context and reported event in a way that is cogently related. Moreover, speakers tell stories to make a point: the purpose of the narrative can be referential (i.e., convey a message) but more often it is a moral evaluation and critical judgements about the world (Polyani, 1985). If the teller wants to focus on revealing her biases and skewed perspectives then storytelling is a powerful way to direct the listeners to those aspects of the story. And when skillfully performed, it provides a vivid way to impute blame onto others, deflect blame from self, even before direct accusations are made (Hirsch, 1998). When poorly performed, it is seen as a "self-indulgent" attempt to "put oneself forward" (Polyani, 1985: 187). A pragmatic perspective on storytelling takes the position that narrative is interactional between speaker and hearer: the audience takes an active role in the shaping of the narrative (Gulich and Quasthoff, 1985; see also Goodwin, 1986).

"Conversational narratives" as they appear on *COPS* for data is invaluable for such reasons. Since the texts are recorded live using audio and video equipment, the data are captured as they "naturally" occur, thereby preserving their locally produced character. *COPS* is filmed and recorded in real time, during moments of interaction, rather than as a historical text. In other words, the narratives in *COPS* are not isolated. For example, when suspects tell their narratives to police, they are removed from the ordinary conversational format and the interactional setting and context: they are placed in a room and told to either write or verbally articulate their story (see Inbau et al., 1986). *COPS* data, however, are produced as part of the situationally and interactionally emergent context of ordinary conversational narrative (Polyani, 1985). Moreover, since *COPS* often captures the stories of participants in the context of disputes, its "verbal dueling" and collaborative character is preserved (see McDowell, 1985). And before participants relate their main narratives to the police, they have to negotiate basic rules of social (conversational) interaction, such as turn taking. Hence, not only are the principles of narrative analysis (Labov and Waletsky, 1967; Polyani, 1985) relevant, but also conversation (Atkinson and Heritage, 1984; Button and Lee, 1987; Sacks, 1992).

Stories are relevant for this research because the data originates from television; and as many scholars have noted, television, too, tells stories (Allen, 1987; Collins, 1987; Kozloff, 1987; White, 1987); it does so in a dominant and pervasive way, permeating into the lives of all people, irrespective of class, race, and gender (Gerbner et al., 1980). Some even conceptualize television as a source of culture rather than a manifestation of it (see Collins,1987; Fiske, 1996; Signorielli, 1990; Signorielli and Morgan, 1996). *COPS*, also, tells stories— entertaining ones. Furthermore, its "liveness" corresponds more closely to the oral storytelling format. Sometimes the conflict between the participants in the context of a call for service is settled with fists, but most of the time, it is managed with words. More importantly, *COPS* is also a narrative text: each episode or call for service is "self contained," meaning that it is ordered temporally and sequentially (Kozloff, 1987); moreover it is shaped by its rules of discourse. This requirement has significant implications for the way the story is told: it sets parameters of acceptability and is directly related to the editing problem which critics find so problematic.

If a call for service to a scene of a domestic disturbance between a married couple constitutes an episode of *COPS*, then the editors will not—cannot—show footage of a high speed vehicle pursuit. There has to be a correspondence between image and narrative. The correspondence cannot be random; it has to be progressive and orderly. What is shown on screen—police officers arriving in a trailer park, finding empty beer cans strewn about the floor of a trailer home, shirtless man and scantily clad woman screaming at each other—must match what is heard on screen. Hence, Doyle (1998) notes that the sounds and images on *COPS* are edited to give a sequential and linear appearance. And researchers such as Oliver (1996, 1994) and Oliver and Armstrong (1995) use such images that appear on *COPS* to examine the role of ideology in television. Accordingly, Oliver (1996, 1994) concludes that the show presents a skewed view of police work, one that is biased toward order, crime, and justice. Oliver examines officers' physical behaviors and overtly aggressive words and codes them into preexisting classification schemes. That is to say she does not use the participants' actual words as units of analysis in their own right.

But this type of content analysis overlooks the fact that words (language) are forms of social action rather than mere representation of it (Maynard, 1988). And editing—technological mediation—cannot affect the grammatical, semantic, and pragmatic structure of language because it is already sequential, progressive, and orderly: editors cannot cut and alter the meaning of language without destroying its internal coherence. In this work, I am principally interested in what is heard on screen, the words that police officers say to the disputants, the things that they say to the police, to each other, and what the responding officers say to them, to each other and to the viewers—the internal order of language on *COPS*.

"Domestics" is one of a variety of calls that the police receive on *COPS*. There are traffic stops, suspicious person stops, burglary, narcotics, prostitution stings, thefts etc. As I have explained using the domestic example, in all these calls, the primary "medium" and my main unit of analysis is language: *what do all of the participants say?* Moreover, *how do they say it and in what sequential order and context? How do they take turns when they do this? What are they trying to accomplish with their narratives?* And because the "tool" they use to accomplish this is language, and the things they tell are stories, despite the fact that their telling occasion is technologically and editorially mediated, the episode is self contained, coherent, and orderly, hence, follows the conventions of a narrative. My analysis of those types of extended talk will be (1) to analyze the descriptive structure of the narratives themselves and (2) as a performance in the accomplishment of legal (e.g., getting the other disputant arrested) and moral (e.g., portraying oneself in a favorable light) tasks (see Hirsch, 1998).

COPS, Technology, and Talk

In *COPS*, the viewer participates as an observer of police in a technologically mediated way. Viewers consume the final product of the mediation (technological, editorial) on TV; and as communication researchers and cultivation analysts have noted, television is one of the most ecological technological developments since it seeps into so many aspects of daily life (Gerbner et al., 1980). The nexus of *COPS*, technology, and language lies in the fact that the "medium" within the medium (TV) is language—talk. The technological innovation that makes television possible is not language or ideology but the video camera—another piece of technology; this is especially true for *COPS*, for without it, the "live" and realistic aspect of police work could not be captured. Video cameras, like the audio tape recorder, have influenced how researchers conduct their business. In *COPS*, language and technology intersect in two ways.

In the first, and as already noted, language is seen as a type of technological apparatus, a machine of sorts. Sacks (1984: 413) first asserted the cog-like character of language, talk, and conversation: "naturally occurring talk can be subjected to analysis that will yield the technology of conversation…we are trying to find this technology out of actual fragments of conversation." In Sacks' view, conversation is technology-like, but in a concrete and material sense, it is not. Beach (1990: 198) notes the mechanical character of talk when he uses videotape recordings of focus group meetings; the question he asks is related in a technology-like way: "how…does the work of language as technology, in a technological occasion, get accomplished?" In this view, although language is still the primary unit of analysis, the role of technology is still secondary, "occasioned."

In the second, technology is not only "occasioned," but implicative. Technology here is not linked to the abouts of the occasion, but the means— technological mediums such as video recorders, audio recorders, and computers. The key distinction between the two points is that in the first, technology is metaphorical; in the second, it is material. That is, there are actual computers, and video recorders and these are somehow relevant—sequentially implicative—to the talk at hand. The main question in this view is: how does technology configure in the production and "coordination" of conversation? That is, technology is not metaphorical but constitutive: the work it does in talk is sequential and procedural. In other words, technology is not a neutral medium that objectively records and facilitates interaction, but it influences, shapes, and changes the trajectory of the interaction—"procedurally consequential" (Schegloff, 1992b). This "procedural consequentiality" of technology is displayed in turns, more specifically, in the "delivery and receipt of talk"—in the line by line, turn by turn, and utterance by utterance organization of conversation (Heritage and Watson, 1980). For example, in doctor-patient clinical interviews, the patient orients his/her turn to the doctor's actions with the computer. Patients withhold their turn while the doctor is entering the prior turn's information into the computer; patients begin their turn at talk when they perceive that the doctor is near completion or finished with data entry (Heath and Luff, 2000). And this turn taking organization, much like ordinary conversation, is accomplished endogenously, in an orderly manner, sequentially, in context. The computers in these interactions are not just a technological medium; they interact in the doctor-patient visits implicatively in the next turn for the next speaker. Conversation analysts and ethnomethodologists who study language and technology all examine this implicative link between the two, in medical settings (Heath and Luff, 2000; Heath and Watson, 1989), focus group meetings (Beach, 1990), air traffic control (Heath and Luff, 2000), police communication system (Benson, 1992; Whalen, 1995), computers (Greatbatch, Heath, Luff, and Campion, 1995), architecture (Heath and Luff, 2000), news-rooms (Heath and Luff, 2000), and control-rooms of an underground railroad (Heath and Luff, 1996). In all these settings, talk unfolds and interacts in the context of technological work mediated by a technological medium.

As this set of questions pertains to *COPS*, the logical question to ask is: "how is technology implicative for talk in *COPS*?" I stated that technology (editing) cannot affect the internal structure of narratives in *COPS*, for to do so would make the product unrecognizable for what it purports to be, a story. The second question pertains to the medium within the medium. How does the video recorder relate to the business of implicativeness in *COPS*? I have already implicitly provided an answer: *the viewer participates as an observer of police in a technologically mediated way, as nonpresent recipients and consumers of talk.* The answer to the second question lies in the word participation.

There are four distinct recipients of talk in *COPS*: citizens/witnesses, suspects, police officers (including supervisory personnel), and the viewing audience. In other words, the communicative structure of *COPS* is not a simple dyadic exchange between speaker and hearer. This is a point Goffman (1981: 137) observes about talk in general: "an utterance does not carve up the world beyond the speaker into precisely two parts...but rather opens up an array of structurally differentiated possibilities, establishing participation framework in which the speaker will be guiding his delivery."

Simply put, *COPS* is not a single event. It is contextually shaped by different recipient design and participant structure, in relation to utterances, and the performer and audience (Goodwin, 1986). *Recipient design* can be defined as a "multitude of respects in which talk by a party in a conversation is constructed or designed in ways which display an orientation and sensitivity to the particular other(s) who are the co-participants" (Sacks et al., 1974: 727). A related idea is Goffman's (1981: 3) notion of *participation framework*: "when a word is spoken, all those who happen to be in perceptual range of the event will have some sort of participation status relative to it." As Goodwin (1990:10) iterates, participant frameworks "align participants toward each other in specific ways...and this process is central to the way in which activities provide resources for constituting social organization within face-to-face interaction." Consequently, although we may be situated in a conversation, we may not necessarily be direct participants, ones to whom talk is addressed; the talk may be addressed to someone else; we may merely be bystanders (over-hearers) to the talk—"unratified" to participate.

For Goffman (1981) not only do participants in a conversation have the possibility of being "bystanders" to others' talk, but they can also, in a way, be bystanders to their own. Goffman's notion of *footing* refers to the fact that, sometimes, speakers are not the true persons (principal) behind their words: "A change in footing implies a change in the alignment we take up to ourselves and the others present as expressed in the way we manage the production or reception of an utterance. A change in our footing is another way of talking about a change in our frame of events" (Goffman, 1981: 128). For instance, a speaker may simply physically articulate words (animator), without having composed them (author). These three concepts form Goffman's *production format* and also illustrate the fact that a speaker's role/identity is not static but continually crafted in the speaking moments, in relation to co-present speakers and in relation to our own utterances (Matoesian, 2001).

That language can be used to describe itself (e.g., one's own utterances) and events in the world illustrates another function of language, the poetic function (Jakobson, 1960). The reflexive capacity of language to refer to itself makes it possible to highlight, dramatize, and emotionally charge a message, to draw attention to itself for rhetorical effect, in addition to its content transmission (Matoesian, 2001: 38; Lucy, 1993). As an example, when a woman who has been battered by her husband tells the responding officer, "He hit me. He hit me on my face, he hit me on my stomach, and he hit me when I was down," the apparent victim does more than just communicate the message that her husband assaulted her. In this woman's account, she formulates her account in a structurally similar—parallel—pattern (he hit me + [in my face], [on my stomach], [when I was down]); and by superimposing her message through poetic and stylistic devices such as parallelism and repetition, the victim is able to foreground and punctuate the batterer's culpability by rhythmically listing the charges in incrementally posed categories of gravity. That is, he hits her on the most visible part of her body, her face, then her stomach—while standing up; and he hits her even when she is down, defenseless and most vulnerable. In form, then, the battered woman "emphasizes and dramatizes" the content of her message, and in the process, she discursively constructs her husband's identity as a malicious batterer, and poetically impeaches his moral character.

As the quadratic communicative structure configures in *COPS*, there are moments in the episode when the officer primarily addresses the audience: they become the "ratified participants" (Goffman, 1981). Consider the following example of a narrative that an officer provides for the viewers at home:

Excerpt 15 (*COPS* data: Jimmy Dean)
147 The scales digital scale the baggies (the weed) uh right now
148 right now looks like we got packaging material digital scales
149 in there looks like he's been selling uh dime bag
150 marijuana from here there's enough marijuana here
151 to charge him with felony possession with intent
152 they put it on there weight it out cut it up separate
153 it then bag it and they'll sell ten dollar increments
154 what he looks like he has right now

In excerpt 15, the viewing audience enters into a direct speaker-listener relationship with the narrating officer. The officer is narrating to the viewers at home as he is searching a suspect's car. When the officer questions, interviews, or interrogates citizens, witnesses, or suspects, the audience becomes unratified—indirect—participants (bystanders) while the speakers on the show become ratified—primary—participants. When officers talk to each other, their patrol supervisor, or concludes the encounter by giving a summary to the audience, the participant structure changes again. When police officers talk with one another, the citizens, suspects, and the viewing audience become "eavesdroppers" on their conversation. Consider the following account that an officer formulates for his fellow officers on scene:

Excerpt 16 (*COPS* data: Jimmy Dean)
122 PO: Looks like we have a domestic assault um possibly
123   provoked by him but looks like right now mutual
124   combat and it looks like there's a little uh marijuana
125   involved also from the description she gave me
126   I saw the possible bag in the car in his truck
127   also apparently he attacked her for him moving his stuff
128   out that apparently belonged to her and uh she her
129   statement was that she bit him to get him off of her
130   okay that's what we have right now

When police officers address the camera, the viewing audience at home, other officers and citizens and suspects become bystanders to the talk between the narrating officer and the viewing audience. In other words, recipient design and participant structure—whom the current speakers and listeners are—are structurally implicative for the way narratives are organized and enacted in talk (Duranti, 1997).

Recipient design is not only structurally implicative but sequentially so. Depending on who the recipient is, talk is reformulated so as to meet the situational and recipient exigencies. The sequential implicativeness of narratives on *COPS* is displayed not on a turn by turn basis but within a turn: what topics are introduced, if introduced at all, how topics are placed and varied within a turn, and how topics are grammatically crafted with the invisible audience in mind are all managed within a single extended turn. But these conversational features are not preordained but produced locally, in the context of performing, managing, and settling disputes, traffic stops, and other assignments—in situ.

COPS is a valuable source of data precisely because it allows access to such a diverse array of talk, from lexical level utterances to extended narratives and single turn units to multi-turn sequences. Moreover, the interactions between the police and citizens are embedded in multilayered—across several time periods, contexts, speakers and listeners—participation frameworks. Thus, depending on the researchers' choice of primary unit of analysis, the analytical goal and method of analysis will vary. For instance, for those who wish to narrow their unit of analysis to lexical items, address terms that citizens and police officers use toward one another during their talk may be one of the ways deference and demeanor can be studied. Those who wish to examine the turn taking and preference organization of P-C encounters may find it worthwhile to study the sequential structure of conversations between the police and the public. And for those who are interested in examining how participants in a domestic dispute allocate and deflect blame, and portray themselves in a morally favorable light, the descriptive and pragmatic structure and function of their extended narratives may be a way to attain that goal. *COPS*, as a research site, is only limited by the creative and analytical vision of future researchers.

Conclusion

In this chapter, I have introduced basic conversation analytic terms that underlie the assumptions behind this study. Concepts such as *turn taking, adjacency pairs, preference, sequential implicativeness*, and *repair* operate not only in ordinary talk but also in institutional ones, such as the ones between the police and the public. Moreover, from a linguistic and sociological standpoint, I have provided a rationale for examining the talk between the police and citizens apart from the relevant police literature. In other words, taking a linguistic turn in police-citizen encounter research is warranted not only according to the criteria set by prior police researchers, but independent of them.

The rest of the chapters to follow offer a gross view of talk between the police and citizens. That is, I examine how concepts such as *turn taking, adjacency pairs, preference, sequential implicativeness*, and *repair* operate and are embodied in the talk between actual police officers and citizens.

Notes

1. Schegloff (1988b: 61) drives this point home: "it is clear that temporality and sequentiality are inescapable; utterances are in turns, and turns are parts of sequences; sequences and the projects done through them enter constitutively into utterances like the warp in a woven fabric."

2. These two methodological points, memory and interpretation, will be addressed in greater detail in chapter 2, as they pertain to the nature of the data.

CHAPTER 2
DATA AND METHODOLOGY
Data Collection and Data Analysis

For this study, I use twenty P-C encounters as they appeared on the reality-based TV show *COPS*, ranging from traffic stops to domestic disputes for data. These encounters were recorded on video and audio tapes. This study also uses twenty actual audio-recorded P-C encounters, mainly traffic stops. These data were made available to me for secondary analysis by officer "Clean Harry" of "Midwest City" Police Department and Officer "Hebert" of "Southern City" Police Department.[1] All of the recorded P-C encounters—mass mediated and actual ones—were transcribed. In chapters 3, 4, and 5, where the data are analyzed and findings presented, P-C encounters which appeared on *COPS* are noted as "*COPS* data." They are followed by a topical phrase that provides an identifiable reference to the encounter that is being analyzed and discussed (e.g., *COPS* data: Jimmy Dean). The actual P-C encounters—traffic stops—are identified as "X city police" + traffic stop #. In addition to the two data sources, I use excerpts of conversations between officers and citizens that other police researchers in prior works have captured. These excerpts, which are buried in footnotes and appendixes (i.e., John van Maanen), and several P-C conversations that are well known in other non-police related works (i.e., Dr. Poussaint), which have remained unanalyzed as data in their own right, are also used for data in this study.

Before I analyze what police officers and citizens actually say to one another in the mass-mediated P-C encounters, I will show how an encounter is organized and framed, and the linguistic work that is performed in it (chapter 3). After I have shown how P-C encounters on *COPS* are structurally and segmentally organized, I will compare them to actual P-C encounters to demonstrate that the structure of language found in mass-mediated P-C encounters on TV is recognizably identical to actual ones. After I have done that, I will analyze the varieties of calls that patrol officers on *COPS* respond to and settle.

Description of the Data

In recent years the fictional nature of TV police officers has slowly been waning: in the name of authentic and realistic programming versions of fictional police have appeared. These figures that have emerged are not the products of a creative and imaginative writer, but real police officers performing their duties. I am referring to the TV show *COPS*. As the first of its kind to blend entertainment and reality, *COPS* purports to show what policing is really like, as seen and experienced by actual police officers. Consequently, there are no actors on the show: it shows the "men and women of law enforcement" responding to actual calls for service, chasing suspected drug dealers, burglars, and petty thieves, in their squad cars and on foot. Moreover, the show does not neglect to air the more mundane and routine assignments that are common in police-work, such as domestic disturbances, disputes between neighbors, and even the occasional snake in the backyard.

The authentic flavor of *COPS* is achieved by the presence of a cameraman who accompanies officers throughout their patrol shift and faithfully records their actions; some of the things that the camera captures and shows are not found in fictional programs. For example, not all police officers who appear on *COPS* embody the idealized images of masculinity and police work. Furthermore, *COPS* captures and shows the actual words that officers, citizens, and suspects speak: speech errors, impromptu retorts, improvised accounts, ad hoc formulations, profanity, and confusion are just too much like ordinary conversations (and police work) to be scripts.

One warrantable question that could be raised in the use of *COPS* as data is that it is edited. In this regard readers may pose a quite legitimate issue: *Isn't COPS edited for TV? Don't the editors slice and cut raw footage to show what they want to show?* Readers are warranted in raising these points; but what skeptics and critics might find disagreeable about using *COPS* for data is that it is an edited product, told from a particular view, created by someone with a vested interest. That vested interest is commercial, driven by prospects for higher rating, hence, financial gain, not by a desire to pursue truth and knowledge. Simply put, *COPS* is neither impartial nor natural data.

Using an edited program such as *COPS* differs from other televisual data, such as video recordings of news and talk show programs. There are other conversation analysts, ethnomethodologists, sociolinguists, and linguistic anthropologists who study discourse as it appears on television (Clayman, 1992, 1989; Greatbatch, 1992; Gruber, 1998; Hutchby, 1998), and on video (Duranti, 1997; Heath and Luff, 2000). "Their [reporters] work practices are commonly broadcast "live" without the benefit of editorial review, and are thus open to the immediate scrutiny of fellow journalists, government officials, social scientists, and a mass audience…accordingly, news interviewers continually face the problem of sustaining the accountability of their conduct under widespread scrutiny" (Clayman, 1992: 163-164). The problem of editing, as it relates to my work, is precisely that. *COPS* is editorially reviewed, cut, and sliced as the editor desires, and it is not open to immediate scrutiny. Hence, this study is similar to other works in that the source of the data originates from a common medium (television), but the editing process and the product's immediate unavailability differentiates *COPS* from other television programs which are used for data.

The problem of editing, showing reduced and partial version of events in its entirety, and using that edited product for data may appear troublesome. But this "problem" is not necessarily as relevant as might be thought for a language-oriented project such as the present one, and can be further illustrated from a similar study. Maynard and Manzo (1993: 171) used a video taped recording of an actual jury deliberation, which lasted about 21/2 hours, to study how juries "define and use the concept" of justice; that same jury deliberation was "reduced and edited" for a one hour television program (*Frontline*). Consider the following excerpt from Maynard and Manzo's (1993: 178) data:

Excerpt1 (12: 59:01)
> Juror#3: Okay, I feel that the defendant is guilty uh on all three accusations technically. But I guess I feel that we should also take into consideration the fact that he does have a reading disability, as well as maybe some other disabilities. I'm not trying to play on your sympathies or anything but it is something that I have to consider and right now I haven't determined whether I should name the defendant guilty or innocent.

Maynard and Manzo (1993) were interested in discovering how jurors used the notion of justice as a "situated" and "practical" phenomenon to socially organize their perceptions about the defendant in their deliberations. Thus, rather than using justice as an abstract and theoretical category, they sought to examine how that concept embodied and emerged in the concrete and fine-grained details of the jurors' talk. That is, how the order of justice was locally produced by the jurors themselves within the context of their deliberation via talk.

Although the temporal order of jurors' turns was varied, when the entire tape was compared to the edited one, their accounts remained the same.[2] It is that "internal order" of conversations and accounts that police officers, citizens, and suspects give to one another—independent from the occasion itself—that constitutes a valid source of data in its own right. Consider the following two excerpts from P-C encounters, one from *COPS* and the other from an actual encounter:

Excerpt 2 (Midwest City Police Traffic Stop #2)
15   D: my insurance I got off my other car
16   I just bought this vehicle
17   (.)
18   PO: how long ago did you buy it?
19   (.7)

```
20  D:   about 2 days now (.6) here's the insurance
21       (2.0)
```

Excerpt 3 (*COPS* data: "Games")
```
129     PO1:     What was the last address you lived at?
130              (.8)
131       BM:    My last address?
132              (1.0)
134     PO1:     Where do you get mail?
135              (.8)
136     BM:      I don't really get mail...
```

In excerpt 2, a "real" P-C encounter, a police officer (PO) questions a motorist (D) about the ownership of the car; the PO is checking to make sure that the car is not stolen. In excerpt 3, a P-C encounter on *COPS*, an officer questions a possible suspect (BM) about his living arrangements. Had I not identified the sources of the data, I imagine it would be nearly impossible for readers to discern the origins of the verbal data. In both excerpts, the talk is sequentially organized and orderly: one party speaks at a time (turn taking), turns at talk are interactionally managed at transition relevant places (turn transition), and the first pair part projects the relevant response in the next turn (sequential implicativeness; conditional relevance); that is one party asks a question (line 18, line 134), the other provides an answer (line 20, line 136). When one party (BM) does not understand the preceding talk, or encounters trouble in talk, that problematic source is repaired through repetition and clarification (line 131).

The readers would find the two excerpts difficult to differentiate because there is no difference. Examined in terms of its discourse structures—turn taking, sequential organization, repair mechanism—the two are exactly alike. Talk is talk whether it occurs in "real" life, on television, or radio because conversations, as a social activity, have a formal and structural character that is independent from its occasion and setting (Schegloff, 1984a). The talk between the police and citizens on *COPS* is coherent—follows the patterns of language—because as discourse it is governed by rules of language production and use, not rules of editing; hence, the verbal accounts and sequences of talk are orderly.

Validity and the Politics of Data Collection and Data Analysis

There are two broad methods of conducting research in P-C encounters, quantitative and qualitative. In quantitative studies, a researcher goes on ridealongs with the police, makes observations about officers' encounters with the public, and then codes the behavior of cops and citizens alike into coding sheets. For example, researchers (in the Balesian tradition) code—reduce—citizens' behaviors into categories such as *polite, impolite, hostile, friendly* and so on. Results of the coding are the observers' impressions and characterizations: it is the their interpretation of the cues that influence how the encounter will be classified. In essence, then, the products of coding are not the action proper of the citizens but the observers' interpretations. Stated in a resounding vocabulary of modals, Bayley (1986: 332) admits "this required a judgment on their part and may have caused some of the richness of the police response to be lost." And as Schegloff (1996: 166) echoes, ignoring "acts" (in this case the spoken words during the P-C encounter) "leaves actual recorded conduct as a kind of scientific detritus." In quantitative police research, the observation process is, from the beginning, filtered through and colored by, the subjective judgment of the coder. Now, consider the following encounter that an officer recounts:

Excerpt 4 (Baker, 1985: 21)
I was on my first post. A young fellow walked up to me—he had his load on— and made some snide remark to me. I deflected it. He came back again and made some very personal remark about my family and I started to ignore that, too. I looked around and I was aware that everybody was watching me. I realized that if I didn't make this situation in hand right away, there would be nothing but I could accomplish.

I pretended to walk past him, but before I had gotten by, I kneed him right in the balls and dropped him to the ground. I picked him up gently, very gently, sat him on the stoop and walked away.

I never had a problem on that post. I didn't beat him up or leave any scars. I didn't enjoy it. I didn't put myself in a situation where people would feel I was getting my rocks off. I just made my point. I had given him the opportunity to get his rocks off and leave. He didn't take it and that was that.

This excerpt illustrates the role of a citizen's demeanor on the outcome of the P-C encounter. Had a researcher accompanied the officer above on his post and witnessed the citizen's behavior, s/he most likely would have coded the citizen's behavior as "hostile," "unfriendly," and "antagonistic." A researcher who might have conducted a field observation would capture detailed notes such as excerpt 4. An ethnographic account like the one provided above provides readers with more detailed information about the encounter than merely classifying behavior into pre-classified coding schemes. That is, this type of qualitative approach is more interactional than the quantitative methods. Instead of merely offering a category of demeanor (a label), this excerpt provides the contextual details of the interaction; furthermore, it captures the emergent nature of the categorization process. The citizen makes a snide remark, the officer "deflects" it, and when he makes another personal remark about the officer's family— challenges and disrespects the officer's authority—the officer sanctions him with physical punishment.

Generally, qualitative research is more interactional and process-oriented than quantitative ones; it broadly captures the emergent character of demeanor:

with their primary emphasis on the cultural background of language use, the ethnographers of communication generally have not developed analyses that combine a focus on the organization of specific sequences in social interaction with a treatment of the understandings and practical reasoning that inform these sequences and are engendered by them (Drew and Heritage, 1992: 16).

The accounts ethnographers offer are rich in descriptions. However, they do not necessarily capture the depth and detail of interactional practices because the interaction itself is preinterpreted by the ethnographer. For instance, in excerpt 4, readers get a detailed description of what happened, but after a certain point, the account, too, becomes subjectively impressionistic. What exact words did the citizen use in his "snide remark?" How did he say it? Was it loud, raised in tone and stress? Moreover, what is involved in "deflecting" such a snide remark? What are the exact contents of "personal remark about my family?" How did he say it? How did the citizen escalate the encounter through his self-initiated encounter? What exactly is 'starting to ignore'? How does that unfold, and in what sequential context?[3]

In order for researchers to make objective coding classifications, they must first observe the interaction between officers and citizens and make a judgement as to what instance of categorial behavior they witnessed. Simply put, it is the researcher's sole interpretation of observed events that lay at the bedrock of objectivity (see Garfinkel, 1967: 76-103). All the hours of training in observing and coding, multivariate and regression analyses only make it look as if coding as a method were objective when in essence the entire procedure is subjective—subjective objectivity (see Maynard and Schaeffer, 2000). Underneath all quantification lies the inevitable work of interpretation and judgement—*ab initio*. To counter this assertion, quantitative researchers could introduce the notion of coder interreliability, meaning that several researchers observed and coded the same phenomenon independently of each other. But again, this involves the same interpretive process; this time several people do it and the authority and objectivity arises not from the rigorous adherence to protocol but from counting heads.

In qualitative police research, ethnographers ride along with police officers on their beats, and instead of using a coding sheet, they carry a small notebook and record the happenings during a patrol shift (see Herbert, 1996a; Muir, 1977; Rubinstein, 1973). The fieldnotes are developed into full narratives after they are finished with the observation; they then look for themes and patterns in the notes and finally, construct a coherent narrative. In police ethnographies it is impossible to record everything that goes on. Second, the very act of note taking arouses suspicion from the subjects of the study; hence, the subjects are not likely to act as they "ordinarily" would (van Maanen, 1978b). Therefore, researchers are reluctant to write at length during ride-alongs. Usually, they jot down brief notations and key phrases that will later jog their memory when the time comes to write a detailed version.[4] Third, full narratives are never developed on the spot during the observation; ethnographers have to wait until they get home. Memory and diligence then are warrantable threats to validity. Finally, in both quantitative and qualitative studies of demeanor in extant police studies, the researcher's impressions of the encounters between officers and citizens serve as the basis of data description, collection, and analysis (Maynard, 1989):

The audience only have access to the researcher's necessarily selective and incomplete descriptions of what went on in a setting, and to his additional analytic interpretations of the described events, which, in that they have to be described prior to any analytic comments, have already been organized by his
own descriptive work. Readers and hearers of ethnographic reports are therefore totally dependent on the researcher's descriptive competences both for
what they get to know (and not to know) about the data, and for their understanding of the analyses of the things they get to know about from the report
(i.e. the 'data analysis'), just as the researcher had also depended on them in
getting to the final writing-up stage of the research. For the ethnographer, then,
the problem of coming to terms with the ethnomethodological constraint
against the unexplicated reliance on members' competences in doing research
is particularly acute (Atkinson and Drew, 1979: 25).

Both quantitatively and qualitatively oriented scholars could raise the point
that the methods I have advocated—using members' own descriptions and actions as data—"only postpones the judgements that must be made, transferring
them to a later place and time, and perhaps affording those not *in situ* to offer
their judgements."[5] The word 'judgement' is used twice in the preceding sentence, but the work it does in the sentence is quite different. 'Judgement' in the
first part of the sentence refers to interpretive—descriptive, representational—
judgements about the data; this usage illustrates the coding problem that I have
been discussing; that is, researchers must first make an interpretive judgement as
to how to classify the phenomenon that they observed. The second occurrence of
that same word later in the sentence appears to do the same work since "sooner
or later, those 'verbatim' representations must be reduced to something resem-
bling the 'impressions' of field observers that have been recorded in detailed
narratives and coded protocols prepared later at the research office."[6] In other
words, 'judgement' in the second part of the sentence is like the former one, an
interpretive one, since the only thing that recordings do is delay interpretation of
the observed (now recorded) phenomenon. But conversation analysts, ethnomethodologists, sociologists of talk, and linguistic anthropologists rarely argue about 'judgements' in an interpretive, descriptive, and representational
sense because the data are publicly available for inspection by all researchers,
including professional analysts and lay people (Hutchby, 1996; Sacks, 1992).

For analysts who use video and audio recordings of social encounters for
data, the judgement is usually not about the accuracy of the representation of the
phenomenon captured on the medium, but analytical. Simply put, the representation rarely has analytical or political consequences. The second 'judgement' in
the sentence works in that way, as an analytical judgment, one that is up for debate, open to criticism, disagreement, and persuasion—political. For analysts
who use the methods I use in this study, the "rawness" of the data is rarely dis-
puted. The video and audio recordings are, in a sense, unmediated, authentic,
and "real": there is seldom a dispute about representational judgements because
the data are available for all to see and describe, not just one person (Silverman,
1998).[7] Hence, availability and repeatability of data sidesteps a historical constraint of ethnography (Sacks, 1992). When disputes arise amongst sociologists
of talk the judgement is an entirely analytical one, which just means that judge-

ments are political, but not political in the representational sense. And the quantitative police scholar who makes such a criticism against verbatim representations does so because he or she conflates—confuses—an analytic activity with a representational one. Furthermore, he or she confuses politics with something else.

There is one more move or question that a quantitatively minded scholar can raise: don't analytical judgements also require interpretation? The answer would be an unequivocal yes. But interpretation in relation to what? Analytical interpretations of data and disagreements about them are what academics do, and those disagreements constitute the discipline (see Fish, 1980). If scholars were able to make infallible analytical interpretations, (1) they would be Superscholars in a divine sense (2) they would no longer be scholars in the human sense. And (3) much to the chagrin of the academic community, there would no longer be an academic community and advancements, except the one or few scholars whose scholarship would be considered sacred, because there would be no disagreements and controversy.

All research—the analytical kind—no matter what one researches, who conducts it, and how one does it, is always and necessarily constrained by the problem of interpretation (Smith and Deemer, 2000). But that problem is not really a problem since it is the norm, not a deviation. Interpretation does not proceed from a groundless epicenter: judgements about a phenomenon do not begin with unmolested observations. Before one can judge, interpret, and assess, one must have something to interpret with because facts, data, and other phenomena in the world do not interpret themselves (see generally Fish, 1989, 1980, 1967). What make interpretations about phenomena and experiences possible are assumptions, premises, and presuppositions (see Lewis, 1948). All research is governed by assumptions; but it's just that those assumptions and dimensions of assessment are all held by those with a finite perspective, that is to say fallible, hence, limited, perspectival, biased, and vested with interest—edited (Schwandt, 2000). Simply put, there is no way around the problem of editing and interpretation, for nothing is ever raw, that is plainly visible; if things were self-evident, clearly held out for all to see—raw—then no interpretation would ever be necessary (Atkinson and Drew, 1979). All research involves editing and politics, with reference to analytic judgements—rhetoric—of some sorts, from the cutting room floors of a production room of a Hollywood studio to ivory towers and halls of the academy—all the way up.

A final argument could justifiably be made that running a tape recorder, a video camera, and/or the presence of a researcher with a notebook and pen—any observation—will influence the behavior of the subjects of the study, even talk itself. That is, the presence of a camera exerts an obtrusive effect: reactivity. The presence of a camera might (and does) lead to blatant camera behaviors such as "camera recognition salutations like staring into the camera and smiling" (Duranti, 1997: 118). However, as Duranti (1997: 118) states:

> People do not usually invent social behavior, language included, out of the
> blue. Rather, their actions are part of a repertoire that is available to them independently of the presence of a camcorder. One might even argue that the pres-

ence of the camera may be used as an excuse for certain types of social actions that might have been done anyhow like when people point to the camera to provide a reason to be polite or be generous. I believe that most of the people are too busy running their own lives to change them in substantial ways because of the presence of a new gadget.[8]

Likewise, ordinary citizens and police officers who appear on *COPS* have to initiate and close conversations; they have to take turns to achieve intersubjective understanding and produce social order. Moreover, they have to make their intentions known, make claims, counter those claims, negotiate, contest, and put themselves forward in order to go about living their ordinary and institutional lives, despite the presence of a camera. Ordinary people may be too busy running their own lives to change their behavior in substantial ways, but police officers do change their behavior in substantial ways, especially if those social acts are criminal. And this position, as it relates to observation, reactivity, and police work, leads to an "unsettling" notion of validity.

It would be naive to believe that the presence of observers will not have an effect on the behavior of subjects. While the effect may be difficult to measure, reactivity is an inevitable factor that is present in the participant-observation method (Leo, 1996a, b); both qualitative and quantitative research suffer from this dilemma. But how does the presence of the camera, the activity of observation itself, and the viewing audience affect talk itself, not only its content, but its structure?

A more general methodological question that is relevant to this study and the possible objections is: do observers have an intrusive effect on the subjects they study? The classical view—purist, positivistic, objective—of observation attempts to exclude the observers' moral, social, political, and emotional standpoint from the observation process. In the dialogic view—interactional, postmodern, empathic—of observation the observers' moral and political stance, their methods of documentation, and representation are included not only in the observation process but in the analysis. Consequently, observation is not a pure and distant activity conducted by neutral observers; it is a reflexive and collaborative project (Tedlock, 2000). Observation is generally defined as a data collection method in which the researcher "attempts to examine the activity of subjects while keeping her or his presence either a secret or to a minimum, so as not to interfere" (Hagan, 1997: 244-245). But is there a way that the police can be "naturally" observed? Is there a way to collect data that is free of bias and beset by the problem of reactivity?

The two types of observations, as they relate to police work, are based on a principle of exclusion and inclusion. Natural observation is another phrase for disinterested observation, one where subjects are not affected by the observer's presence. Although academics and researchers usually purport to neutrally observe, the subjects of their observation do not always share that belief (the problem of collusion). In this view, members of the subject population must be excluded as observers to accommodate the validity of the observation. A partisan observation is an observation conducted by a native, a member, someone with a vested interest; and as a result, reactivity is not a problem, but validity is (Angronsino and de Perez, 2000; Gubrium and Holstein, 1997). In this view, validity is excluded to include members.

In the explication of the two types of observations I provided above, there appears to be a tension between validity and reactivity as a consequence effected by the very activity of observation. But as I noted, the two definitions, as well as the definition of observation in general, assume behavior outside of observation. That assumption, however, is false, especially as it relates to police work, because patrol officers are never outside of observation: they are observed by citizens on the street; they are observed by patrol supervisors; they are watched by shift commanders for signs of activity; and they are observed by internal affairs and federal agencies (see Rubinstein, 1973). Most significantly, police officers are observed by other officers (Bayley and Garofalo, 1989; Muir, 1977). Simply put, police officers are already and always observed: there is no such thing as a "natural" observation, and "natural" activity, if by natural, the definition means disinterested, neutral, unmediated—objective. Neutral observation is a construct (Duranti, 1997). The principle of inclusion and exclusion, as they relate to reactivity and validity, then, is not really a problem at all since the problem is the norm for everyone who observes the police. The police are always, in one form or another, in front of someone's eyes or lens—*on* (see Goffman, 1959). The problem of reactivity then is not a categorical one (does it or does it not happen?) nor is it is a gradient one (how much?), but a categorial and an intentional one—who is observing and for what purpose? The only way to truly and authentically capture the behavior of subjects would be to do so in secret, which is not ethical or possible for academic researchers. There is no "reactivity-free" way to observe the police, in any way, shape, or form.

Transcript Symbols

Transcript symbols are used in CA in an effort to reproduce and capture the properties relevant to conversations (i.e., tone, pitch, intonation, interruptions). Readers who are familiar with transcription conventions will have noticed that there are always slight variations from author to author. For instance, Conley and O'Barr (1998) use a simplified version of the one originally developed by Gail Jefferson. They eliminate many "non-standard" English features that aren't relevant to the discussion. For the purposes of this work, I attempt to recapture the conversational details as much as possible, and will include those details when analytically relevant.

Simultaneous Utterances
Simultaneous utterances refer to utterances that begin at the same time. They are marked with brackets and equal signs at the beginning of the utterances.

Excerpt 5 (*COPS* Data: Jimmy Dean)
PO: Okay you have some ID?
BM: =[Mine's over there in my (van)

BW: =[Go check his truck cuz he's got weed in it

Latching (Contiguous) Utterances

Latching or contiguous utterances refer to talk that has no gap between two utterances:
Excerpt 6 (*COPS* Data: Naked Enough)

M: You have no reason to search me=you got no reason to touch me

Overlapping Utterances

A single left hand bracket indicates the point where first speaker's utterance starts to overlap with the second speaker's utterance. Right hand brackets are used to denote where the overlap ends.

Excerpt 7 (*COPS* Data: Naked Enough)
PO: Didn't you just tell me [you didn't have a wallet?
M: [You have no reason to search me

Timed and Untimed Intervals

Intervals between utterances can be timed and noted in parentheses for those that are in seconds and tenths of seconds. A period enclosed by parentheses (.) indicates that the interval is a tenth of a second or less, not measurable.

Excerpt 8 (*COPS* Data: Games)
PO: Why you have all these tools if it's just laying in an open lot?
        (.9)
S: Cuz

Characteristics of Utterances (volume, stress, prolongation, rapid delivery)

To indicate utterances that are louder than normal tone of voice, capital letters are used. Underlining is used to indicate a word or a phrase that is emphasized or stressed. And to indicate sounds, especially vowels, that are stretched or prolonged, colons are used; the more colons used, the longer the sound. To indicate utterances that are articulated at a faster than normal pace, "greater than" and "less than" signs are used.

Excerpt 9 (Matoesian, 1993: 54-55)
DA: WERE THE ITEMS
DA: WHY:::
DA: Did he force you to get in- to his automobe:::; in the parking lot?

DA: <u>WHAT HE WAS ABOUT</u> >except that he was good looking<

Excerpt 10 (*COPS* Data: Driving a Baby)
PO: FEMALE PUT YOUR HANDS UP
PO: Where'd you get the car mae::ing?

Excerpt 11 (*COPS* Data: Games)
PO: <u>And that thing's just cut</u>

Excerpt 12 (Midwest City Police Traffic Stop #2)
PO: How you doin >see your driver's license en proof of insurance?<

Other Transcription Conventions

Difficulties in the transcription, such as inaudible and indecipherable utterances, are enclosed in parentheses. To give descriptions of physical actions during the course of a talk, double parentheses are used.

Excerpt 13 (*COPS* Data: Naked Man)

PO: What's goin on man ((officer puts his hand on his weapon))

Speaker Designation

In a courtroom a speaker's identity is designated "officially" by the institution itself. For example (Matoesian, 1993: 55-56):
Judge = J
Victim = V
Defendant = D
Defense Attorney = DA
Prosecuting Attorney = PA
Witnesses = W

To an extent, this is also true in P-C encounters in general and on *COPS*. Obviously, police officers convey their institutional identity and affiliation through uniforms, badges, guns, and their marked police cruisers. Hence, designating police officers as speakers is quite simple:
PO = police officer
If there is more than one police officer present on the scene, they are designated by the order in which they speak:
PO1 = police officer # 1
PO2 = police officer # 2
PO3 = police officer # 3
Designating the other speakers' identities is a bit more problematic since citizens, witnesses, suspects, and other directly involved parties in P-C encounters wear no visible markings and carry no overt signs of their identities. More-

over, it is those very identities that are ascribed, negotiated, contested, and accomplished through talk during moments of talk with the police.

Sacks (1992) first observed that the way people refer to each other in talk is organized into collections (Pn adequacy). Once a person has been categorized by members as X (e.g., doctor), that same person can also be referred to as Y (e.g., mother, Asian, etc.). Simply put, why is one term chosen over an equally available and appropriate one? Schegloff (1992b: 108) refers to this dilemma as the *problem of relevance*: "Some principle of relevance must underlie use of a reference term, and has to be adduced in order to provide for one rather than another of those ways of characterizing some member." For example, in one of the episodes on *COPS* ("Games"), an officer receives a call about a man who may have committed a burglary, and as he is approaching the scene, he witnesses a black male who is pushing a water heater down the street. Now, there are numerous ways to designate the man's speaker identity: he could be designated as a burglar (B), a male (M), black male (BM), a citizen (C), a guy wearing an overcoat (GO), a suspect (S) etc. Out of all these possible choices, is there a principled way to go about designating the speaker's identity?

Schegloff (1991: 50) proposes two solutions to such a problem. In the first, the way to "warrant one is the success of the way of characterizing them in producing a professionally acceptable account of the data being addressed." Thus, a uniformed police officer who sees a black man pushing a water heater down the street at two o'clock in the morning can be operationalized as an encounter between a police officer and a burglar, or at best, a suspected one, since the officer receives a call about a commercial burglary in which a man is seen leaving the business pushing a hot water heater in a cart. In this solution the context's obviousness guides the designation process.

The second solution to the problem of relevance would be to characterize (designate) the participants in a way that is most relevant for the participants, at that moment. It should be kept in mind that the black man's identity/role as a possible burglar is precisely what is at stake, especially for him. And in the "Games" example I just discussed, it would too analytically presumptive to merely designate the speaker's identity 'burglar' to the black male who is seen walking down the street with the allegedly stolen items in tow. The goal of a CA oriented analysis would be to show how that identity emerges from the details of the talk itself. Thus, throughout this work, speakers' identities are designated on grossly general and identifiable characteristics, such as gender: male (M), female (W); ethnicity and race: black (B), Hispanic (H), white (W) Asian (A) etc., and other gross features: driver of a car (D). Of course, this is not to say that gender and ethnicity is the overriding variable that is affecting the outcome of the encounter. Race, ethnicity, and gender may or may not shape how the contour of the talk itself unfolds; but that would have to be empirically shown in the analysis, first through the participants' own turn and sequential organization and, second, through the analysis (Moerman, 1988). And for me to offer a definite speaker category prior to any empirical expatiation would violate the central precepts of my presuppositions about a phenomenon; hence, I try to be as unmotivated and faithful to the members' own descriptions, doings, and designations as possible by withholding that category till they have produced it themselves.[9]

Limitations of the Data and Analytical Aim

A possible and warrantable limitation of the data presented here that I have excluded from my analysis is gestures, gazes, and other physical acts that occur during the course of a talk. These are possible topics of analysis in their own right; and other researchers routinely do use physical gestures and gazes as units of analysis in relation to talk (see Duranti, 1997; Heath and Luff, 2000; Schegloff, 1984b). However, it's just that I have not included it in this study, for that would have taken the study in unwanted—not unjustified—directions. These limitations, perhaps, could be filled in by other researchers who are interested in examining those types of things. For this work, the aim is linguistic.

Notes

1. It should be noted that both names are pseudonyms.

2. I am grateful to Doug Maynard for this point.

3. A sequential level analysis of utterances is important precisely because intention and meaning make sense only in their sequential context. That is, words are uttered in relation to a previous one—procedural, historical—and make sense only when the totality of the speech context is taken into consideration (see Schegloff, 1968; Schegloff and Sacks, 1973).

4. For a discussion of the problem of collusion that arises in police ethnography, see Herbert, (1996a); van Maanen, (1978b).

5. The quantitative scholar I've quoted in this footnote is a well-known scholar in police-citizen encounter research. The quote comes from the review of a paper that I submitted to a reputable journal in the field. Although the reviewer's methodological orientation is never explicitly stated in the review itself, from the criticisms s/he offers and assumptions s/he holds, his/her methodological orientation is obvious.

6. This sentence occurs just before the sentence I used in the preceding footnote by the same reviewer.

7. It could be argued that the point I make here is tantamount to something like methodological "fanaticism" since I appear to preclude the possibility of disagreements that might arise over the representation and analysis of the data. It could also be stated that the claims I make are rather strong, and possibly, inaccurate, since two people disagree about the very same things they have witnessed. This observation would be true if my claims were merely methodological and epistemological since two individuals could observe the same phenomenon and come to an entirely different interpretation of what they perceived as a function of their presupposed first premise, not as a function of different methodologies and ways of knowing (Fish, 1967). So far, ethnography and video-recordings are on the same epistemological plane.

My rather strongly worded critique of observation-based research, including quantitative ones, is not epistemological but metaphysical and ontological. A researcher who uses coding sheets and an ethnographer who uses pen and paper faces a similar constraint: they have one chance at observation. Once a phenomenon has occurred, there can be no arguments about the validity of representations because the constitutive moment of interpretation belongs solely to the present researcher/observer. With video and audio recordings, however, it is possible to disagree, challenge, and contest the validity of the representations because the moment is reproducible; the interpretive moment does not belong solely to one researcher. This means that recorded phenomenon can be played ad nauseam, possibly until the captured reality begins to take on a reality of its own (Baudrillard, 1988). Thus, the invention of audio and video technology effectuates an ontological and a metaphysical—not epistemological—difference between traditional ethnography and video recordings (Sacks, 1992; Schegloff, 1989).

The methodological consequences brought about by the transformation in ontology vis-a-vis technology highlights another interpretive process prior to the one assumed by members of the criminological community. Again, disagreements over data and inferred conclusions about them are what constitute the academic disciplines (Fish, 1980). We might call this *analytic interpretation*. These types of interpretations lie at the center of debates in various disciplines and have significant intellectual (political) consequences. No academic discipline is immune from this condition.

The interpretive activity that actually precedes this one might be termed *representational interpretation*. But this type of interpretation is possible only because of the existence of technology—the ability to suspend reality for indefinite periods; an anthropologist who studied exotic peoples in a far away land a century ago need not worry about this type of interpretation because his/her observations and impressions would form the foundation of his/her representation; and we would find this initial interpretive move—representation—in the form of fieldnotes. However, there would be no way for anyone to contest and challenge those representations (fieldnotes) because there is no way to verify the researcher's observations. We would just have to take his/her word for it; and that is the key difference between ethnography and video/audio recordings; with the latter, we do not have to settle for the researcher's word because the availability of the phenomenon (and data) prior to representation adds another dimension to interpretation, one that is just not possible in the former. This *essence* of the criterion that differentiates observational data from technologically mediated ones—availability—is ontological and metaphysical, not epistemological.

8. Ian Hutchby (1996) makes the same argument about his source of data (talk radio) and analysis. He argues that the shows would have gone on with or without his recordings. The same argument could be made for the presence of the camera in police-citizen encounters: cops and citizens still have to get through their encounters, with or without the presence of a camera. Of course, as I argue, the presence of the camera and viewing audience does affect talk in noticeable ways.

9. Designating or labeling speakers in transcripts has never appeared to be a problem in CA thus far. Throughout the CA literature, we see a variety of ways speakers are labeled: by name (e.g., Marsha), institutional roles (e.g., police officer, therapist etc.), and letters (e.g., A, B, etc.). There has been little discussion about the implications of such speaker designations, because, there is thought to be none. In CA, the designations are thought to be secondary to what is actually "going on" between speakers. However, Billig (1999a, b) charges that designating a speaker in a particular way presupposes a certain social relation, one that is diffused with power, an explanatory variable that CA researchers have not adequately addressed. To illustrate his argument, Billig (1999a) offers a hypo-

thetical—and spectacularly imaginative—scenario of a man raping a woman. He asks how the speakers in that hypothetical setting would be designated: as A/B, man/woman, rapist/victim? Billig's (1999a, b) challenge to researchers in CA, particularly Schegloff, stems from the their claims to unmediated and direct access to the social reality of participants, on their own terms, without any presuppositions. The debate between researchers in Critical Discourse Analysis (CDA) and CA is centered around CA's claims of epistemological and methodological naivety. The charge against CDA is that researchers in this tradition "discuss more loosely, but also more freely, the many ways power, dominance and inequality are expressed, enacted and reproduced in discourse, both in its structure and its contents" (Van Dijk, 1999: 460). I realize that this controversy between CA and CDA is far and beyond the scope and aim of this work; but there is still the problem that any analyst must face, and that is how to label or designate a speaker's identity. My approach has been to make minimal assumptions. For the full debate, see Schegloff (1999b, c).

CHAPTER 3
TELEVISION AND TALK IN *COPS*

In the preceding two chapters I presented the main problem that *Language and Demeanor* attempts to answer, as well as a brief introduction to the logic, method, and analytical strategy this book assumes. In this chapter, using the interaction phase of mass-mediated and actual P-C encounters I demonstrate the essential sameness of their verbal exchange by scrutinizing the question/answer sequences between the police on *COPS* and actual police. While the question/answer sequences are essentially identical, the *COPS* data also differs from the actual ones in that the P-C encounters on *COPS* are structurally divided into three distinct segments: (1) framing narrative (2) interaction phase (3) debriefing narrative. The primary difference between mass-mediated encounters and actual P-C encounters lies in the metalinguistic functions of the first and last segments. Drawing on the reflexive studies of language, this chapter demonstrates how framing narratives serve a valuable "prepping" function while the debriefing narratives serve a "summarizing" one in the discourse of *COPS*. That is to say that the triadic narratives are intertextually linked, both synchonically and diachronically, to maximize viewer interest through editorial authority.

The Triadic Segmentation of Police-Citizen Encounters on *COPS*

The Metapragmatic Function of Framing Narratives

A P-C encounter on *COPS* (a "vignette") lasts about six to seven minutes, and is composed of three segments. In the first segment, a police officer—"host cop provides autobiographical information, so the viewer gets to know the host personally. The officer will talk about why he—or occasionally she—joined the force, how long he/she has been a cop and so on" (Doyle, 1998: 100). Consider the following account that an officer in a southern part of the U.S. gives the viewing audience in the beginning moments of a vignette:

Excerpt 1 (*COPS* data: "Games")
We're studying in college and uh I took a criminal justice class and the instructor was at the front of the class and he looks at everybody and he'd he'd been a police officer since nineteen forty something. He'd served in the MPs in world war two and he just took it for granted that if you took his class that's what by golly that's what you were gonna do is be a police officer and he looked at everybody in the room and said 'someday when you're police officers you'll understand why I'm saying these things'.

In this first—opening—segment of *COPS*, the recipient design seems dyadic since the viewing audience at home and the narrating officer enter into a direct speaker-listener relationship. But although the speaking moment is in the present (moment of narration), there is another context that is embedded in the structure of his utterances when the talk with the viewing audience is taken into consideration. The contents of the officer's extended talk are rather simple: he tells the audience why he became a police officer; he states that an instructor of a criminal justice course he took in college was an instrumental reason for choosing his profession. The narrative does indeed personalize the "host cop" since it provides the viewing audience with some of the particular details of his life; his story also offers a commentary about the often bastardized functions of a criminal justice education and a glimpse into the attitudinal—ideological—assumptions of his ex-police officer/teacher. The host officer reports the speech of his mentor in college when he says, "someday when you're police officers you'll understand why I'm saying these things." If the utterances themselves are taken as the objects of analysis, the obviousness of the content of talk disappears.

The officer in excerpt 1 quotes his ex-WWII-MP-criminal justice professor: he brings the words of another to life by using a past tense quotative verb to report speech that took place in past time (Bakhtin, 1981). The reporting involves taking an utterance that took place in a college classroom in the past and bringing it into the current speaking context of giving audience the biographical details of how he came to be a police officer. There are several linguistic components in excerpt 1 that are used to animate the story that is being told, such as the historical present (HP), tense variation, reported speech (direct quotes), knowledge claims, and affective stance; in all these practices the past is brought into the present and made relevant through a stylistic, poetic, and grammatical manipulation of discourse.

Within the reported utterance ("someday when you're police officers you'll understand why I'm saying these things") is a plural demonstrative, an indexical expression. Of course, just what "these things" are is not clear, for there is no prior referent; moreover, the speaker is situated not in the current context of talk, but in a college classroom several years past. Perhaps the "things" he is referring to are impressions and characterizations of people and events that stand out during his teacher's tenure as a police officer; but the noteworthy point is that although the host cop is the one articulating the words, the emotion and attitude which are injected into the talk are his mentor's. The officer is merely the *animator* of his teacher's talk (Goffman, 1981). The author is invisible and elsewhere.

Thus, even within one turn at talk, situated in a direct speaker-listener relationship with the viewing audience, we can see that there are other contexts and speaker-listener frameworks within the present one. Within a single turn, the host officer has taken the viewing audience to a college classroom and has framed them as direct recipients of his ex-WWII-MP-criminal justice professor's lecture. Notice how this past and current speaker-listener relationship is embodied in the poetic features of discourse. The host cop's descriptive scene opens in the present progressive (HP), thus enlivening the past events into the current talk, narrating the story as if it were taking place at that particular moment (Wolfson, 1978). This tactic is employed again as a preliminary cue signaling a shift in participation framework. That is, the viewing audience is on the verge of being a direct recipient of the instructor's talk rather than the officer's; but before doing so, the host officer takes the viewing audience to the college classroom as the ratified recipients of the instructor's gaze through the HP, thus visually and grammatically prepping the invisible participant toward a reconfiguration in the participant status.

Viewed in this light, the simple dyadic structure of communication on *COPS* is misleading: the viewing audience and the host cop are not only situated in the present speaking moment, but they are embedded in another one, in a prior context and time. As noted in a prior chapter, there are several speaker-listener frameworks on *COPS*. In prior works, participation framework and recipient design are generally defined as the alignment that speakers assume in relation to other speakers, the alignment a constitutive element in the social organization of face- to-face interaction (see Goodwin, 1990: 10); that alignment however is implicitly presupposed to be physical and constrained to direct face-to-face interaction. For instance, Goffman's (1981:3) definition of participation framework delimits an interactant's participant status relative to the speaker's "perceptual range"; similarly, for Sacks et al. (1974) a participant's status relative to the ongoing talk rests on his/her capacity to "display an orientation and sensitivity" to the presence of others. As I have shown here, however, *COPS* highlights the complex and multiple nature of participation framework and communicative contexts, one that transcends the definitional boundaries of social interaction.

In excerpt 1, the past is brought into the present, and the present lived in the past. Furthermore, the parameters of face-to-face interaction (perceptual range, orientation and sensitivity to others' presence) are redrawn through the technologically mediated nature of the interaction. Thus, despite the invisibility of other participants (audience), their absence (face-to- face) and presence (technological) are implicative for the social organization of talk. Simply put, the talk itself and the interaction is dialogic, multicontextual, and self-generative

(Bahktin, 1981). Consider the following narrative that another police officer gives the audience:

Excerpt 2 (*COPS* data: "You tryin to fight me")
I'm finishing up my eighth year ( ) certain calls stick in your mind and the one that I think I'll never forget is a call where there was two guys fighting, ended up shooting each other and then when I got there, investigated (laughter) the call, it was all over onions on a hamburger. I went home that night thinking to myself if onions were that important that he would shoot his own family member, this world's in trouble (laughter). I, people will do amazing things. And that one just stands out. I think I'll never forget it.

This officer, too, talks about things—amazing things—citizens do. In this excerpt the officer recollects one of the most memorable assignments that he responded to in his eight-year tenure as a police officer. In excerpt 2, the officer incidentally provides a substantive topic matter for criminology, theory of interpersonal violence, in addition to his attitude toward the people involved in the call. In this episode, the officer is dispatched to a family disturbance where a man assaults his brother and mother while fighting over the remote control. When the officer goes into the suspect's residence to arrest him, he encounters a hostile subject who refuses to be taken into custody: numerous officers have to fight and wrestle him to subdue and arrest him.

This time, the host officer does not take us into his teacher's classroom but into the officer's trek home; and this time the reported utterances do not belong to another speaker, it is his own. The officer recounts, "If onions were that important that he would shoot his own family member, this world's in trouble." Those words, however, have never actually been uttered in historical time; they are imagined, made up in the officer's mind and silently uttered in it, years ago, but articulated for the first (and only) time in the present. What we—the viewing audience—are treated to is the officer's affective stance back then, as he is going home after having answered the call. The viewing audience is transplanted into the speaker-listener relationship with the officer's mind. Again, the viewing audience is transported to the past, and the past relived in the imaginative narrating moments through the officer's inner dialogue; that the officer's hypothetical utterance is used to describe his own thinking speech illustrates the reflexive capacity of language to dramatize a message—its poetic function (Jakobson, 1960; Lucy, 1993). That is, the host officer animates his past thinking speech for the viewing audience and foregrounds the current narrative to maximize its rhetorical effect; this poetic representation of his past affective stance, placed adjacently to how he has understood the domestic dispute then and now, provides a rhetorically powerful summary: laughter. Again, the viewers are situated in multiple contexts and multiple participation structures.

This encounter also exemplifies the role of language in *COPS* in a pragmatic way. The narrative does not contain just autobiographical information and socialization cues; it implicitly prepares the viewing audience for what is to follow; moreover, the narrative covertly provides a framework with which to understand the ensuing encounter. Thus, the sheer absurdity of a fraternal dispute over condiments in an ordinary domestic situation "sets up" the farcical actions of a man who slaps his mother and punches his brother because he could not watch the TV program of his choice (football game). Conceptualized this way, as a preliminary narrative before the main sequence of interaction (the actual encounter with police), it serves a valuable function of prepping the viewer for what is to come: the autobiographical information and the stories the officer tells in this segment do not have a purely referential (informative) function. I refer to these narratives told at the beginning of the vignettes as *framing narratives*.

The first segment is not orphaned: it is situated—editorially framed—in a triadic network of relational segments. As a "background" frame for what is to follow in the second segment, and as a way of reporting lived experience, it is governed not only by rules of editing but also by the principle of social—discursive—organization (Goffman, 1974). That is, frames allow to see "the connections between things, or between present things and things we have experienced before or heard about" (Tannen, 1993: 15). But there is no natural or inherent connection between things we have experienced (the first segment: e.g., an officer's absurd encounter with a family dispute involving condiments on a hamburger) and what we are about to experience (the second segment: e.g., an officer's encounter with a family dispute over the remote control). That connection is editorially and arbitrarily effected, a result of placing images and words in a particular slot. Thus, that the connection is editorially manipulated leads us to restate the framing in talk, on *COPS*, as a structur*ing* of expectations rather than a "structure of expectations" (Tannen, 1993). The initial framing narratives provide—constructs, structures—a dimension (structure, schema, framework) of assessment before the actual story takes place. In other words, the framing structure does not exist prior to talk, but it is actively shaped by the utterances. The viewers' expectations on *COPS* do not exist before hand (i.e., independent schemas or structures); they are created (structur*ed*) through the first segment.

I call it framing because that's what the stories do; they provide a dimension of assessment before the actual story takes place. The opening segment not only "opens" the episode and the P-C encounter, but it implicitly provides the viewing audience with a particular set of assumptions—assumptions about the nature of police work and what is to follow in the next segment. But it is not the superimposition or arrangements of shots or frames of images—editing—in a particular way that makes this complex preinterpretive process possible; it is language. It is what the officer says, which cannot be manipulated, without altering its discourse structure, that makes framing possible. The framing narratives illustrate an important aspect of language use. Pragmatics is the study of how language is used (see Green, 1996); but the capacity of language to represent, report, and refer to events in the world is not limited to the physical world. Language can also be used to represent, report, and refer itself: it becomes the object of reference (Bakhtin, 1981); in other words, language is reflexive (Lucy, 1993).

When officers articulate their narrative in the first segment, they are not talking to themselves; the message is intended for a viewing audience. Hence, although the interlocuter of the officer's speech is never seen or heard (invisible), the host officer is already situated in a communicative structure and a participation framework, in an interactionally complex speaker-listener relationship.

There are two principal distinctions within metapragmatic—reflexive—studies of language: *metalinguistic* and *metacommunicative* messages. Metalinguistic messages describe instances where the subject of speech is speech itself. For example, when an officer tells an exciting story about one of his encounters during his shift, after work in a tavern, and a listener replies, "that was a good story!" that utterance is not a commentary about the internal events within the story, but an explicit comment about the medium—story—as an object of reference. In metalinguistic messages, the relationship is linked to other utterances; in metacommunicative messages, however, the relationship is between speaking agents; hence, messages are designed to structure discourse before it happens, to facilitate and assist listeners to interpret the message they are hearing in a particular way. In other words, metacommunicative messages are action oriented (see Lucy, 1993). Thus, if the same officer tells his audience, "I've got a good story to tell," before he tells the actual story, then the utterance not only serves as an object of reference, but it also performs a "guiding function" (Lucy, 1993: 11).

And guiding is precisely what the framing narratives in *COPS* do. Thus, as Goffman (1974: 22) also notes, frameworks provide "background understanding for events that incorporate the will, aim, and controlling effort of an intelligence, a live agency, the chief one being the human being. Such an agency is anything but implacable; it can be coaxed, flattered, affronted, and threatened. What it does can be described as 'guided doings'." Although we do not know what the ex-MP-criminal justice professor means when he says "someday when you're police officers you'll understand why I'm saying these things" in the framing narrative, the viewers have already been metacommunicatively signaled as to how to appropriately interpret "these things" and what it might mean in the next segment. After this brief framing narrative, the host officer usually receives a call for service, or self generates one. The next segment shows what officers do when they receive an assignment or generate one.

The Sequential Structure of the Interaction Phase

The second segment of a P-C encounter on *COPS* captures the interaction between the police and the public. This segment can be conceptualized as what prior police researchers have termed the "interaction phase" of P-C encounters—one minute or three or more verbal exchanges between police officers and citizens (Mastrofski et al., 1995). Prior research has conceptualized this verbal sequence as an instance of a *field interrogation* or *field interview* (FI). Field interrogations are often compared to criminal interrogations (see Leo 1996a,b) because the sequential organization of the verbal interaction—question/answer format—is essentially the same. That is, officers usually ask questions and suspects and citizens answer them. Consider the following excerpt from the criminal interrogation of a murder suspect:

Excerpt 3 (Watson, 1998: 92)
P=police officer
S=suspect

1   P: Why did you shoot at this G...?
2   S: He's a nigger
3   P: Did you eh were you alone when you er shot at him?
.
.
.
31   P: Well then did you know that you were shooting ar G...or did you
32   shoot at him just because he was colored, period?
33   S: He's a nigger.
34   P: And that's why you shot him and er.
35   S: That's why I shot him.
36   P: Did you intend to kill him...or?
37   S: Yes...!
38   P: Yer
39   S: Do you think I'd fire at somebody if I didn't intend to
40   kill them?

Criminal interrogations differ from field interrogations in an obvious way: the latter take place on the street while the former take place inside the police station. Often, the criminal interrogation room is enclosed, private, and contains minimal amount of furniture; furthermore, directions exist for specific arrangements and manipulation of furniture and personal space, which serve as techniques that interrogators use to their advantage (see Inbau et al., 1986; Royal and Schutt, 1976).

Leo (1996a, b) notes that American police interrogations resemble confidence games in that the police manipulate and betray the trust of suspects. First, Leo states, the police "qualify" or "size up" the suspect; then a "cultivating" process takes place where interrogators attempt to establish a "pattern of psychological dependence on the interrogator that leads to a 'yes or submissive mood'" from the suspect (Leo, 1996a: 271). Interrogators then "con" the suspect, tricking the suspect into believing that a confession will improve his/her situation. After the con has been purchased, Leo (1996a: 283) observes that the police "cool out" the suspect: the police "compliment the suspect for his actions" and "portray" the confession as the best course of action.

Watson's (1998) analysis of police interrogations is ethnomethodological, linguistic, and micro-sociological. He uses police interrogations to examine how the descriptive practices of suspects and their victims are organized in talk to reveal a motive for the offense in question. For example, notice the way the victim's descriptions are given in excerpt 3. In line 1, the officer refers to the victim as G (name) when s/he attempts to elicit a motive through an open ended WH question (why). In the next turn, the descriptive category the suspect uses indexes pejorative connotations (nigger); and as Watson notes, a motive is imputed through that descriptive term since it implicitly pairs the author behind such words with categories such as 'those who hate blacks' (category bound). That is, 'those who hate blacks' engage in acts that are consistent with the given descriptive category (kill blacks) (Sacks, 1992).

The primary difference between a field interrogation and a criminal interrogation, however, lies not in the setting of the talk but in the assumptions speakers hold about the other speakers. Leo (1996a, b) notes that most American police interrogators believe suspects to be guilty of the offense of which they are accused. As instructors at the Federal Bureau of Investigation (FBI) state, an interrogation seeks to elicit the "truth" from a subject (McIlwane, 1994). Or as another FBI instructor puts it, the goal of an interrogation is "to obtain truthful admissions or confessions" (Vessel, 1998:3). In criminal interrogations, then, the police begin with the assumption of guilt already in place; in a way, the questions the police ask during criminal interrogations are accusatorial. Interviews gather "facts," interrogations an admission of guilt. The difference, then, lies not in the discourse structure of criminal and field interrogations, but in the assumptions police officers and interrogators make about the speaker prior to any talk (Walker, 1985).

But aside from the descriptions that participants use and the assumptions speakers hold about one another, there are other features in excerpt 3 that is independent of the occasion of the talk that is worth mentioning. First, both the suspect and the interrogator take turns. One speaker speaks at any one time; turns are switched at the end of a prior speaker's turn or at transition relevant places. Second, the turns are sequentially organized. The first pair part projects the relevant next turn action: thus, an answer follows a question (lines 1 and 2; lines 31-33; lines 36-37). Confirmation and repair of misunderstandings are accomplished through clarification seeking repetition (lines 34-35). These context free structures of talk are essentially the same, in field interrogations, criminal interrogations, and ordinary conversations.

Field interrogations take place on the street, in plain view of all curious onlookers, and in a way, it can be viewed as a street performance; and unlike criminal interrogations, field interviews are conducted by patrol officers, not by trained interrogation specialists. In the following excerpt, the host cop receives a call about a man who is seen "pushing a hot water heater in a cart down the street." Excerpt 4 examines the question/answer sequence between a black man (BM) suspected of burglary and several police officers (POn). The following is a transcription of the actual spoken words between officers and a suspect on an episode of *COPS*:

Excerpt 4: (*COPS* Data: "Games")
14   PO1:   HEY come here partner (1.9) Where'd you get this at?
15   (.5)
16   BM: See that vacant lot right there? (.7)
17   Somebody just dumped it a few minutes ago?
18   (.6)

19	PO1:	The thing's still leaking water man
20		(.)
21	BM:	Yeah
22		(.6)
23	PO1:	Somebody just dumped it and you just picked
24		it up at two o'clock in the mor[ning
25	BM:	[Uh-huh
26		(1.0)
27	PO1:	<u>And that thing's just cut</u>
28		(.6)
29	BM:	Yeah (.5) They just dumped [it

This segment—field interrogation, a P-C encounter—begins when the officer self-initiates a summons hailing the suspect into the encounter. The "hey come here partner" (line 14) is like a ringing of the telephone in that it beckons the other party to interact (Schegloff, 1968). The summons is followed by the use of a WH question with a contracted operator which raises questions of property acquirement (ownership) (line 14: "where'd you get this at?"). The WH question is, on the surface, a constative/locutionary act, a "police-initiated fact seeking sequence," which perhaps is seeking to elicit an account (Sharrock and Turner, 1978; Antaki, 1994). But in addition to issues of ownership, the context of the interaction (call for service regarding a possible theft) and the identity/role of the questioner (police officer) connotes an alternative interpretation of the question, one of accusation.

The question—where'd you get this at?—is an embodiment of the role of the speaker as an official representative of the institution of law (legitimacy). And that legitimacy is demonstrated in the next turn by the next speaker: the suspect who is selected as the next turn speaker provides a sequentially relevant response, as demonstrated in the next turn type (line 17). That the black male has provided an answer to a question such as "where'd you get this at?" already signifies the legitimacy—and power—of the speaker to ask such a question in the first place. Moreover, the speaker demonstrates his understanding of the officer's assumptions—intention—by voluntarily providing the responsible agent (someone) for the patient (water heater) and the theme (theft). That the speaker has "heard" the officer's WH question (line 14) as an accusatorial one is displayed in his response: the speaker distances himself from the problematic topic (leaking water heater; the anteceding referent of 'this') by tacitly denying and accusing someone else. Analyzed sequentially, then, the WH interrogative is an implicitly blame imbued and accusatorial way of covertly initiating a problem. As for its sequential implicativeness, the police officer might as well ask "Did you steal that?" because the answer the black male gives is equivalent to "I didn't steal it, someone else did." To summarize, within the first two turns of this P-C encounter, the officer has implicitly accused the BM of theft; and in return, he has managed to shift responsibility to someone else, thereby aligning himself in a morally favorable light. The moral work is accomplished two ways, agentically and sequentially.

The question/answer format is particularly relevant for police officers because most police work involves asking questions—to citizens, witnesses, disputants, and suspects—about who, where, when, what, and how something happened. And when participants in P-C encounters remain silent, act "cool and detached," use disrespectful or deferential language, act friendly, or ridicule the police in response to their questions, the second pair slot after the first pair part—question—is a sequentially provided place for participants in P-C encounters to display their moral stance toward the police. The citizens' moral attitude toward the police is made relevant by officers in the next turn, where they assess the citizen's "governability" or rebelliousness (see Muir, 1977). As prior research on P-C encounters have noted, those who disrespect police authority and legitimacy are more likely to receive official sanctions. Thus, showing deference and cooperation to police officers is a strategic move for citizens and suspects if they do not want to anger the bureaucratic leviathan. And showing deference and a cooperative attitude is precisely what the suspected burglar does. When the officer asks him a question, he does not remain silent or challenge the officer; he answers it right away. In form and content, the suspect has thus far complied with the officer's requests; he follows the contours of the police-citizen interaction that the officer has sketched: a police officer orders him to come, he comes; the officer asks a question, he answers—swiftly and crisply.

The alternating question/answer adjacency exchange format comes to a halt after the second turn (lines 16-17). The third turn (line 19) is a declarative statement, an acknowledgment of the previous turn; however, the acknowledgement is a "problematic" assessment—disagreement—of the prior turn. The officer receives a call about a man pushing a hot water heater down the street; the call is already encoded as a possible burglary and the BM's answer that someone "just dumped it" does not achieve topical coherence for the officer. This incredulity and inappositeness of the response is embodied in the officer's assessment (line 19) of the BM's prior turn (lines 16-17).

In line 21, the BM appears to provide an agreement with the officer's assessment (yeah); the BM's second turn (line 21) occurs after the officer's assessment in line 19: the BM's agreement in line 21 appears procedurally relevant to its immediate antecedent—the officer's problematic assessment (It's still leaking water). And that candidate understanding is supported in line 25, where the BM again provides an agreement to the officer's second—intensified—assessment. Notice that in line 23-24, the officer recycles a portion of the suspect's previous answer into the first part clause of a declarative assertion; and in the second clause he appends a temporal dimension of the situation to transform the declarative statement into a question (somebody just dumped it at two o'clock in the morning): the suspect answers with a glottal affirmative in line 25. The officer again acknowledges the response with a problematic assessment (line 27: and that thing's just cut). In the final turn, the suspect provides another agreement with the prior utterance and, after a slight pause, he reiterates the declarative proposition that attempts to absolve personal agency from his property acquisition (line 29: they just dumped it).

To summarize, the first turn is a WH interrogative (line 14), the second turn is an answer to that question (line 17), the third turn provides a problematic assessment of the prior turn considering the circumstantial evidence (line 19), and the fourth turn provides agreement to the prior turn (line 21). The next four turns (lines 23-29) essentially mirror this format. There is one component of the preceding talk—suspect's agreement with the officer's problematic assessment— that is a bit puzzling: what interactional work do the agreements perform?

The officer's first assessment occurs after the BM's second turn, in line 19 (The thing's still leaking water man), after the BM's story about someone who just dumped the water heater a few minutes ago. The BM's agreement in line 29 is preceded by an assessment that takes into consideration the physical evidence that is present (line 27: that thing's just cut). Notice the incremental character of each assessment: the BM's initial claim is hierarchically assessed and challenged by the officer within each subsequent turn. For example, after the BM's initial claim, the officer in his turns comments on (1) the leaking water (initial evidence) (2) two o'clock in the morning (time) (3) just cut (overwhelming evidence). In other words, the officer's assessments are subsequently upgraded and intensified (Pomerantz, 1984). The officer's final assessment is prefaced with a continuous marker 'and', thereby framing the utterance as the final item in a list; the upgraded character of the utterance is prosodically marked with accompanying stress.

Now, notice what the BM agrees to, after three upgraded problematic assessments. His agreement is marked in line 29, first grammatically (yeah) then prosodically: the 'yeah' is articulated with a rising intonation, as if stating it emphatically. The 'yeah' is produced in relation to the prior turn; but after a (.5) pause, notice what follows: they just dumped it (line 29). Although the suspect appears to agree with the officer's assessments since the agreement markers are produced in the sequentially relevant slot, in a well-established adjacency pair format, the only assessment he agrees with is his own initial story, and the only person he agrees with is himself. In other words, the agreements are not produced in relation to the officer's assessments; on the contrary, the agreements are agreements to his initial story about somebody just dumping it—his first turn. So what practical function do his repeated agreements have?

As other police scholars have noted, those who disrespect the police are more likely to receive official sanctions while those who flout, challenge, and resist police authority are candidates for street justice, that is, "unofficial" sanctions. Therefore, presenting oneself to be a deferent and a cooperative self is a strategic maneuver designed to create a favorable impression management (Goffman, 1959). Showing deference and a cooperative attitude is precisely what the suspected burglar does. If, however, all of the suspect's agreements in the excerpt do nothing but agree with his own assessment and story, therefore, disagree with the officer's claims, then the agreements only affiliate to disaffiliate—agree to disagree. That is, although the explicit markers of agreement grammatically correspond to affiliation, they do the interactional work of disagreement and denial: a 'no' disguised in the form of a 'yes', a hostile attitude under the cloak of a cooperative attitude. Consequently, the BM is able to avoid direct disagreements—opposition—in the second turn, and minimize a potential escalation into conflict talk with the officer (Grimshaw, 1990; Maynard, 1985a).

With the initial opening sequences of one P-C encounter, as they appeared on *COPS*, I have shown the linguistically complex ways that a suspect and an officer make claims, counter those claims, attribute and deflect blame— negotiate the encounter. The suspect in this encounter on *COPS* never challenges or fights the officers; he is compliant, respectful, and cooperative all the way through, even as he is arrested. An ethnographer who accompanied this officer would have noted that as the host officer was driving to the scene, s/he witnessed a black male in a long coat pushing a water-heater inside a cart, away from the scene of the burglary. S/he would have added that the officer questioned the BM about where he acquired the water-heater, and that the suspect stated that he "just found it."

Had another researcher used a coding sheet or a notebook and observed this encounter during his/her ride-along, s/he most likely would have had two coding possibilities: (1) s/he could have been sympathetic and generous in his/her classification of demeanor and categorized him as being civil. (2) S/he could have been cautious and parsimonious in his/her definition and classified his demeanor as non-hostile[1] since the suspect never says or does anything that can be construed as hostile—that is, he doesn't physically attack the officer; he doesn't use profanity; and otherwise "disrespect" the officer in an obvious way. The BM answers the questions asked of him and produces no disagreements to signal his oppositional stance to the officer.

But this ascription would have had to abstract and gloss over an instance of communicative action and miss the verbally rich and sophisticated ways that the suspect uses language to align himself in a morally favorable light to the officers throughout the encounter. I characterize the suspect's verbal behavior as "sophisticated" because the way he uses language captures the semiotic nature of communicative action: his impoliteness is veiled as deference; he uses agreement markers to cover his disagreement; he employs affirmations to do the work of a denial. He says one thing to mean another (see Black, 1980). But this insight, if made at all in the current paradigm, would have been a solipsistic derivation, meaning that the interpretation would have preceded the analysis. By capturing the actual words, in sequence, viewers and readers are treated to a complex performance of linguistic evasion that the BM animates.

It is precisely the type of analysis done here that adds another layer to the observations already made by extant researchers in police studies. A quantitative stance would have used the occurrence of a word (e.g., sir, ma'am, pig) as a representation and a reflection of demeanor; an ethnographer would have described the words used, along with the spirit of their articulation (e.g., the officer snidely remarked 'have a good day sir'), but the description and analysis of the encounter would have been his/her sole possession, the analysis preinterpreted. However, by capturing the verbal details of the encounter, we are able to see line by line, word by word, turn by turn, how demeanor emerges from the interaction in the way that demeanor is enacted in the form of an agreement to "do" disrespect; to avoid conflict with the police by agreeing adjacently with the prior turn (and the police), only to reaffirm and signal his commitment to his original story, ultimately, assuming an oppositional stance.

If the structure of talk in *COPS* is compared to actual encounters, we would see that there is no essential difference. Consider the following excerpts from an actual traffic stop:

Excerpt 5 (Midwest City Police Traffic Stop #2)
```
8   PO:      how you doin >see your driver's license
9            en proof of insurance?<
10           (.7)
11  D:    I got it in my jacket can I get it?
12           (.)
13  PO:       Yeah
14           (5.0)
15  D:    my insurance I got off my other car
16           I just bought this vehicle
17           (.)
18  PO:       how long ago did you buy it?
19           (.7)
20  D:    about 2 days now (.6) here's the insurance
21           (2.0)
22  PO:       you know why I stopped you?
23           (1.0)
24  D:    No not re[ally I
25  PO:              [I clocked you doing 44 in a 25
```

In the above excerpt, the motorist is pulled over for speeding. The officer, however, does not make the official justification topically relevant until nine turns later in line 25; the preceding thirteen lines of interaction is the initial opening sequence of a traffic stop. The exchange format of this encounter does not differ unrecognizably from the encounter on *COPS* in terms of their sequential organization. The way the talk itself is managed is quite orderly. Each speaker (police officer, driver) takes turns, one after the other; the officer asks questions, the driver provides an answer. The officer makes a request, the driver grants the request.

Excerpt 6 (Midwest City Police Traffic stop #3)
```
35  PO:      so what did you u:h get out of jail for?
36           (1.0)
37  D:    uh why did I get out?
38           (.)
39  PO:       yeah (.) what were you in for?
40           (.4)
41  D:    uh aggravated battery
42           (.5)
```

43 PO: for what=what d'ju do?
44   (.5)
45 D: uh I beat up some kids when I was younger (1.5) 22

In excerpt 6, the officer pulls over the motorist for speeding; in the prior 34 lines, they go through a similar question/answer opening sequence found in excerpt 5. When the officer runs the motorist's driver's license in the computer, it shows that the motorist has a prior record. The excerpt above is the exchange that takes place after the officer returns to the driver.

Excerpt 7 (Midwest City Police Traffic Stop #4)
37   (1.4)
38 PO: where you goin?
39   (.9)
40 D: to see my girlfriend [keu ha heh heh
41 PO: [oh okay]
42   (1.4)
43   Goin out for dinner [or?
44 D: [luv no lover's lane
45   to get my other girlfriend a birthday gift

In excerpt 7, the motorist (a woman) is also pulled over for speeding; they have negotiated through the opening sequence and the official justification for the stop; and 1.4 seconds pass before the officer resumes his field interrogation. Again, the sequential structure of the encounter is essentially the same as ones that appears on *COPS*. That is, the officer asks questions, the citizen answers them. The driver's answers are sequentially and conditionally relevant in that they are a function of prior turns. But the type of questions officers ask, as well how they ask them, depends on the context. It is here, in a discussion about contexts, that those who criticize *COPS* as data can raise issue about the problem of interpretation and proliferation: if there is no overriding meaning or context (neighborhood, attitude of the officer, motorist, recent and historical trends), how can any sense be made from the data? To answer that, I would again question how a context is defined.

A traffic stop or any P-C encounter is a physical context in itself; and police researchers have noted three contexts within P-C encounters: contact, processing, and exit (Bayley and Bittner, 1984; Bayley and Garofalo, 1989). In other words, what the police do at the beginning, middle, and end of the encounter is interactionally different. As a conversation, traffic stops and other P-C encounters contain multiple contexts which operate concurrently in talk—how officers open, negotiate, and close the encounter, as Bayley and Bittner (1984) observe. The three contexts that Bayley and Bitter (1984) use leads to my next point: conversations within P-C encounters on *COPS* are segmentally and sequentially organized. Simply, what goes on in each segment is a context in its own right; moreover as I have shown using the framing narratives, there are other numerous contexts within a context. The logical question to ask, then, is: what goes on in each step of the encounter? What are the participants trying to do?

The types of question and answer sequences between police officers and citizens and suspects, both mass mediated and actual—the kind I've shown here—are what would be found if encounters were recorded with video cameras. But in addition to the main sequence of interaction *COPS* adds two other dimensions to the encounter. As stated earlier, *COPS* provides the viewing audience with a *framing narrative*. And after the interaction phase, the host officer must explain and justify his or her actions to other officers and patrol supervisors on scene. Furthermore, each encounter on *COPS* is concluded with a "debriefing" by the primary officer on scene, the third segment of a P-C encounter on *COPS*.

The Intertextuality of Debriefing Narratives

In a typical debriefing narrative, officers usually explain, step by step, what actions they took and why they took them in their encounters with citizens and suspects after an assignment is completed. Usually, debriefing narratives are not replete with bureaucratic argot; instead, the narratives are filled with figurative and metaphoric expressions, humor, and other creative uses of language. As I will show in later chapters, the form and content of those utterances vary in accordance with participation structure and recipient design. Consider the following example of a debriefing narrative on *COPS*:

Excerpt 8 (*COPS* data: "Games")
PO1: We got this guy pushing this hot water heater down the street (.) at two o'clock in the morning (.9) obviously it doesn't look right (.) He says he just found it (.6) in the uh alley (1.6) and the water's still steaming and there's fresh filings in the ( ) where he's cut it so its walk back here ther's just a solid trail of water leading from that hot water heater (1.6) all the way back through this alley (2.3) It doesn't take much more than common sense to figure this crime out (1.2) Looks like he stopped right here and rested a little (4.1) It's all the way back in through here (3.1) You could still see it (.) startin' to dry up a little bit.....

(brief dialogue with a supervising officer)

Well (.8) just right here maybe (4.6) and the water trail comes all the way on in here (through) this business (3.4) loops back around to this bathroom (1.6) where you can see (3.3) where they all (1.4) everything he touched right here (1.7) and he had everything to cut this stuff (.) he had (.) uh tin snips (.9) to cut this and then uh lookslike maybe he rinsed that off there to try to cover this up to stop the water (.8) and uh here's the vent (.) he just ripped it all out and he's carrying (.) a piece of the vent pipe and everything else right along with it (.4) he's brought (.8) like most burglars he brought all the tools he needed with him (.8) and he can improvise with anything else

.(radio call)

>That just goes to show you you never know what you're gonna come across at two thirty in the morning a guy carrying a hot water heater< (1.0) now he's in hot water I guess

This account of the preceding P-C encounter is close to "verbal reports of cognitive steps taken by police officers" in their decision making (see Worden, 1989: 704). It is in this monologue account that viewers first get a further peek at the hidden premises of the officer's decision-making processes. As the officer states, "it doesn't look right," that "it doesn't take more than common sense to figure this crime out"; but the noteworthy point is that the officer's "hidden premises" and "cognitive steps" are linguistically encoded in his account. For instance, after he repeats the assignment ("guy pushing a water heater down the street at two o'clock in the morning"), and before he lists the circumstantial evidence, he prefaces it with an epistemic adverbial (obviously), which provides an important insight into the officer's stance toward the details surrounding the alleged crime. Seven lines before the clip ends, he finally reveals the presupposed bureaucratic identity of the citizen: "like most burglars." So what features of the interaction lead the officer to discursively construct this particular call as "not looking right"? The police routinely look for things that are out of place (Sacks, 1978): a dirty license plate on a shiny new car; a man who wears a long trench coat on a hot summer day; minority persons in a white neighborhood; white, middle-class people in minority neighborhoods (Rubinstein, 1973).

The debriefing account essentially describes a call for service that involves an agent ("this guy"), patient ("this water heater"), space ("down the street"), and time ("at two o'clock in the morning"). The four constitutive elements of the proposition somehow conflict and appear incommensurate with the officer's existing interpretive framework. The issue of agency can be narrowed down to identity; the theme can be narrowed down to relations of property exchange; space and time with common sense notions about them. It is because these four elements somehow "don't fit" (incongruous) that this crime is solvable through invocation of "not much more than common sense."

Police officers on the street discern incongruities and inconsistencies in the speech of citizens and immediate settings as a prevalent strategy for constructing common sense; this "common sense knowledge" is a primary compass that guides the officers' actions (McNulty, 1994). Hence, common sense is seeing something that shouldn't be there, and conversely so—an exercise in detecting incongruity (Sacks, 1978). The noteworthy point of the conversational data in excerpt 4 and 8 has been its repeated reference to the questionable means of property acquisition. The suspect's denials and justifications are replete with the assertion that he "just picked it up" because somebody "just dumped it." The officers on scene do not believe the suspect's statements because the evidence present on the scene contradicts the suspect's statements.[2]

I have said that the third segment of a P-C encounter on *COPS* is the place where some of the creative aspects of language use emerge. One such creative usage is metaphoric and idiomatic expressions. Idiomatic and figurative expressions such as "break a leg," "she's under the weather," "he's in hot water now," are pervasive in naturally occurring talk, and give natural conversations their "colloquial character" (Drew and Holt, 1998). Furthermore, it has been found that idiomatic expressions are used to establish affiliation and formulate complaints (Drew and Holt, 1988). The latter case is particularly so when the subject matter of complaint possesses an "egregious character" to it. In addition, figurative expressions and idioms serve noteworthy interactional functions: they are used as topic termination and transition devices; they are used to provide summaries of complaints and cases (Drew and Holt, 1988). When used as interactional resources in conversations, idioms and figures of speech are constructed so that they "fit" with the characteristics of the circumstances of the situation (Drew and Holt 1998, 1988).

In the "games" episode on *COPS*, after the officer's framing narrative, he receives a radio call from the dispatcher. After he listens to it, he tells the viewing audience:

"We got a guy pushing a hot water heater in a cart down the street and we're gonna see what's up with this."

In this episode, officers spend most of the interaction phase trying to get the suspect to confess that he stole the water heater. Despite overwhelming evidence against him—i.e., the presence of a water trail linking him to the scene of the crime, his possession of burglary tools, his story about an unknown subject who "just dumped" the water heater—the suspect never admits his guilt. He repeatedly denies any knowledge or involvement. And after he is arrested and placed into the wagon the host cop addresses the audience with the following summary account in the debriefing narrative as the segment comes to an end:

That just goes to show you that you never know what you're gonna come across at two thirty in the morning, a guy carrying a hot water heater. Now he's in hot water himself I guess.

There are three features of the preceding spate of talk that I want to note. The first is contextual, the second, situational, the third, conversational. The contextual relevance of the call is the water heater; that is, the call of a possible theft of a water heater from a place of business generates the official police business. Second, the water heater is a significant patient throughout the encounter because the hot water trail—literally—links the suspect to the crime. Third, the water heater becomes a linguistically generative object of reference and creativity. I want to focus on the third.

"He's in hot water" is an idiomatic and figurative speech (pun), one that is used in situations when someone is in trouble, experiencing a problem, or caught in a quagmire of some sort. Thus, a husband who is caught in a hot tub with someone other than his wife, can said to be, literally, in "hot water"—in trouble. As a metaphoric expression, "he's in hot water" essentially captures the contextual and situational details of the "Games" episode: the suspect allegedly stole a water heater; he is linked to the crime through a trail of hot water; now he's in trouble. Next, I want to note the sequential and structural position of the utterance, and the work that it does. The metaphoric expression is found in the third segment of the encounter; it is also the final words the officer utters within the third segment. As the 'final word' the officer utters in the segment, it provides a succinct and creative summary of the encounter. More significantly, the work that the metaphoric expression does in the episode is no different from the work that metaphoric expressions as a class of general utterances in mundane, ordinary talk do: summarizing and topic terminating.

These types of expressions are creative because the utterances are not scripted or planned in advance, but contextually and situationally invoked and produced spontaneously by the officers. I refer to the interactional function of metaphors and their endogenously produced character as *metaphoric synchronicity*. The third segment is furthermore linked to the framing narrative in a historical way, synchronically and diachronically. I conceptualize the utterances, especially the creative aspects of language use, in the third segment as being diachronic because they are intertextually tied to the framing narrative. The utterances are intertextually linked—diachronic—because the speaking context of the framing narratives, the interaction phase, and the debriefing narratives is temporally different. The utterances are also synchronic in that they are imported into the current speaking context and used as a resource as an object of reference in the succeeding talk.

Prior work on intertextuality of *COPS* has examined the way *COPS*, as a media product, under the auspices of media logic, "shapes the meaning of consumers of other products" (Doyle, 1998: 108). For example, Doyle (1998) observes that *COPS* is intertextually tied to other law enforcement related programs on the same network by its structural location in a linear time span. Some of the programs like *America's Most Wanted* cross over and spill into another so that two or three programs will be connected in time and theme. This observation is correct, but it overlooks another important aspect of intertextuality, one that is linguistic in character. Intertextuality can be embedded across contexts, but it is also embedded intracontextually, within the medium and context itself. If an episode of *COPS* is a context in itself, tied to other contexts (other crime and justice related programs) in a historical and temporal way, then an episode of *COPS* can be linked to internal speaking events within itself as an object of reference—metapragmatics. I have already described what metapragmatics is and how it works linguistically, but what exactly is intertextuality and how does it work metapragmatically?

According to Matoesian (1999: 77) intertextuality refers to the "vast repertoire of metadiscursive practices for shaping the interrelationship between past and present discourses, such as direct, indirect, and free quotations, the historical present tense and other types of transpositions." Moreover, truth is constructed, power and authority invoked and established through various intertextual strategies (see generally, Bauman and Briggs, 1990; Briggs and Bauman, 1992; Briggs, 1993). The quintessence of intertextuality—taking an utterance from a prior context and embedding it in another—is exemplified in reported speech.

Notice how reported speech and intertextuality work in the next two excerpts. In the following framing narrative an officer describes what police work is like for him:

Excerpt 9 (*COPS* data: Mentally ill)
It can be dangerous at times there's a lot of times when an incident will start out dangerous, but I mean you get it under control then you you know pretty much have a good time

with it, but like I said iih it's funny at times ( ) there's some things that people do that's kind of off the wall I mean you sit back after and you think 'man' you know heh heh it's crazy but no uh uh it's a good time it's a good time

After this framing narrative the officer receives a radio call; he tells the audience:

Excerpt 10 (*COPS* data: Mentally ill)
We got a sergeant says that uh vehicle that's been blowing through red lights; he's in an unmarked vehicle and he needs a marked vehicle to respond

After the host officer pulls the suspect's car over, he interrogates the female driver about why she blew through the red lights. The woman answers that aliens and other "people" are plotting to kill her and her family. The woman shows classic signs of mental illness, such as paranoia and bizarre speech patterns. As the officer arrests the woman and loads her into the wagon, she starts yelling and screaming at the officer. In the final segment, as the episode ends, the officer's last words are: "she's got a lot of anger in her ha ha ha heh heh heh" (laughter), with laughter as the " last word." There are several linguistic and non-linguistic phenomenon at work in the preceding excerpt, but I am mainly interested in the intertextual link between the framing and the debriefing narrative.

Notice how the framing narrative implicitly supplies clues as to what will follow; hence, providing an implicit and subtle interpretive frame before the actual encounter with a mentally ill person takes place. The officer refers that it [calls for service; police work in general] can start out dangerous but "once under control you have a good time with it." The dangerousness of the encounter on the episode is a mentally ill person who drives a car at high speeds and flagrantly violates traffic signals, putting citizens and other pursuing officers' safety in jeopardy. He later gains control and manages to restrain her. During the interaction phase, the "funniness" of police work is given a concrete face when the woman gives bizarre and fantastic responses to the officer's questions. This officer, too, talks about things that people do; and the officer characterizes that thing as being "off the wall"—a paradigmatic metaphor for mental illness; he uses another lexical item—it's crazy—to again characterize the nature of calls and the people he encounters in police work—a "good time."

The intertextuality of the debriefing narrative is interwoven with its positional final utterance in the overall structure of *COPS* and in the positional final utterance in the framing narrative. The last word—laughter—serves as a topic summary of the interaction phase. The preceding encounter with a "crazy" woman who claims that aliens are trying to persecute her unfolds in segment two. And the officer summarizes the entire encounter succinctly, in a contextually and situationally relevant way: laughter. Now notice how the two utterances, in two different segments in one episode, in two different temporal orders within one context, synchronically manifest in a spontaneous and endogenously generated production. Laughter is the iconic, both verbal and nonverbal, representation of "having a good time." People who have a good time enjoy themselves—they laugh. The two utterances, "have a good time with it" and laughter, are somehow magically positioned in the last utterance slot of the first segment as a metapragmatic topic summary and in the last segment as a topic summary. But the noteworthy point is that the summary is given in the first segment, before anything has occurred. The officer has yet to receive a call, but by placing the utterances in that slot, the intertextuality of the debriefing narrative is magically constructed.

The magic lies in the metadiscursive authority of the editors to arrange segments of talk to create what they desire: a metaphorically synchronous vignette that is entertaining. Notice that the editors cannot alter the internal structure of the verbal accounts. The editors cannot edit the officer's subjective understanding of police work, as he verbally constructs them; nor can they alter the topic summary and the topic transition work that figurative expressions perform. What they can do is vary the placements of the accounts in the overall structural organization, or they can exclude them. But their editorial discretion is entirely external, in accordance with the intertextual strategies available to them, as dictated by the conventions of editing and framing, not language. The ability to frame and arrange segments on *COPS* is a function of editorial power. The editors cannot alter the internal coherence and internal structure of language; their magical ability to produce highly entertaining episodes lies in their intertextual, not discursive, authority. The editors create the episode and the segments which comprise it; they also create the intertextuality of *COPS*. But that is a consequence of their editorial power—power to cut, slice, and arrange shots and frames—not a consequence of their power to ascribe value and meaning to the utterances they record and use as data, and as members of a speech community.

Conclusion

In this chapter, verbal transcripts of actual P-C encounters and mass mediated P-C encounters as they appeared on *COPS* were compared. The P-C encounters on *COPS* were classified into three segments: (1) framing narrative (2) interaction phase (3) debriefing narrative. Consequently, I argued that there are multiple speaking contexts within one P-C encounter. Drawing on the work of reflexive studies of language, I demonstrated how framing narratives serve a valuable metapragmatic function.

Using the interaction phase of mass mediated and actual P-C encounters as data, I demonstrated the essential sameness of their verbal exchange format. The creative language usage found in the debriefing narratives was used to argue that the structure of verbal accounts cannot be affected by rules of editing. The only rules applicable to discourse, I argued, are the rules of language.

I showed how the narratives in *COPS* are intertextually linked, synchronically and diachronically, locating that link in metadiscursive and editorial authority of editors. However, I argued that editorial power still cannot affect the internal coherence of language production and use.

Notes

1. I am indebted to Kelly Marzano for her "cautious" and "sympathetic" observation.

2. In this episode of *COPS*, from the accounts given by officers and the alleged suspect, along with the evidence that is presented (recorded and framed), the BM appears guilty of the accused crime. One variable I have not included in this portion of the analysis is his race and how that variable is implicated in the officer's talk. For now, I just want to emphasize the obvious point that a black male transporting property during early morning hours does not necessarily mean that he is stealing. Then, from where does the officer's interpretation of the situation and his view of property exchange relations come from?

According to Herbert (1996b), machismo and capitalism are dynamics that shape the contours of urban policing; and through a detailed analysis of the officer's common sense, it is possible to delve further into capitalism's influence on the hidden premises of common sense. Although unlikely in this case, it is entirely possible that materials and goods could be exchanged using alternative modes of property exchange. But the master status that is given to capitalistic mode of exchange is evident in the officer's cognitive framework. The officer's repeated reference to temporal dimensions of property acquisition alludes to a consumer-based logic of capitalism: goods are not exchanged at two o'clock in the morning; goods are exchanged in stores, during set business hours, by merchants and consumers. The rigid adherence to such subtle—hidden—premises make alternative interpretations impossible: it suggests that property exchange relations that do not abide by the dominant mode of consumption are illegitimate and illegal means of acquiring goods. In other words, what is touted by this officer as common sense is really capitalist-consumer common sense.

CHAPTER 4
POLICE TALK: CONVERSATIONS BETWEEN THE POLICE AND THE PUBLIC

As already noted, the primary deficiency in prior police research has been its use of language as a conduit for representing and describing some external reality. This fact is particularly noteworthy since language is the "cornerstone" of police work. Yet, despite this linguistic mooring in the theoretical and practical infrastructure of police studies, how the police use language has been virtually neglected as a topic of analysis in its own right. To remedy that gap in the literature this chapter examines the structural features of talk between the police and citizens as an embodiment of demeanor in traffic stops and other routine P-C encounters. Aside from merely describing the contents of the talk between the police and the public, its context free and mechanical aspects are examined. This chapter is concerned with presenting some of the gross conversational features of talk such as turn taking, repair, preference, address terms, and silences which operate in talk, and how they contribute to the speakers' interactional aims.

Turn Taking

In an earlier chapter, I noted two salient differences between openings in ordinary telephone conversations and in emergency calls for service: (1) reduction and (2) absence of recognitionals and greetings. In what follows, using calls to emergency services as a backdrop, I want to note some further differences between calls to the police and P-C encounters.
Excerpt 1 (Zimmerman, 1992: 428)

```
1    CT: Nine one one what is you emerg-((cut off by
2         transmit static))
3         (.2)
4    C:  GO::D MY WIFE JUST SHOT HERSELF (.3) TWENTY
5         TWO SIXTY EIGHT (GRANT) AVENUE HURRY U:::::P
6         (.2)
7    CT: What happened?
```

According to Whalen and Zimmerman (1987) and Zimmerman (1992), calls to emergency services, such as fire, police, and paramedics, are socially organized into the following core components: (1) prebeginning (2) opening/identification/acknowledgement sequence (3) request (4) interrogative series (5) response (6) close. Prebeginnings refer to the—unobservable components of call making—physical act of picking up a phone and dialing the other party's number (911), "thereby summoning another to interact" (Whalen and Zimmerman, 1987: 180). In emergency calls to 911, the callers generally remain anonymous: the task of self-identification falls to the institution. Asking what the emergency is immediately after the categorical self-identification, according to Zimmerman (1992: 419), initiates "interrogation prior to a request for assistance."

Whalen and Zimmerman (1987) note that when citizens call emergency services it begins with a categorical identification by the dispatcher (e.g., Mid-City Emergency, nine-one-one emergency). That is, the identities in calls to emergency centers are organized such that the call-taker (dispatcher) chooses "identification-oriented" recognition over "recognition-oriented" response to the telephone summons. When citizens call emergency services for exigent problems or pressing troubles they may have experienced or witnessed, the format of talk is constrained in such a way that the business of the institution is built into the structure of the talk itself (i.e., institution speaks first). Thus, following the first sequence, citizens make a request for service (police, fire, paramedics), state the reason for the call (e.g., somebody just vandalized my car); or the request and the categorical self-identification component of the call is collapsed into the opening first turn (e.g., nine-one-one, what is your emergency?) As already mentioned, these requests can be formulated by the callers as: (1) descriptions (2) direct or indirect requests (3) ambient events. The call-taker then asks a series of questions to find out the exact nature of the problem, help is promised, acknowledged by the citizen, and the call is terminated.

The work that the police do begins in two ways: citizen-initiated or police-initiated (see Manning, 1988; Wilson, 1968). When citizens contact the police through 9-1-1 emergency centers, the request for assistance is symbolically encoded into organizationally relevant codes and assigned to the police (Manning, 1988). The talk between the police and citizens also begins in a similar way: 1) citizen-initiated 2) police-initiated. In the first, after a citizen has called the police, and requested assistance, the police eventually show up to the caller's residence and initiate the interrogative series, such as "Did you call?" or "What's going on?"

Excerpt 2 (*COPS* data: "Am I resisting?")
12   PO1: what's goin on man? ((puts his hand on his service weapon))
13   (1.8)
14   put your hands up

In excerpt 2, a woman calls the police to complain about her son who is in her garage, naked, and under the influence of drugs. Three officers respond to the call, and as one of the officers approaches the garage, he sees the naked man and initiates the interrogative series.

Sometimes, the parties who contacted the police initiate the talk by moving to the reason for the call, the first topic. In the following excerpt, an officer is dispatched to a domestic disturbance; when the officer attempts to establish the identities of the involved parties, a black woman (BW) not only identifies herself as the involved party (line 13: yes), but also preemptively moves to the reason for the call (line 13: he came into mah house):

Excerpt 3: (*COPS* Data: "Jimmy Dean" sausage)
12 PO: You the involved ma'am?
13 BW: (Yes he came into mah house)

When the talk between the police and citizens is police-initiated, more salient differences—and controversies—emerge. Self-generated police activity such as suspicious person stops, traffic stops, and vehicle searches intrude into the lives of citizens; such actions hinder free movement and, therefore, contradicts the principles of democracy (Skolnick and Fyfe, 1993); moreover, these types of activities usually involve members of the minority, hence, they are fraught with controversy (e.g., HEY, Come here!). A good example of a police-initiated encounter is the traffic stop—for driving through a red light, running a stop sign, speeding, driving with broken taillight etc.

Excerpt 4 (Midwest City Police Traffic Stop #2)
8   PO: How you doin >see your driver's license
9   en proof of insurance?<
10   (.7)
11   D: I got it in my jacket can I get it?

Excerpt 5 (Midwest City Police Traffic Stop #3)
12   PO: how you doin >can I see your driver's license
13   and proof of insurance?<
14   (.5)
15   D: sure

Overt Problem Initiation

In traffic stops, the police initiate the encounter—"summoning another to interact"—by activating their sirens, horns, and flashing lights. In other words, the summons is visual and aural—semiotic (see Schegloff, 1968). And just as callers to emergency centers initiate contact "to get assistance for troubles they have witnessed or experienced" (Zimmerman, 1992: 418), the police, much like callers to emergency centers, initiate contact with motorists concerning a particular "problematic" relevancy—what the stop is about.   However, unlike emergency calls to 911, ordinary traffic stops shoulder no exigent burden: just what the exact nature of the problem is has to be introduced and announced during the course of talk. Sometimes, that process of introducing and announcing the reason for the stop shapes the contours of the talk itself in legally and morally implicative ways.

If activation of sirens, flashing lights, and horns constitutes a summons, then the answering of that summons is the act of pulling over. Thus, traffic stops begin with a "prebeginning" where the officer activates the squad's lights, much like the way callers to emergency services pick up a phone and dial 911; but notice what is absent in the officers' first turn in excerpt 4 and 5: there is no categorical self-introduction. The bureaucratic/official "request" to see a driver's license is the officer's first turn utterance (line 8-9, 12-13). That is because in traffic stops the summons/answer sequence and identification/recognition sequence found in ordinary talk are reduced to one. By virtue of their uniforms, squad cars with flashing lights, and other "occupational accoutrements" (Niederhoffer, 1967), the task of verbal self-introduction and categorical-identification are not necessary since they are semiotically conveyed.[1] The semiotic summons already identifies the "caller" as the police. Thus, in a traffic stop, the summons/answer sequence and identification/recognition sequence— first semiotic turn—are achieved visually and aurally, thus further reducing the opening sequences noted in prior work (see Zimmerman, 1992). Furthermore, a fundamentally social act of beckoning another for availability of interaction is usurped for institutionally motivated reasons, one which shapes the responses of citizens to police action.

The police possess the authority to legitimately intrude into the lives of citizens, and theoretically, that intrusion is justified solely on legal grounds and in good faith. Thus, when the police initiate a traffic stop with a semiotic summons to halt, it is already an indication of a problem. This semiotic prebeginning in a traffic stop is what I refer to as *overt problem initiation* (OPI). There is surely nothing subtle or covert about flashing lights and blaring sirens in one's rearview mirror. Overt problem initiation is the first step in the opening sequences of a traffic stop. That motorists are being legally summoned then already carries the pragmatic sting of an accusation. That is to say, they are directly accused— with sirens, flashing lights—regarding some problematic relevancy, without a ratified knowledge of what that might be.[2]

However, can sirens and flashing lights be construed as accusations in addition to being a summons? Niederhoffer (1967:1) writes, "The policeman is a

'Rorschach' in uniform," that his "occupational accoutrements—shield, night-stick, gun, and summons book—clothe him in a mantle of symbolism that stimu-lates fantasy and projection." The police are often baffled by some of the atti-tudes and behaviors of citizens; they do not understand why—without turning into pop psychoanalysts—citizens "stiffen with compulsive rage or anxiety at the sight of a patrol car" (Niederhoffer, 1967:1); for that matter, the uniform. For instance, in an informal gathering with police officers, one patrolman related to me how he had pulled over a motorist to warn her about low tire pressure, only to be greeted with severe indignation. Or as Baker (1985) notes, a highway patrolman offers a ride to a hitchhiker on Christmas Eve, only to be violently cursed at and attacked. Why would such seemingly friendly gestures engender such hostile responses?

It is tempting at this point to offer a reductionistic, simple, and obtuse psy-chological explanation for motorists' apparently bizarre behavior. Thus, we could say that motorists and citizens who act out toward the police are not the models of mental health, that they are paranoid, crazy, antisocial, and have a deep-seated hatred of their fathers. And it is tempting to stop here; but if we examine the phenomenon sociologically, the act of being summoned, pulled over, greeted, covertly interrogated, and having the problem announced as se-quential steps in the opening sequences of a traffic stop, then we can salvage the analysis from psychology and psychoanalysis by grounding our analysis in ob-servable, demonstrable, and empirical action that subjects engage in. Overt problem initiation is overt in the sense that there are flashing lights and sirens, but there is little else overt about it. Citizens know that there is *a* problem, but they may not know what *the* problem is. In the first sequence, the semiotic summons, citizens are indirectly accused in a direct manner: "*As you are driving down the highway, suddenly there are flashing lights in the rearview mirror and the whoop of a siren in your ears. A small dose of adrenaline surges into your blood stream. Your heart beats faster; your palms sweat. You feel guilty whether you've consciously done something or not*" (Baker, 1985: 249).

Thus, when motorists and citizens act belligerently to officers' apparently friendly and concerned overtures—telling citizens about a tire dangerously low on air, offering a ride to a hitchhiker on Christmas Eve—their reactions seem to point the finger at the squad car, flashing lights, officer, and his/her uniform. If we adopt a five part sequential explanation of traffic stops, a citizen's violent reaction is a reaction to the direct and blatant manner of accusation—the sum-mons—not the uniform.

In ordinary social life ignoring a summons incurs only a morally account-able sanction (Schegloff, 1968). That is, if someone or something (telephone ring) calls us and beckons us to interact in an ordinary social encounter, we can refuse, albeit, at a moral expense (s/he snubbed me!). However, when the police summon us (civilians) to interact and we do not answer it, the accountability we face is not only moral but also legal. We can be sternly commanded to do so; they can physically grab us and force us to interact, and should we physically resist, the police can use pain compliance holds and strikes to make us interact (Bittner, 1978; Skolnick and Fyfe, 1993). As Skolnick and Fyfe (1993) posit, the police need not use those types of methods; their mere presence, sometimes, deters crime and forces citizens to change their behaviors. Hence, the police also need not issue a summons at all nor do they need to directly and bluntly accuse; their mere presence—the uniform and identity itself—sometimes achieves that purpose. When the bureaucratic summons is made, however, it's just that the Rorschach is no longer clothed in a "mantle of symbolism that stimulates fantasy and projection"; instead the Rorschach is cloaked in a uniform with a badge and a gun. Simply put, the Rorschach no longer exists as a fantasy and a projection in our minds; it roars to life in real-time action. The summons is the first step in giving that fantastic Rorschach a concrete face and an audible voice.

The Conversational Opening: Greetings and Requests

After the first part has been initiated (car pulled over) notice how the next stage is conversationally organized. Consider the following opening sequences from a traffic stop in which motorists have been pulled over for speeding:

Excerpt 6 (Midwest City Police Traffic Stop #2)
8   → PO: How you doin >see your driver's license
9   en proof of insurance?<
10   (.7)
11   D: I got it in my jacket can I get it?

Excerpt 7 (Midwest City Police Traffic Stop #3)
12   → PO: how you doin >can I see your driver's license
13   And proof of insurance?<
14   (.5)
15   D: sure

Excerpt 8 (Midwest City Police Traffic Stop #6)
3   → PO: How you [doin may I see your driver's license and=
4   D: [Hi
5   PO: = proof of insurance?
5   Do you have your insurance card?
7   D: (   )

Excerpt 9 (Midwest City Police Traffic Stop #5)
3   → PO: How you doin may I see your driver's
4   license and proof of insurance?
5   (.7)
6   D: Hi

The officers' first turns in excerpts 6-9 from ordinary traffic stops display some of the characteristics of *institutional talk* (Drew and Heritage, 1992). Each officer self selects him/herself as the first speaker; he/she selects what to talk about; he/she determines how much of the "topic" to talk about (Psathas, 1995). In this sense the first opening lines of a traffic stop are "pre-structured" in that speaker and topic selection and turn size are preallocated as a function of the officers' institutional authority. However, they are also different from requests found in calls to the police in that there is an "inversion" of requests: when citizens contact the police, they request assistance for their troubles (Sharrock and Turner, 1978; Whalen and Zimmerman, 1987). When the talk is initiated by the police, they make the request—the request in traffic stops "belongs" to them. This inversion has tremendous moral, social, and linguistic implications. The bureaucratic request is the second step in the overall structural organization of traffic stops, a statement which opens and conversationally initiates the encounter with the citizens.

There are two observations in excerpts 6-9 in the officers' first conversational openings in ordinary traffic stops that I want to mention since it is related to the prior work on institutional talk in a law enforcement related context. The officers' first turn utterance is composed of two clauses, two distinctive speech acts. The first clause is what could ostensibly be called a greeting, the second a request. It is noted in prior work on institutional talk, emergency calls for help (911), that unlike ordinary conversations where parties engage in greeting sequences to mutually recognize, ratify, and accomplish an intersubjectivity of sociality (see Sacks, 1992; Sacks et al., 1974; Schegloff, 1996, 1992a), greetings and "how are you" sequences are absent (Whalen and Zimmerman, 1987; Whalen, Zimmerman, and Whalen, 1988; see also Whalen and Zimmerman, 1990; Zimmerman, 1992). What we find in the empirical details of talk between patrol officers and motorists is that officers do open the traffic stop with a greeting appended to the request, as numerous ethnographic accounts of police work have already noted (e.g., Baker, 1985; Bayley, 1994; Black, 1980; Fletcher, 1990; Muir, 1977; Rubinstein, 1973; van Maanen, 1978a).

The first observation: the second clause is topically related to the problematic relevancy since the motorists' license and proof of insurance are organizationally and procedurally consequential for what follows next: if a driver does not have a license or proof of insurance then the motorist can be issued a ticket, arrested, or told to arrange for a ride; or should motorists refuse to give up their driver's license, the police can exercise their coercive power to gain their compliance (Bittner, 1978). Simply put, issuing statements such as "May I see your driver's license and proof of insurance?" is the discursive and sequential embodiment of police power. Only the police possess the theoretically legitimate capacity to issue such statements without the words crumbling under the weight of their own "unhappiness" (Austin, 1962). However, in addition to its institutional and bureaucratic function, there is a moral component to the request. The officers' first turn is the sequential environment where they can conduct an "attitude test."

The bureaucratic request made by the police is a way of initializing the talk with citizens, but it is also an officer's way of educing the moral character of the motorist—as a "governable" or a "rebel" (Muir, 1977). Depending on the motorists' demeanor to the officer's request, the officer changes his/her demeanor toward the motorist, hence, the outcome of the encounter (van Maanen, 1978a; see also Black, 1980). Thus, motorists shape the moral contour of the P-C encounter through their verbal behavior in the second turn. The second pair slot, the turn after the initial conversational opening in a traffic stop, then, is the first sequential opportunity for motorists and citizens to do discursive moral work. The request is a "perspectival display" of moral character where "one party solicits another party's opinion and then produces a report or assessment in a way that takes the other's into account" (Maynard, 1991: 458; see also Maynard, 1992). In traffic stops, however, it is not the other's opinion the patrol officer solicits, but the motorist's driver's license; and more importantly, what is also concurrently solicited is the motorists' demeanor—attitude toward the police.

Now, notice how each motorist in the given excerpts displays his/her understanding of the officers' verbally loaded utterance in the next turn. In excerpts 6 and 7, the motorists comply with the officers' request: the officer asks motorists to produce a driver's license and proof of insurance, they accede. No overt challenge to authority takes place. Consider the following data:

Excerpt 10 (Midwest City Police Traffic Stop #6)
```
3        PO: How you [doin may I see your driver's license and=
4   →    D:          [Hi
6            PO:        = proof of insurance?
7                       Do you have your insurance card?
7        D: (    )
```

Excerpt 11 (Midwest City Police Traffic Stop #7)
```
6        PO: How [you doin may I see your driver's license=
7   →    D:        [Hi
8        PO: =and proof of insurance?
```

In excerpt 10 and 11, an overlapping utterance—talk that occurs simultaneously between two or more speakers—occurs toward the end of the officer's first part clause. How are the motorists' apparently divergent responses (excerpt 6, line11; excerpt 7, line 15; excerpt 10 and 11, lines 4 and 7) to the officer's first turn—apparently a request—to be accounted for?

In ordinary conversations greetings are found in sequentially predictable places as the first and second pair parts of greeting sequences. This type of exchange format is so well established in mundane, everyday talk that it is referred to as an adjacency pair (Sacks et al., 1974). Greeting sequences, however, are not the only turn types in which sequentially preferred responses are systematically found: questions precede answers, requests are usually followed by granting of requests; denials follow accusations; invitations are usually accepted (see chapter 1). And at first glance the motorists who interject into the officer's first turn request may appear to be interrupting the officer's spate of talk, in a disaffiliative sort of way, as most interruptions do. However, if the motorist's response (hi) is seen as a response to the first clause, then the overlapping greeting does not work as a disaffiliative move, a challenge to the officer's request or as a sign of "uncooperativeness." The motorists' greeting responses merely orient to an utterance that temporally (historically) precedes the second one.

That motorists in the above excerpts are not disaffiliating to the officer's request shows the importance of speaking contexts (temporal, procedural, indexical)—even the miniscule syntactic structure of an utterance—in understanding and explaining how language is used in the micro details of P-C "talk-in-interaction" (Schegloff, 1987). Moreover, the motorists' overlapping greetings also hint at a poignant facet of social life in general. By orienting to the officers' greeting with delay absent—overlapping—responses, those utterances display the sociality of communicative behavior and the rigid structure of conformity and normative expectation that is embedded within the mundane social world. Moreover, we can see how even in a bureaucratically occasioned intrusive social interaction, the primordial rules of social intercourse permeate into the micro details of discursive action.

A greeting such as a terse 'hi' or 'hello' is morphologically and phonetically simple, but the social and moral work it does is tremendous. When someone says hello we are normatively held accountable for a similar return, and that expectation is almost like a knee-jerk test. When speakers violate that expectation the inference that the violation generates is moral. By flouting a reflex-like response, the rebel speaker disengages him/herself from the social world in a most simplistic, but profoundly brutal way. Prior police scholars have noted that there are citizens who remain "cool and detached" or stay silent to the questions posed by police officers during encounters, and as a result, they were characterized as being hostile or disrespectful (see Worden and Shepard, 1996).[3] The observers' characterization arises from the violation of a normatively accountable communicative—social—trust (Garfinkel, 1967).

Compare the motorists who orient to the first clause of the officer's utterance to those who orient their turns to the second clause. In excerpt 6 when the motorist responds "I got it in my jacket can I get it?" the indexical expression (it) has its referent in the prior turn—driver's license and/or proof of insurance. In excerpt 7 the motorist's "sure" is a response to the second clause request, for 'sure' as the second pair part of a 'how you doin' makes no sense; more so for 'I got it in my jacket can I get it?' Why do motorists orient to different fragments of the same sentence and base their next turn on that particular understanding? My point is that that's what police officers and citizens do: officers ask a seemingly simple question, but one group of subjects bases their understanding of the utterance as a greeting, in a socially lubricative sort of way, while the other group of subjects orients to the question in a more official business-like way, shaping their turns around the first turn utterance as a bureaucratic request, not a greeting.

This leads to my second point. As stated, there are two distinct types of utterances which are interwoven—interlocked—into the officer's first turn. In excerpt 6 and 7 the first turns are articulated with little pause between the two speech acts; the greeting and the request are delivered rapidly, in almost one breath. How that loaded first turn is understood by the motorists vary, for some orient to the prior turn as a request, some as a greeting. For those who respond to the "How you doing may I see your driver's license and proof of insurance" with a "hi," the [greeting + request] is treated as a greeting, for "hi" is an adjacency pair to another greeting (Sacks et al., 1974). Those who respond to the "How you doing may I see your driver's license and proof of insurance" with a "sure"—request granting—are treating the [greeting + request] as a request, the sequentially preferred next turn response. "Hi" as a response to "May I see your driver's license?" borders on the absurd; it only makes sense if the utterance that preceded it is another greeting. Similarly, "can I get it it's in my jacket" is meaningful only if the utterance which preceded it is a request, not a greeting.

In a way, then, although the greeting is there, prior to the request, it is not there (absent) because some motorists do not "hear" the greeting, that is treat it as one. Thus, what some of the motorists and police officers display supports prior research on institutional talk, that greetings and other recognitionals are absent in institutional talk (Whalen and Zimmerman, 1987; Zimmerman, 1992). Even that absence, however, is performed collaboratively and reflexively: (1) the rapid manner in which the greeting is articulated, compressed into the official business at hand with little room for a transition relevant place, suggests that the greeting is present merely in form but not in intention and function. The officers give no sequential opportunity or turn space for the other speaker to respond by articulating the greeting in an overly perfunctory manner, thus prosodically imprinting their preference for institutional and bureaucratic organization of talk. (2) The way in which the motorists respond to the first turn demonstrates that the officer's intention can be heard two ways: as a greeting and as a request. That some citizens respond to the [greeting + request] with a 'hi' demonstrates the way motorists orient to the social aspects of the encounter, not its institutionality, thus revealing a preference organization toward a non-institutionalized format of talk. However, both the presence and absence of greetings require sustenance from police officers and motorists: police articulations and citizens' understandings of the bureaucratic—loaded—first turn are mutually and collaboratively performed in the institutional opening first turn, and citizens' response to it in the second turn. Greetings, as an activity that mutually ratifies and lubricates the social engine, come to be through a particular manner of police articulation, and only through the motorists' understanding of the officer's intention in that way; and they must display that understanding in the turn after the initial request.

That the motorists' understanding of police greetings is a function of their articulation leads to the question: how do the police articulate greetings that in form (appearance) and intention perform the conventional task of mutually recognizing, ratifying, and establishing intersubjective social relations? Consider the following data:

Excerpt 12 (Southern City Police Traffic Stop #2)

1 →	PO: How you doing sir?
2	D: Alright, I guess
3	PO: Alright, can I see your license and registration and
4	proof of insurance?

Excerpt 13 (Midwest City Police Traffic Stop # 4)

| 1 → | PO: how you doin? |

2   (.3)
3   D: not good uh heh heh [heh
4   PO: [ye eh heh
5   you work for Park Ridge or?

In these two traffic stops, the officer's first turn utterance is not interlocked with another speech act (request). The greeting—how you doing—is uttered in the first turn slot by itself; and in the next turn, drivers respond to that first pair greeting as a greeting with "conventional" responses (line 2, 3). However, that the greeting sequence—perhaps even the interaction itself—portends "trouble" is indicated in the drivers' second turn responses. That is, "Alright, I guess" (line 2) and "Not good" (line 3) as the second pair parts of a greeting sequence display features of dispreferred responses: in terms of their sheer turn size, they already extend well beyond the preferred monosyllabic response "fine" and "good" (see Jefferson, 1980; Raymond, 2000; Sacks, 1975). Contextually, "not good" and "I guess" both use the prior sequence in the interaction (the summons) as a resource in the production of their current turn at talk; that is, the "bad news mood" that the semiotic summons forecasts is recycled into the second turn response to the greeting (Maynard, 1996).

In excerpt 12, when the motorist responds to the greeting with a dispreferred response, the officer repeats a portion of the answer as an acknowledgment token and proceeds to the bureaucratic request. In excerpt 13, the driver laughs after her "not good" response. By doing so, she transforms the somber and "bad news" mood of the interaction through a juxtaposition of affect: she admits that she is in some sort of trouble (speeding), but she also uses humor to cast a different emotional perspective on the encounter. The driver's laughter invites the next turn speaker (officer) to join in the laughter (Jefferson, 1984). As a result, through laughter and the social and normative expectancies it generates, the driver alters the footing of the interaction from a negative (accusatorial) one to a positive one (laughter) (Goffman, 1981).

If some motorists hear the isolated (not interlocked) greetings as they are meant to be heard (e.g., excerpt 12 and 13), some motorists, despite the turn constructional isolation and the sociable intention, do not hear the greeting as such. Consider the following data:

Excerpt 14 (University Police Traffic Stop #1)
1 →   PO: Good evening how you doin (man?)
2   D: You got a problem?
3   PO: Yea, it's a big problem
4   what chu in a rush fuh?

Just in case the motorist might not understand the intention of the officer's first turn utterance, this officer compounds his greeting into two parts. The response to the officer's greeting, however, is far from an expectable and conventionalized one. In fact, it isn't even heard as one. The motorist responds with a question that attempts to preemptively move to the reason for the stop (first topic) in a way that challenges—opposes—the officer's authority (see Goodwin, 1990). The officer, in line 3-4, intensifies the motorist's initial assessment (Pomerantz, 1984) and suggests just what the problematic relevancy might be (in a rush—speeding). But the key point is that the motorist never accepts the uptake of the officer's greeting; instead, he uses it to display a hostile and an uncooperative attitude.

If hostility is a moral category that the rebel speaker produces, through silence and other verbal behavior, then its converse, conformity, hence, order, is something that ordinary speakers also produce. Ordinary speakers in everyday speaking contexts negotiate turn taking, allocate and switch topics, open and close conversations, reformulate and clarify misunderstood utterances, and repair and correct speech errors (see Schegloff and Sacks 1973; Sacks et al., 1974; Schegloff et al., 1977). The same conversational machinery operates in P-C encounters. Institutional authority derives its force from ordinary authority, one that all members of the social world mutually orient to and collaboratively establish. If rebel speakers challenge police authority, hence social order, by not talking when they are normatively held accountable to do so, then police authority and social order is also spoken into existence in the micro details of communicative action through the citizens' verbal behavior—providing answers when they are asked questions, granting requests when requested, obeying commands when commanded, greeting the officer back when he/she says hi. And those rules that guide social life, including moral and linguistic ones, are empirically demonstrable in the actual moments of members' production and use (action), turn by turn, line by line, utterance by utterance—not in observations and descriptive accounts about their action.

Covert Problem Initiation

With the first two turns—first two lines—of a prototypical P-C encounter, I have shown how the two parts of an utterance are differently intended, understood, and implicative in the next turn for the next speaker. Now, I want to show how the third sequence is conversationally organized and the work that is performed in it.

Excerpt 14 (Midwest City Police Traffic Stop #3)
```
12       PO: how you doin >can I see your driver's license
13            And proof of insurance?<
14            (.5)
15       D:   sure
16            (16)
17   →   PO: you know why I stopped you?
18            (.7)
19   →   D:   why sir?
```

Excerpt 15 (Midwest City Police Traffic Stop #5)
```
3        PO: How you doin may I see your driver's
```

```
4              license and proof of insurance?
5                      (.7)
6        D:   Hi
7                   (  )
8     →  PO:  You know why I stopped you?
9                   (  )
10    →  D:   (No)
```

Excerpt 16 (Midwest City Police Traffic Stop #2)

```
8        PO:  how you doin >see your driver's license
9             en proof of insurance?<
10            (.7)
11       D:   I got it in my jacket can I get it?
12            (.)
13       PO:  Yeah
14            (5.0)
15       D:   my insurance I got off my other car
16            I just bought this vehicle
17            (.)
18       PO:  how long ago did you buy it?
19            (.7)
20       D:   about 2 days now (.6) here's the insurance
21            (2.0)
22    →  PO:  you know why I stopped you?
23            (1.0)
24    →  D:   No not re[ally I
```

In excerpts 14 and 15 after the semiotic summons is acknowledged and the initial conversational opening sequences are mutually worked through, the officer asks another question, and true to the form and function of an interrogative, it appears to require a simple yes/no answer. In excerpt 16, after a brief "side sequence" (Jefferson, 1972) about insurance and vehicle ownership, the officer asks the same yes/no question found in other excerpts ("you know why I stopped you?"). Again, although the question is syntactically constructed as a simple yes/no question, one that, on the surface, requires the next turn speaker to dichotomously confirm or negate an epistemological state, there is an implicit hint of something else—blame.

Grammatically, these types of polar interrogatives (yes/no) project as a relevant next turn response a yes or a no (type conforming answer) (Raymond, 2000). Furthermore, they are unmarked and contain minimal amount of presupposition. It has been found that in these types of sequences, there is an overwhelming preference for preferred—type conforming—responses over nonconforming ones (Raymond, 2000). Raymond (2000) finds that if nonconforming responses are given, it may allude to some sort of trouble, hence, are likely to be expanded (Raymond, 2000). I refer to this third part as *covert problem initiation* (CPI). The question is covert because, obviously, it differs from the overt way *a* problem—indefinite—is initiated. Motorists know that something is wrong, but do not yet know what *the*—definite—problem is. And the "Do you know why I stopped you" initiates just what that specific problematic relevancy might be before the officer actually informs the motorist of his/her blameworthy action in subsequent turns (Pomerantz, 1978). Furthermore, when the officer asks the motorist who has been pulled over as to why he or she thinks the officer did so, the officer gives the motorist an opportunity to give an account—an exoneration—of why s/he has been legally summoned before the officer does (Antaki, 1994). Since the problem has yet to be announced, the covert problem initiation can be thought of as a "preliminary" (Schegloff, 1980) to a *problem announcement*, the fourth-part of the opening sequences in a traffic stop.

If "I stopped you because you were speeding" or its variation such as "I clocked you doing 50 in a 25 zone" can be viewed as an "official" problem announcement, an official accusation that describes "the addressee as the agent of an offensive act" (Goodwin, 1982: 78), then the "Do you know why I stopped you?" can be seen as a pre-blame of sorts (Pomerantz, 1978). That's because the "Do you know why I stopped you?" (CPI) does not announce the problem; it grammatically projects the preference organization of the next turn response toward a type conforming one (Raymond, 2000). Let me provide a concrete example. "Do you know where Waldo is?" is on the surface an epistemological question which requires a responder's display of knowledge state (Yes I know where Waldo is /No I don't know where Waldo is). However, as Schegloff (1988b) notes, that literal interpretation is not what is meant in ordinary conversation; it is an indirect request for information—where is Waldo?[4] How is this indeterminate and indirect sense of utterances to be applied to the covert problem initiation? What function does the covert problem initiation serve?

There are two interpretive possibilities to the "do you know why I stopped you?" question, one that is premised on (1) ordinary social structure and (2) an institutional social structure. In ordinary talk, as a preliminary to a problem announcement, the question is a request/offer/invitation to tell an account, an extended turn at talk (Antaki, 1994). And conceptualized as an invitation to tell a story, the officer's yes/no interrogative—much like "Do you know where Waldo is?"—projects an extended turn at talk as the preferred second turn response to the indirect request for information (Levinson, 1983: 336). However, if the polar interrogative is conceptualized as a blame-imbued question, then an extended turn at talk (e.g., an admission of guilt) would be the dispreferred response; the preferred response to such blame imbued and accusatory question would be a denial (Levinson, 1983: 336).

Now, notice again the motorists' responses to the officers' yes/no questions:

Excerpt 14 (Midwest City Police Traffic Stop #3)
17   PO: you know why I stopped you?
18   (.7)
19   → D: why sir?

Excerpt 15 (Midwest City Police Traffic Stop #5)
8   PO: You know why I stopped you?
9   ( )
10 → D: (No)

Excerpt 16 (Midwest City Police Traffic Stop #2)
22   PO: you know why I stopped you?
23   (1.0)
24 → D: No not re[ally I

   If the polar interrogative was meant as an invitation to give an account and uttered in that way, the motorists have not heard its illocutionary and pragmatic sense. The "Do you know why I stopped you?" is not heard as an invitation, but as a confirmation-like question of an epistemological state. In other words, the question is heard in a purely formal and grammatical way, as a yes/no question. But notice that the motorists' responses in excerpts 14-16 are rather curt (line 19: why sir?; line 10: no; line 24: not really). As the dispreferred response to an invitation/request/offer to give an account, it is done without the turn delaying features such as mitigations, accounts, and excuses (Pomerantz, 1984). However, if the "do you know" question is viewed as a covert way of initiating blame (pre-blame) and pre-accusing (Pomerantz, 1978) then it acts as a way of implicitly securing "recognizability and understanding" of what the motorist—the other speaker—knows (Schegloff, 1980:115). That implicit prior "recognizability and understanding," of course, is sequentially and institutionally derived. The "do you know" question occurs as the third part in a five-part sequence; hence, motorists have already been given clues and signaled via the summons (OPI) and the bureaucratic request of a problematic relevancy. It's just that the problematic relevancy is phrased in an equivocal and unmarked way, organized in a manner that projects a preference for motorists' articulation (see Schegloff, 1988a).[5]
   Viewed as an accusatory and blame-imbued question, the responses to the "do you know" question display the preferred features of an accusation/denial sequence. Although the "no" or its equivalent negation tokens fulfill the grammatical relevancy requirements of the yes/no questions, the "no's" not only deny the conditional relevance of its preceding turn, but they also deny the occasion—the problematic nature of the encounter. The "do you know" question already makes minimal assumptions about the motorists' state of knowledge; however, to view those questions as being "unmarked" is a bit misleading, for the prior two sequences (OPI, request) institutionally, contextually, and sequentially, "mark" the unmarked question. To give a negative answer, then, is not only a way of negatively providing a response, but it is also a way of challenging the presupposition embedded in the grammar and in the institutional context. And the way the motorists' blunt responses follow swiftly, immediately and early in their turns support the following conjecture: the sequential structure of "Do you know why I stopped you?" and "No" in its turn after suggests that

those two adjacent turns bear a strong structural resemblance to accusations and denials (see Atkinson and Drew, 1979; Garcia, 1991; Komter, 1994).

As already noted, the semiotic summons establishes the means and availability of both parties to interact; the officers' [greeting + request] is the statement that conversationally "opens" the encounter; and the "do you know" question covertly initiates the problem/topic. Not all traffic stops, however, follow this "routine" form. The topic/problem can be preemptively moved or challenged by motorists through questions such as "what's the problem officer?" "Is there a problem officer?" Or "What did I do?" Consider the following data:

Excerpt 17 (Southern City Police Traffic Stop #4)
```
1        PO: How you doing sir?
2        M:  Alright, I guess
3        PO: Alright, can I see your license and registration and
4            proof of insurance?
5   →    M:  Yes, was I speeding or something?
6        PO: No, once you give me the information provided
             that I asked for I'll let you know why I stopped you
```

In this traffic stop, the officer does manage to go through two sequences, the summons and the [greeting + request]; but before the officer can continue to the next step, the motorist initiates another action (topic selection) and interrogates the officer, thereby momentarily realigning the participation structure of the P-C encounter. Thus far (lines 1, 3) the police officer has been the one dictating the contours of the interaction: he asks the questions; the motorist answers them. However, in line 5, the motorist temporarily breaks that institutional frame and asks the officer a question of his own. There is, again, an uncanny parallel between the opening sequences in traffic stops and openings in ordinary telephone calls. As Schegloff (1968) notes, in telephone calls it is the caller who canonically initiates topic (the reason for the call) after the completion of the second "how are you" sequence—the anchor position.

The "caller" in police-initiated encounters such as traffic stops is the police; similarly, as a general rule, the police "make the call" using sirens and lights, initiate talk, and determine the topic of talk as a function of their institutional power. However, that motorists, like some callers, can and do preemptively launch into the first topic slot does not mean that the sequences I've presented thus far are not valid. That the motorists have not violated the turn taking order by preemptively moving to the first topic, and instead treat the traffic stop as a "routine" one attests to the fact that its "routineness" is mutually oriented to by both participants. As Schegloff (1986: 117) writes, routines are "achievements arrived at out of a welter of possibilities for preemptive moves or claims, rather than a mechanical or automatic playings out of pre-scripted routines."

Notice how the "routineness" goes awry in this Southern City traffic stop when the motorist preemptively moves to the reason for the stop (first topic slot): the officer tells him to first give him the requested documents, and then the officer authoritatively tells the motorist that he will tell him why he stopped him.

In not so many words, the officer lets the motorist know who is in charge, and in a blatant way, socializes the motorist into the institutional order of talk in traffic stops, and in encounters with the police in general: the police ask the questions, motorists and citizens answer them. In excerpt 17, when the motorist preemptively moves to the topic slot, the "smooth" and "routine" character of the traffic stop fades and a more rigid, formal, and stern bureaucratic order appears. As this data illustrates, the "routinessness" of traffic stops, as a conversational activity, is a collaboratively accomplished one, one that requires joint effort of both parties; furthermore "routineness" is not something that automatically just happens in a ritualistic manner; routines are accomplished and chosen from a range of "structural" possibilities" (see Schegloff, 1968; 1986).

That motorists forgo a sequentially and institutionally provided slot to give an account and reject the question's sensibility through a denial hint at the legalistic constraints the motorists face in traffic stops. To accept an invitation to announce the problem—give an account— differs from ordinary invitations—to come to a party, to go out for dinner, to go out on a date—in that the acceptance of those mundane invitations carries no possibility of a legal sanction. I conceptualize the turn after the invitational question as an opportunity to confess because that's what the announcement is tantamount to, an admission of a legal violation. For example, if the officer asks, "you know why I pulled you over?" and a motorist replies, "I was speeding," then the problem announcement—I was speeding—is not just an announcement but an admission—a confession. And this statement is legally recognized as an admission of interest, which can be used against motorists in a court of law.

Motorists, then, are caught in an irresolvable paradox and equivocalness of police power: (1) The legal nature of talk precludes citizens from admitting and stating the problem since it automatically imputes their bureaucratic identity (law violator; speeder). (2) As a result, the legal consequences of the preferred second pair part preclude conformity to the preference organization found in ordinary talk (invitation→acceptance). (3) The moral nature of the occasioned talk disfavors declination and rejection of the invitation since it interactionally shapes their moral identity (cooperative versus hostile citizen). Theoretically, motorists are stranded either way: if they admit and announce the problem, they are imputed the label of being a law violator; if they reject the invitation to announce the problem, they are labeled as being uncooperative and improperly demeaned. Practically, however, if motorists admit their guilt and confess, they create a positive impression management: they are seen in a morally favorable light, one who is honest, properly demeaned, corrigible, and penitent (Emerson, 1969).

Problem Announcement and Excuses

The participants have thus far negotiated three stages—overt problem initiation, the greeting + request, and covert problem initiation—of a five part opening sequence in traffic stops. Consider how the fourth part of the traffic stop occurs in the following data:

Excerpt 18 (Midwest City Police Traffic Stop #3)
17   PO: you know why I stopped you?
18   (.7)
19   D: why sir?
20 → PO: I clocked you doin 48 in a 25

Excerpt 19 (Midwest City Police Traffic Stop #5)
8   PO: You know why I stopped you?
9   ( )
10   D: (No)
11   ( )
12 → PO: I clocked you doing 44 in a 25

Excerpt 20 (Midwest City Police Traffic Stop #2)
22   PO: you know why I stopped you?
23   (1.0)
24   D: No not re[ally I
25 → PO: [I clocked you doing 44 in a 25

In the excerpts above, the officer pulls the motorists over, makes a request, covertly initiates the problem, the motorists deny their wrongdoing, and do not give an account; consequently, the officer announces the problem, the "bad news" (e.g., I clocked you doing 44 in a 25). And after the officer announces the problem, notice what happens in the next turn:

Excerpt 21 (Midwest City Police Traffic Stop #2)
25   PO: I clocked you doing 44 in a 25
26   (1.0)
27 → D: I'm sorry about that officer I'm just
                 trying to get home from Glen Ellen man

Excerpt 22 (Midwest City Police Traffic Stop #4)
26   PO: I clocked you doing 46 back there for 25
27   (.7)
28 → D: I didn't even know I mean it was stupid
29   it was (stupid) I know
Excerpt 23 (Midwest City Police Traffic Stop #4)
28   PO: [Why you
29   going 45 in a 25? ((raised tone))
30 → D: Well I'm sorry sir but I hit my head my head
31   was bleeding I'm just trying to get over there now

Excerpt 24 (Midwest City Police Traffic Stop #6)
14   PO: I clocked you doing 47 in a 30
15   ( )

16 → D: I'm really sorry I'm like so late

The official justification for the traffic stop—problematic relevancy—is finally announced in the fourth part of the opening sequence. Here, the motorists are accused of speeding, and the accounts—the extended talk that was initially projected in the third sequence—emerge in the slot after the accusation, the act that is legally "offensive." In the turn after the problem announcement, the motorists offer excuses for why they were speeding. But notice that the excuses come only after the officer announces the problematic relevancy and accuses the motorist of a traffic violation.[6] The excuses are also delayed across turns, and they do not occur as extended turn constructional units until after the motorists have treated the covert problem initiation in an institutionally preferred way (denial).[7] That sequential environment, post problem announcement, however, is not the first opportunity for motorists to give their excuses; the first sequential opportunity occurs after the first, second, and third sequence, but well before the fourth, problem announcement. Motorists in the discussed excerpts never take advantage of their sequential opportunities to announce the problem, thereby shaping the contours of their moral identity. And notice in the following excerpt how a motorist who has been pulled over for speeding accomplishes the excuse by violating the turn taking order:

Excerpt 25 (Midwest City Police Traffic Stop #1)
3   D: Hi I just got into an accident I'm an I was just trying
4   to get to my boyfriend's work so I can[
5   PO: Let me see your license[

In excerpt 25, the motorist does not wait for the officer to approach the vehicle to initiate the opening sequence; she self selects herself as the first turn speaker, and after the summons, she provides an excuse for why she was speeding. But the key point is that she initiates the sequence before the officer announces the problem. She gives an excuse even before the officer announces the problem, thereby metapragmatically confessing to a legal violation before any substantive verbal communication. Notice the work that is performed in the slot after the problem announcement, and its similarity to the "I'm washing my hair" line that young high school girls commonly give to boys who ask them what they are doing Saturday night (preliminary to a request for a date): the mean-spirited high school girl says it to weasel out of a date, the motorists a ticket. But the work they do is the same—give excuses. Thus far, we have seen the diverse—and endless—excuses that motorists give officers when they are informed of their infraction (speeding).

Artists can learn volumes from the way motorists creatively and ingeniously formulate excuses; however, listening to them does not have to be an exercise in exasperation. Excuses can be topically constrained by the officer in an interactionally tactical way for the officer's benefit. Consider the following traffic stop data:

Excerpt 26 (Southern City Police Traffic Stop #7)
1   PO: Hello. Can I see your driver's license please?
2   Good evening ma'am, my name is officer X with
3   the Southern City Police Department. The reason
4   I'm stopping you is you are doing 42 in a 30.
5   Is there any medical emergency you're in a hurry for?
6   D: (driver shakes her head; officer begins to write the citation)

In excerpt 26 the officer summons the driver and pulls the car over for
speeding. In his first turn, the officer greets the motorist (hello), politely makes a
request (can I see your driver's license please?), deferentially goes through another greeting sequence (good evening ma'am), introduces himself (my name is
officer X with the Southern City PD), announces the problem (the reason I'm
stopping you is that you are doing 42 in a 30), and asks if there is an emergency
that might be causing her to speed. The motorist in the next turn shakes her head
to indicate that there is no emergency: the officer begins to write the citation.
    What is noteworthy about this traffic stop is the way the opening sequences
are densely "compressed" into the officer's first turn at talk. The motorist has
little sequential room or turn space to respond to the different utterances that are
embedded in the first turn. To be sure, there are two questions in the officer's
extended turn (lines 1-5), a request and a yes/no "emergency" question, that give
the impression that the motorist will have a chance to explain himself. It is misleading, however, to believe that these two interrogatives give the motorist a free
reign to verbally respond to the officer's questions in an unrestricted manner. In
traffic stops, the preference organization of next turn response to requests is
physical (giving the officer the necessary documents), as well as verbal (sure)
(Dore, 1978; Garvey, 1975). Likewise, although the officer greets the motorist,
she is given no opportunity to respond to the greeting as such. The officer also
does not give the motorist an opportunity to give an account (excuse) through
covert problem initiation (CPI); the officer preempts that sequence and directly
moves on to problem announcement. And when the next interrogative is asked,
it is grammatically and semantically constrained in a severe way.
    Phrased as a yes/no question, it projects the preference organization of the
next turn response towards a type conforming one (yes or no) (Raymond, 2000).
Hence, the motorists are faced with two grammatically possible answers: (1) yes
+ account (2) no. If motorists answer affirmatively to "Is there any medical
emergency you're in a hurry for?" the forthcoming account is semantically constrained to the one projected in the question, one that is related to a medical
emergency. In excerpt 26, the female motorist shakes her head to indicate no.
Now, consider the following data:

Excerpt 27 (Southern City Police Traffic Stop #5)
1   PO: Can I see your driver's license please?
2   My name is Officer X with the Southern City Police Department.
3   The reason I'm stopping you is you are doing 44 in a 30.
4   Is there any medical emergency that you're in a hurry for sir?

5   M: Actually uh we have a Chinese restaurant and I'm the
6   only driver and I'm the only one and the other ones
7   didn't come in and I've got like eight orders
8   PO: No medical emergencies though?
9   M: Oh no

In excerpt 27, the motorist does answer the yes/no question with extended talk. However, the motorist's talk—excuse—is not related to the topical constraint imposed in the prior turn (medical emergency). And notice that the deviation from the grammatical constraints embedded in the prior turn is prefaced with two hesitation tokens that delay the account (line 5: actually, uh), thus lexically marking the dispreferred design of the motorist's turn in progress (Raymond, 2000). In excerpt 27, there is an implicit hint that the delivery guy may be trying to generate sympathy from the officer. This interpretation is suggested in the way the motorist tells his excuse: his co-workers didn't show up; consequently, he's all alone, and he's got eight orders he has to deliver by himself, all within a reasonable amount of time before the food gets cold. These reasons are intrasequentially (within a turn) linked in the account with the coordinating conjunction 'and' in a list-like manner, thereby giving his "overworkedness" a linguistic face. After hearing the Chinese food delivery guy's excuse, the officer in line 8 repeats the emergency question, and in response, the motorist denies that there is an emergency, which is prefaced with a change of state/receipt of new information marker (see Heritage, 1998b, 1984b).[8]

The noteworthy point about this way of framing a question (is there a medically emergency that you're in a hurry for?) is that it has a similar function to covert problem initiation (CPI). However, it restricts the topical range of the solicited account in a specific way, thereby preemptively restraining the limitless and creative excuses that citizens come up with after they are informed of their legal infraction. The officer frames the yet to come excuse as a medical emergency; consequently, he sets that criterion as the only acceptable and legitimate reason for motorists' legal violation. That is, unlike the covert and open-ended "do you know" question, the parameter of the excuse in the "is there an emergency" question is already grammatically and semantically constrained.[9]

To summarize: there are five parts to the opening sequences of a traffic stop, (1) overt problem initiation (summons) (2) [greeting] + request (3) covert problem initiation (4) problem announcement (5) excuses. The noteworthy point about the five part structure in the opening sequences of traffic stops is the extent to which the institutional—police—talk parallels ordinary talk, and in the way the police modify and adapt the discourse structures found in everyday life to conduct and negotiate the social encounter.

The first part (overt problem initiation) derives its sociological force from a pervasively occurring social phenomenon. A summons is a primordial form of social action, one which morally binds the one summoned to interact (Schegloff, 1968). In police work, that moral obligation is adapted in a legalistic fashion. Moreover, summons in P-C encounters is different from those made in ordinary life because they can only be made by a few who have been legitimately conferred that right (see Bittner, 1978); in this way, the first part semiotically materializes the coercive authority of the police, and socializes the citizens into its acceptance (obedience, pulling over).

In the second part, the police give concrete and discursive form to their institutional authority by canonically speaking first, introducing the topic, and exercising their authority to entangle citizens in a bureaucratically occasioned event. They veil their authority to initiate such action through politeness (request), thereby, projecting politeness (request compliance) as the preferred next turn action. And when the conventional sociality of everyday life is adapted to the encounters by prefacing greetings to the requests, they are articulated in such a way that the talk is organized with a preference for its institutional occasion rather than a social one.

In the third part, the police disguise—intentionally or unintentionally—a seemingly simple polar interrogative phrased as an epistemological question to do the interactional work of an invitation and a "pre" accusation. And by packaging the third part as an ordinary mechanism for soliciting an admission and acceptance, the police project a conditionally relevant next turn answer: a confession. That motorists do not announce or admit the problem but provide denials gives empirical support to the accusatorial nature of the "do you know" question.

In the fourth sequence, the police officially state the problem and accuse the motorists of a legal violation; and usually, the motorists give excuses for why they were speeding in the slot after the announcement (fifth), as the step last in the opening sequence in traffic stops.

Throughout all these sequences the police give a semiotic and a linguistic face to the coercive and moral aspects of police power. The police do not give citizens just one chance at impression management but several. And although the police are ideologically imbued with an unimaginably raw power and brutal capacity to exercise physical force, they do not exercise it in a unilateral way. As I have shown from routine traffic stops, the police exercise of power is sequentially and linearly coordinated, mutually and collaboratively brought to order by the officers and motorists alike. Moreover, the citizens are socialized by the police into the bureaucratic and institutional order of talk through various sequentially driven discursive mechanisms.

In the first sequence, how citizens respond to the summons (immediately and swiftly), or do not, communicates their moral character to the police. In the second, the citizens' verbal response to the request also signifies their attitude toward the police, determining the treatment they receive. The same is true of the third sequence. What is noteworthy analytically is that the absolute and coercive authority of the police is not exercised categorically and unilaterally, but sequentially, turn by turn, line by line, fluid enough to be adaptive to the moral contingencies that arise during routine police-citizen encounters.

The Equivocalness of Police-Initiated Interrogatives

A noteworthy feature of WH questions is that they presuppose a major part of the proposition (Jacobs, 1995). That is, certain questions assume the general proposition in them to be factual. For example, "when did you last beat your wife?" already presumes that the responder beats his wife on a regular basis. WH questions can be alternatively formulated using a yes/no interrogative, thereby questioning the truth or falsity of a proposition (e.g., do you beat your wife?). In a courtroom cross examination, for instance, WH questions are used to elicit narratives; consequently, they give witnesses and victims extended turns at talk (see Conley and O'Barr, 1990; Matoesian, 1993); when yes/no interrogatives are asked, the answers are institutionally constrained to provide only the minimally requisite information.[10]

The function of WH and polar interrogatives in P-C talk is similar to the function of WH questions in courts. The purpose behind the questions, however, may be different. The police, by giving citizens and suspects more opportunity to talk, may be allowing them to contradict themselves or giving them options to do otherwise (e.g., confess, deny, give excuses). Or, since the answer is already presupposed in the question—meaning that the suspect is already assumed to be guilty—officers can concern themselves with the problem of finding out only the details of their story. But the noteworthy point is that WH and polar interrogatives do not wear the grammatical cloak of accusations. For example, uttering, "Did you steal that car?" accuses the recipient of the message of a legally offensive act; however "Is this your car?" or "Where did you get this car?" formally suggests no such accusatorial interpretation. In order for the latter to be heard as accusations, they have to be oriented to as such in the respondent's next turn response through a denial, rather than as fact seeking interrogatives.

Being equivocal (and covert) when initiating a problem, however, has a valuable interactional function: "one possible answer relates the employment of equivocal utterances to the issue of responsibility for version. For the record, and if challenged, speaker can claim the literal version as his, and can disavow a pejorative alternative, which is thus made out as recipient's 'misunderstanding' (and hence recipient's responsibility)" (Sharrock and Turner, 1978: 186). That is, officers cover themselves from counter-accusations; alternatively, because they never directly accuse, they can always back out of their purported intention by ascribing a different one. Direct accusations such as "did you steal that car?" make it impossible for officers to back out of their utterances and save face if they are wrong. However, if accusations are phrased indirectly, the officer can always back out: *I didn't mean that you stole it, I just wanted to know where you got it.* This way of covertly initiating a problem—indirect accusation—offers a strategic and tactical way for officers to save face if they are wrong, thus preserving both participants' face and autonomy. Moreover, it saves the face of citizens by desisting them from the act of denying a formal, "official," and face-threatening accusation (negative politeness). Therefore, equivocally initiating a problem and indirectly accusing citizens reconfigures the preference organization of a well-established adjacency pair (accusation/denial) by syntactically packaging the accusative first pair part as something neutral (information seek-ing question).

That citizens understand WH questions in an equivocal way, as requests for information or accusatorial interrogatives, and that the police have the capacity to use them in an equivocal way gives the police much leverage (power) in their ability to contextualize talk. As Sharrock and Turner (1978: 186) note, "to speak unequivocally is to deprive one's remark of just those effects that equivocality accomplishes." Of course, there is no inherent reason why seemingly simple questions work in an equivocal way; that it can and does work in an equivocal and accusatorial manner is an effect of the institution, not language.

Consider the following data from a felony traffic stop. In excerpt 28 officers pull over a motorist for allegedly driving a stolen car. The officers activate their sirens and initiate a felony traffic stop.[11] After they have restrained all of the occupants in the car (except the baby), one of the officers begins the interroga-tive series. There are five principal participants in this excerpt, male Hispanic driver (HM), his wife, two patrol officers, and a baby (the driver's son).

Excerpt 28 (*COPS* data: "Driving a baby")
```
035 →  PO1:    Where'd you get the car mae::ng?
036             (1.4)
037    HM:     It's my car I bought it
038             (.7)
039 →  PO1:    Where'd dju get the license plate that's on there?
040    HM:                             [ Uh
041             I got it from somebody (.) used to live  (1.5) with my friend
042             (.6)
043 →  PO1:    You got it from somebody named who?
044             (1.2)
045    HM:     Uh (.) I don't remember her name-It's a girl
046             (2.6) ((radio call))
047 →          I didn't steal it
048             (1.5)
049 →  PO1:    Well (.) the problem is (.) that the plate's stolen man
```

The officer asks a WH question—where'd you get the car man—in line 35, and in the next turn the motorist (HM) asserts his ownership rights by first stat-ing that it is his car (line 37); he then fulfills the grammatical constraint pro-jected in the question (line 37: I bought it). Although the HM's statements look like a denial, it doesn't "officially" resemble one. In response, the officer asks a more specific question about a car related item (line 39: license plate); the mo-torist provides a nebulous identity of a person who sold him the car (line 41). And next the officer recycles that ambiguous reference and formulates it into a question (line 43), to which the suspect provides another unclear answer (line 45). And after a noticeably long pause (2.6 seconds) the motorist issues a formal denial in line 47: "I didn't steal it." In line 49 the officer officially accuses the motorist of a serious legal infraction (stolen plates)—after the motorist in the preceding turn denies an unannounced official accusation.

Between lines 35 and 43, the patrol officer asks the motorist three WH questions that seem to elicit information. In the first two, the WH questions occur in the sentence initial slot (line 35, 39); in the third, it is transposed to the sentence final slot (line 43). The motorist in excerpt 28 answers the questions the officer asks; however, that the officer has assessed the HM's responses to be problematic can be seen in the turn design of the WH questions in the subsequent turns: the officer begins the interrogative series with a general problem about the car's ownership (line 35); he then narrows the scope of his next question to a particular component of the prior topic (line 39: license plates), and finally, to its previous owner (line 43). The accusatorial force of the questions is intensified and upgraded in each subsequent turn until the officer finally announces the problem in line 49.

If the officer's problematic assessment of the motorist's answers is embodied in the upgraded and intensified form of his questions, then the motorist's accusatorial understanding of those questions is also demonstrated in his responses. The motorist utters a "soft" denial in line 37 when the officer first asks him where he got his car; however, after the officer's third WH question—and before he is officially accused in line 49—he utters a "hard" (indubitable) denial.

The three preceding WH questions in excerpt 28 uttered by a police officer in the context of "official" police business, then, can be said to work like accusations. The work they do, however, is never direct; the officer never comes out and bluntly asks the suspect "did you steal the car?" or "is this stolen?" That proposition is equivocal, covert, and implied in the incrementally posed WH questions. The officer could have intended to ask those questions in a matter of fact way, as information seeking questions, but the suspect's final response (line 47) empirically demonstrates that he has not understood the WH questions in that way. The questions that the officer poses in line 035, 039, 043, then, are not merely factual, information seeking interrogatives. Since the WH questions occur well before the main blame is attributed, they can be viewed as "pre-blames" and preliminary accusations (Pomerantz, 1978; Schegloff, 1980). The questions that the officer asks accuse without actually accusing (indirect); they do the work of saying, "did you steal that?" without actually saying it. And the accusatorial tincture of the questions that the police ask is empirically visible from the way motorists and citizens respond to them, not in any inherent feature of language itself.

Consider the following case where a police officer approaches a "suspicious" looking white male (WM) who is hanging around a parked motorcycle; as he does so, the WM starts to walk away. The officer accosts the WM and begins the interrogative series in the following way:

Excerpt 29 (*COPS* data: "Harley Marijuana")
1   PO: Ok, you don't have anything on you?
2   WM: No

3   PO: Well then you don't mind if I take=
4   WM: =I have no gun
5   PO: Well then you don't just calm down you
6   don't mind if I take a quick search then do you
7   WM: Well I don't I don't have anything on me but
8   PO: Alright
9   WM: I don't really wanna be search either
10   PO: I'm just gonna pat you down on the exterior
11   WM: I don't
12   PO: Ok? What I need for you to do
13   I want you to come over on the hood
14   put your hands on the hood
15   WM: Well, I don't I don't really want to
16   PO: <u>JUST PUT YOUR HANDS ON THE HOOD</u>
17   okay you don't have any weapons on you right?
18   WM: No

In excerpt 29, the officer formulates his utterance as a negatively posed polar interrogative. There is a minimal amount of assumption within that question that the WM does not have anything (weapons, drugs, needles, anything that is mentionable or might cause the officer harm), and that assumption is marked in the grammatical form of the question. When the officer receives information that the WM has nothing noticeably illegal (line 2), he asks a preliminary question to a body search. In response, the WM swiftly states that he has no gun (line 4).

The noteworthy observation about line 4 is that it is an emphatic denial; what makes the denial noticeable is that (1) it is found in the slot after a permissive request (2) the gun has not been an explicit topic in the preceding three turns. What we can state with a fair degree of certitude is that although there is nothing overtly or bluntly accusatorial about line 1 and 3, the WM has understood the "anything" in line 1, and the request for permission to search him as an accusation—"do you have any firearms on you?" or something to that effect.

What is topically noteworthy is that the officer has not mentioned anything about guns; that topic is suspect initiated and the denial comes out of the blue. And notice the effect that the gun's sudden appearance in the WM's talk has on the officer: he first tries to calm the suspect down (line 5); he repeats the permissive request again (line 6); and when the suspect again denies that he does not have "anything" (line 7), the officer acknowledges it, but then radically alters the politeness system of the interaction. In line 7, after the suspect openly states his opposition to the officer's request to search, the officer switches from an equivocal and polite yes/no question to a firm directive (line 10). After the first open opposition, or sign of conflict, the officer just tells him, in a manner that marks the coercive authority of the police, that he will conduct the search, with or without the suspect's permission (line 10). When the WM opposes the directive again in line 11, the officer commands the suspect to physically move to the front of the squad car; and when the suspect again opposes the officer's commands, the command escalates in volume (line 16), prosodically marking the exchange into a conflict-talk sequence (see Grimshaw, 1990; Maynard, 1985a, b).

The interaction in excerpt 29 begins in a routine way with the officer asking a safety-motivated utterance. When the officer requests permission to search the white male, he utters what is unmistakably a denial. This denial comes out of nowhere and, along with the suspect's uncooperative attitude, escalates the seriousness of the encounter. That is, the WM resists the officer's request to perform a body search, keeps issuing opposable utterances (e.g., I don't wanna be searched either), and as a result, the cop initially begins to do an exterior pat down, but one turn later (after another opposition, line 15) he commands the WM onto the hood of the patrol car. After the suspect is placed on the hood, legs spread apart and hands spread out, a similar version of line 1 reappears; this time, however, instead of "anything," a more precise "weapon" appears in the officer's reformulated question (line 17). Of course, this transformation takes place only because the suspect emits a denial about a weapon in the first place (line 4), without the officer's prompt or topic initiation in the prior turn.

As already discussed in an earlier chapter, when the police ask routine and simple questions, citizens respond to them as if they have been accused of a wrongdoing. In excerpt 29, the officer asks if the WM has "anything" (equivocal); the suspect responds with, "I have no gun." Consider again an exchange discussed in the last chapter. An officer responds to a call of a theft from a place of business, and runs into a black male (BM) who is pushing a water-heater down the street:

Excerpt 30 (*COPS* data: "Games")
14   PO1: HEY come here partner (1.9) Where'd you get this at?
15   (.5)
16   BM: See that vacant lot right there? (.7)
17   Somebody just dumped it a few minutes ago?
18   (.6)
19   PO1: The thing's still leaking water man
20   (.)
21   BM: Yeah
22   (.6)
23   PO1:   Somebody just dumped it and you just picked
24   it up at two o'clock in the mor[ning
25   BM: [Uh-huh

In line 14 the officer first makes contact, and asks the BM where he got the water heater (this). The BM refers to a vacant lot up the street and states that somebody just dumped it. This call (a commercial burglary) is received at 2 a.m. in the morning; when the officer arrives on scene he witnesses a black male pushing a water heater down the street. The officer never asks the BM if the water heater is stolen or if he stole it; the officer merely asks where he got it. The BM never fulfills the action projected in the question (an account of where and how he acquired the item in tow); that is left to inference. He does, however, deflect the blame away from himself and manages to accuse someone else for the crime (line 17).

A conjecture: the missing component of the BM's response (how he got the water-heater) may be attributable to the fact that he blatantly attempts to deflect blame away from himself and minimize culpability; consequently, he (tactically) forgets to fully answer the officer's question in line 14. In line 23 the officer fills in what was absent in the BM's answer to the WH question (line 14: where'd you get this at?): somebody dumped it; he picked it up. In the officer's commentary slot (lines 23-24) (see chapter 3) the officer emphasizes the BM's agency and culpability (line 23-24: you just picked it up), which was left out of the BM's turn (line 17). In this sequence, the officer could have meant to ask the literal version of the question, but the BM's responses indicate that he has heard the question in line 14 as an accusation.

The accusatorial sensibility of police interrogatives may be related to actual "guilt" of the participants, but it may also be related to the "roles" of the participants (victim versus "perp"), and how the call originates— initiated by citizens or the police. In the following data, two different officers, in two different cities, and in two different types of police action, ask the same WH question to their primary participants. Contrast the two responses to the same WH question that each officer receives when they investigate the scene.

In excerpt 31 ("Voodoo"), an officer responds to a call about a man and a woman who get into a fight (domestic dispute); in this assignment, however, the female disputant is the suspect rather than the victim. As the officer pulls into the residence, he sees a white male (WM) who is disheveled. In line 12 the officer asks the WH question.

Excerpt 31 (*COPS* data: "Voodoo")
12 → PO: What's going on?
13   WM: She threw me on my back I'm dis I'm totally
14   I'm permanently disabled certified by the state
15   and uh she came into the house and made a big
16   scene started throwin grabbed my by my hair
17   wrestled me to the ground kicked me in my groin
18   I did not go back up there just like you said she
19   came into my house I didn't ask her in she just
20   opened the door and walked in just started
21   screamin and yellin grabbed me by my hair threw
22   me down man I'm disabled

After the officer asks, "what's going on?" in line 12, the WM begins his turn at talk. A noticeable feature of the WM's turn is its extended size. The WM—the alleged victim in a domestic dispute—has heard the WH question as an invitation to tell a story to the officer (what happened), and that the WM continues to tell an account without the officer's interruption attests to the interactional aim of "what's going on?"[12] Now, contrast that narrative response to the WH question in excerpt 31 to the next one.

In the following data, a police officer initiates a suspicious activity stop. He witnesses movement in the backseat of a car in the parking lot of a popular nightclub, and decides to investigate further. As he approaches the parked car and knocks on the window, he (and the TV viewers) sees a young man (M), who has his pants down, on top of a scantily clad young woman. After seeing this, the officer asks the young man (M) what is going on:

Excerpt 32 (*COPS* data: "Naked enough")
21 →   PO: What's goin on?
22   (.7)
23   M: Nothi:ing
24   (.5)
25   PO: Nothing? (.7) How bout we get dressed so
26   I could take a look at some ID okay?

In this excerpt the police officer discovers that inside a parked car in the lot of a nightclub, a couple is engaged in sexual activity. Line 21 is the first line of the interaction after the officer has walked in on their amorous activity. The framing narrative has already set up the next segment (interaction phase) as an encounter that may be related to prostitution/drugs/sexual assault as a possible interactional footing. As the officer approaches the parked vehicle, he sees a dark hair colored young man (M) on top of a young blond woman (W)—with his pants down. The officer knocks on the window, and asks the WH question in line 21. In response to the WH interrogative, the young man (M) utters what appears to be a denial. The "inadequateness" of the single lexical item as a response is suggested in the next turn where the officer repeats the M's response, and then requests to see official identification, thus indicating trouble of sorts (Tannen 1987a, b).

While WH questions are commonly understood as fact seeking interrogatives (or requests for information), there are instances in everyday talk when they function as accusations. For example, consider a child rummaging through a cookie jar only to be discovered by his/her parent, who asks, "What are you doing?" When the child replies "nothing," the response is more than just a curt negation; it is a denial in response to an accusation. That the second part of a sequential pair is a denial suggests that the first part is functioning as an accusation (Komter, 1994). The difference between an overt accusation and an indirect accusation disguised in the WH form lies in the structural—face saving—alternatives such interactional moves allow. For example, had this officer phrased the accusation bluntly (Are you a prostitute? Are you raping her? Is he raping you?), and realized that the situation had been misconstrued, the officer is sequentially limited in his conversational options because the next turn response will most likely be a denial. However, by phrasing the accusation indirectly, disguised in a WH form, the officer is provided with tactical and strategic conversational alternatives: he is able to disengage from the counter accusations and denials and impute a different motive.

In contemporary American vernacular, "what's goin on?" also functions as a type of greeting. In this greeting sequence, "nothing" is the acceptable and preferred second part response. As an example, consider another common greeting form: the "how are you?" To actually give a detailed account of how one really is rather than the conventional 'fine' or 'good' would be a gross breach of social and conversational norm (Sacks, 1975). Again, two interpretations are possible here. 'Nothing' as the next turn response to a 'what's going on?' in an ordinary social structure is normative since those two utterances are adjacently related in a greeting sequence; 'nothing' as the next turn response in an institutional social structure is expectable since the two utterances are adjacency pairs in an accusation/denial sequence. As shown in an earlier section, citizens routinely understand and process bureaucratic talk in a socially lubricative way, demonstrating their preference for social (non-institutional) talk while the police generally orient to utterances in an official way, demonstrating their preference for institutional organization of talk. The possible misunderstandings that may occur between the two parties highlights the differences in the assumptions each party makes about their footing in the social world, not necessarily as evidence of deviant character.

The young male's "problematic" footing is evidenced in the officer's third turn. The officer repeats the second turn with a rising tone; that repetition is followed by two intraturn clauses that further expand the scope of the interaction. While repetition is generally a solidarity building device that is used to produce further talk, to evaluate, and accomplish social goals in a relatively mellifluous fashion in the interaction, it can also serve as a gauge for problematic discourse (Gruber, 1998; Tannen, 1987a,b). In the excerpt above, the repetition, combined with the rise in intonation, evaluates the "inappositeness" of the prior turn. After the repetition, there is a (.7) pause, a transition relevant place for the prior speaker to repair the problematic turn; moreover, the third turn is also the slot where the officer could further comment on the prior turn. When there is no response the officer makes a "request" which further entangles the male participant. It is evident from the intrusive third turn expansion that M has not conformed to the officer's definition of the situation.

For the police the WH interrogative is strategic because it can serve as the equivocal foci for three different activities: he can align the interaction as a (1) greeting sequence, (2) an indirect accusation, and (3) a fact seeking interrogative. The suspect, however, is constrained by the officer's definition of the situation, the officer's contextual power—the power to define the discursive footing of the interaction. If citizens/suspects do not conform to the relevancy requirements projected by the officer's question, then the turn deviates from the adjacency pair format and expands.

Thus, within the first three turns in excerpt 32, we can state that the young man has treated the WH interrogative as a greeting, possibly an accusation, but not as a fact seeking interrogative. Extrapolating from the findings from a previous section (that motorists tend to treat the interlocked request [greeting + request] with a greeting, thus demonstrating their preference for social talk rather than an institutional one) we can speculate that the young man orients to the social aspects of the encounter rather than a bureaucratic one. However, whether the young man treats the WH question as an accusation or as a greeting, we can see that his response has not conformed to the officer's definition of the situation.

There are two points that support this claim. (1) Contextually, what the young man is doing is not nothing; he is caught with his pants down while on top of a young woman. Thus, if his second turn response ("nothing") is viewed as a denial to an accusation, it imputes a non-cooperative attitude to the young man. (2) That the officer is treating the young man's response in an institutional way is demonstrated by his treatment of M's response in line 25: the officer repeats it as a way of signaling a problem with the answer (Gruber, 1998), and within that same turn, he entangles the young man further in the occasioned bureaucratic event by making procedurally relevant his ID.

Why do citizens respond in such a way to seemingly simple questions that police officers ask? One possible interpretation may be that the police occupy a special status (role) in the social psyche of individuals. That is, they are the most visible representatives of the criminal law, and have often been conceptualized as a Rorschach in uniform, a symbolic and pseudo-paternal figure—the father's deputy (Freud, 1945, 1914; Lacan, 1977; Salecl, 1994; Wambaugh, 1987). Niederhoffer (1967:1) states that the tools of the police officer's trade—"shield, nightstick, gun, and summons book—clothe him in a mantle of symbolism that stimulates fantasy and projection." Two common reactions to the presence of the police are anger and guilt (Baker, 1985; Niederhoffer, 1967).

The origin of such unconscious sentiments is a psychoanalytic question; and as one influential theory posits, they originate from our universal desire to commit patricide and engage in incestuous relations with our mothers (Freud, 1914). If the genealogy of the primal guilt is a psychoanalytic question, then its manifestation is a sociological one: as I have shown in this section, there is evidence that those sentiments are embodied in the structural features of talk between the police and the public. Ordinary citizens and suspects who are summoned to interact with the police verbally (pragmatically) behave as if they have been accused of a crime when, formally, no such accusations have been made. They bring that unconscious guilt to life by hearing and responding to simple yes/no questions, WH interrogatives, summons, and sometimes, an officer's mere presence, as accusations. Consequently, the Rorschach is given a structural face in the micro-details of talk-in-interaction between the police and public. That effect is a function of the institution and its symbols, not language.

The Tactical Value of Repair and Turn Inversion

During the course of a conversation, it is entirely possible to not hear or misunderstand an utterance spoken by other speakers. As already mentioned in a previous chapter, misunderstandings, miscommunications, "unhearings" and other troubles during talk are clarified and "worked through" by employing repair sequences (Goffman, 1981: 55; Schegloff, 1992a, 1984a). One way repairs can be initiated is by using single turn constructional devices:

(Schegloff et al., 1977: 367)
    D: Wul did'e ever get married'r anything?
→ C: Hu:h?
    D: Did jee ever get married?

    A: Have you ever tried a clinic?
→ B: <u>What?</u>
    A: Have you ever tried a clinic?

Repairs can also be initiated through a partial repetition of the prior (trouble source) turn, plus a WH question:

(Schegloff et al., 1977: 368)

    B: .hhh well I'm working through the Amfat Corporation
→ A: The Who?
    B: Amfah Corporation

    B: I went to a shower
→ A: To a where?
    B: I went to a shower

    In the excerpts taken from Schegloff et al.'s (1977) seminal paper on repair, the source of the trouble is located in the first speaker's turn. Consequently, repair is initiated in the second turn by the next turn speaker through single turn utterances (e.g., huh? what?) and partial repeats (e.g., the who?). The notion of repair reiterates the local and endogenous nature of talk in the social organization of talk since social members have to find a way to deal with conversational dilemmas that arise in ordinary social life (Schegloff et al., 1977; Schegloff, 1992a, 1991). This is especially true for dealing with the police since misunderstandings could lead to the loss of one's freedom.

    Even in an austere and ceremonious legal setting like the court the well-structured system of turn taking is not always observed. Witnesses exercise some control over the sequential flow of talk (Matoesian, 1993). Likewise, citizens and suspects, too, are capable of inverting the turn taking system, thereby realigning the pre-allocated institutional turn taking system into a more natural conversational model. One of the elementary conversational mechanisms for achieving this goal is repair. Consider the following example:

Excerpt 33 (*COPS* data: "Driving a Baby")
063 → HM: You take care of my baby?
064   (.8)
065   PO2: Guy I've got two of my own I'm you know
066   more worried about you taking care of your baby
067   at this [point (.) there's no car seat in the car

068 → HM: [Why? (1.6) There is a car seat
069   PO2:   Okay (1.2) but the baby needs to be in the car seat man

In excerpt 33, officers have initiated a felony traffic stop; the occupants are removed from the vehicle and separated. The officer has also just removed the baby from his mother's care and is holding the baby in his arms. The suspect self selects himself as the next speaker and proceeds to inquire about the welfare of his baby (line 63). Consequently, the officer in line 65 responds to the HM's question by reproaching and lecturing him about his reprehensible parenting practices (lines 65-67). And in the next turn, the suspect temporarily renegotiates the turn order and launches into repairing the problematic item in the preceding blame implicative talk (line 68).

In excerpt 33 the suspect temporarily guides the sequential organization of talk: he asks the questions, the officer answers. This example demonstrates that suspects possess the sequential power to invert the interactional order of talk in P-C encounters. In the excerpt above the police, at least momentarily, follow the contours of talk the citizen sketches.

Excerpt 34 (Midwest City Police Traffic Stop #2)
8   PO: how you doin >see your driver's license
9   en proof of insurance?<
10   (.7)
11 →   D: I got it in my jacket can I get it?

In excerpt 34, the motorist answers the question with another question. Moreover, the second clause question the officer asks in lines 8-9 is a bureaucratically occasioned (official) request, and instead of granting the request, the motorist answers the request with a counter request. I want to note next some further instances like excerpt 34 where a question is answered with a question, and the tactical effect behind such moves:

Excerpt 35 (*COPS* Data: "Games")
118   PO1:   So where exactly did they dump it?
119   (.6)
120 → BM: Okay you see where he's at right now?
121   (.)
122   PO1:   Yup
123   (.4)
124   BM: Okay (1.1) now watch (.8) right there (.6) where he goes to
125   that lot right there (.4) right there on the corner

Excerpt 36 (*COPS* Data: "Games")
129   PO1:   What was the last address you lived at?
130   (.8)
131 → BM: My last address?
132   (1.0)

134	PO1:	Where do you get mail?
135		(.8)
136	BM:	I don't really get mail I haven't had mail in

Misunderstandings and other troubles that arise during talk are routinely corrected using conversational devices such as repetition (Schegloff, 1988b; Tannen, 1987a, b) and open class repair initiators such as "what?" "sorry?" "pardon?" (Drew, 1997). That is, speaker A produces an utterance that is not clearly understood by speaker B; consequently, speaker B in the second turn repeats the preceding turn, or portions of it, or employs repair initiators to clarify the trouble. And the arrowed lines in excerpt 35 and 36 appear to work that way, as a way of clarifying misunderstandings in talk; the two repair-like turns (line 120, 131) are produced in the second turn slot after the first turn WH interrogative. The question that I want to raise is: is there another interactional purpose behind such sequential moves? What does the second turn speaker accomplish?

The black male (BM) in excerpt 36 is suspected of burglary, and as mentioned in chapter 3, he is stopped by the police as he is walking away from the place of business which has been burglarized, with the alleged stolen item in tow, along with a bag full of burglary tools. As shown in chapter 3, the suspect repeatedly denies his involvement in the crime, thereby disrespecting police authority, while putting on a cooperative face. He never confesses his crime. Now, notice how the suspect uses language to impede the officer's attempts to establish a solid identity. In Excerpt 35, by placing a question in an answer's slot (line 120), the suspect gains control of the conversational floor, and as a result, the officer who is doing the interrogating is momentarily, for one turn, placed into the role of one who is interrogated, forced to acknowledge the suspect's prior utterance (line 122: yup). Furthermore, when the suspect finally resumes his turn and begins to answer the WH interrogative initially posed in line 118, he uses discourse markers and fillers, along with four distinct pauses (possible transition relevant places), to prolong his single turn. By deviating from a commonly occurring sequential organization of talk—answering a question with a question (line 120)—the suspect inverts the turn order and gains an extra turn to formulate an answer to the initial WH interrogative in line 118; moreover, when his sequentially delayed turn does arrive, he controls the trajectory of his talk: he successfully stalls for extra time in formulating his answer in line 124 by varying his turn size.

In excerpt 36, a similar strategy occurs. The officer attempts to find out the suspect's place of residence (line 129); in the next turn (line 131), the suspected burglar repeats a partial component of the previous turn in what appears to be a repair sequence. After a full one second pause the officer asks a variation of the WH question in line 129. Mails are delivered to homes, where there are established postal addresses, and it is still that topic that is being pursued by the officer; but notice how in the suspect's next turn (line 136) that topic—his address—is slyly changed, from a locative orientation (where he lives) to a temporal one (when he gets mail). The suspect's answer is more conditionally relevant to a when question rather than a where question. By repeating a partial

clause of the question and placing it in the second pair slot of a Q/A sequence, in
what looks like a repair, the suspect first gains (.8) seconds after the initial WH
question, then he gains more time by repeating a portion of the preceding turn
(my last address?). A noticeable one full second passes before the officer, in line
134, reformulates the question asked in line 129; that noticeable delay may be
attributable to the way repairs are socially organized: self-repairs are preferred
over other-initiated repairs (Schegloff et al., 1977). By delaying his response, in
what appears to be a repair sequence, the suspect forces the officer to reformulate the question in the next turn (line 134), and another (.8) seconds is allowed
to pass (line 135) before he finally provides an answer—a conditionally irrele-
vant answer. As a way of delaying answering a question, as a way of formulating an answer, and as a way of stalling, turn inversion through repetition and
repair then serves a valuable purpose (see Tannen 1987a). By using repair devices such as repetition, the suspect is able to shift the conversational floor to the
officer, thereby stalling his turn and buys an extra turn to formulate an answer.

In the next excerpt an undercover police officer posing as a "John" in a
prostitution sting uses similar strategies to accomplish a different objective:

Excerpt 37 (*COPS* Data: "Pickup Truck Prostitute")
29		WW:	Ain't you a cop?
30	→	PO2:	What?
31		WW:	Are you a cop?
32	→	PO2:	No are you?
33	→	WW:	Are you?
34		PO2:	No I'm not a cop
35		WW:	Alright, are you sure? I thought you
36			were this young cop that drives around here
37		PO2:	No not at all

In this excerpt the police are conducting a sting operation to "get prostitutes
off the streets." A white woman (WW), an alleged prostitute, is "picked up" by
an undercover officer; however, his identity is immediately cast into doubt when
the woman suspects the anonymous "John" to be a neighborhood beat officer.
That suspicion is posed as a negatively formulated confirmation question in the
opening moments of the encounter (line 29). Within the negatively posed question the presumption that the "John" is a cop is already epistemologically
marked. But more significantly, that question is a direct accusation; and it is in
that sense that the alleged prostitute asks the question. In line 30 the officer
picks up the incongruent sense of a cop soliciting a prostitute, and uses that inapposite sense to initiate what appears to be a next turn repair (Drew, 1997).
Consequently, in the next turn, the presupposed information is softened and
posed in an epistemologically dubious and unmarked form (line 31: are you a
cop?). Notice the accusatorial sense of 'are[not] you a cop?': the officer immediately provides a denial (line 32). The exchanges are sequentially adjacent, and
it is the first part (are you a cop?) that projects the relevant next turn action, a

denial. In addition, the one who has been accused makes a counter- accusation of his own (line 32: are you?).

Throughout this four-turn sequence the woman accuses the John of being a cop five times. The accusations, however, are downgraded within each subsequent turn: (1) line 29: Ain't you a cop? (2) line 30: Are you a cop? (3) line 32: Are you? (4) line 35: Are you sure? (5) Line 35-36: I thought you were this young cop that drives around here. How does the officer deflect these direct accusations and whittle it down to an epistemologically dubious question? One of the conversational mechanisms the officer uses is rhythmically posed incremental denials: (1) line 30: What? (2) line 32, 34, 37: No (3) Line 34: I'm not a cop (4) line 37: Not at all. Within four turns, the undercover officer provides six separate and distinct negation markers in his utterances. But before the officer produces what could be called a formal denial (e.g., No, I didn't kill my wife; No, I wasn't speeding; No, I'm not a cop (line 34)), he first softens the accusatorial force of the first two accusatorial questions (line 29, line 31) by posing his responses as an interjection and repair (line 30: what?), then issues a counter-accusation of his own.

In response to the most forcefully presupposed accusation (line 29), the undercover officer produces an interjection marker (line 30) that also serves to repair a blame-imbued identity (see Goffman, 1981; for open class repairs, see Drew, 1997). When the woman accuses again, he utters a denial; but he does not do it passively. He inverts the turn order, changes topic, and turns the accusation back at the woman (line 32). The effect of this type of accusation/counter-accusation sequence can be seen in the alleged prostitute's gradual diminution of knowledge: are you? (line 33), to which the undercover officer provides a full fledged denial—no I'm not a cop.

These excerpts I have used demonstrate that although the format of talk in P-C encounters is pre-structured and pre-allocated, the encounter still has to be collaboratively brought to order by both parties. I have already stated that the coercive power the police possess is exercised sequentially and linearly, not in an absolute manner. We can see a similar type of sequentially progressive character in repairs. Repair sequences and their tactical usages, however, tear the abstract veil of another philosophically abstract concept in a palpable way.

The notion of power, as possessed and exercised by the police, is theoretically conceptualized as a distinctly specific, punitive, and highly authoritarian social control mechanism in a thoroughly Weberian sense (e.g., guns, nightsticks, handcuffs). Its converse view, however, situates power not in a nameable thing/person/mechanism but under the rubric of a generalized, psycho-politico-legal discourse (Foucault, 1977, 1979). In this thoroughly deconstructionist philosophical view, power is vague, amorphous, and decentered (Bracher, 1993; Taylor, 1984):

> Power is exercised rather than possessed; it is not the 'privilege', acquired or preserved, of the dominant class, but the overall effect of its strategic positions—an effect that is manifested and sometimes extended by the position of those who are dominated. Furthermore, this power is not exercised simply as an obligation or a prohibition on those who 'do not have it'; it invests them, is

transmitted by them and through them; it exerts pressure upon them. This means that these relations go right down into the depths of society, that they are not localized in relations between the state and its citizens or on the frontier between classes and that they do not merely reproduce, at the level of individuals, bodies, gestures and behavior, the general form of the law or government; that, although there is continuity (they are indeed articulated on this form through a whole series of complex mechanisms), there is neither analogy nor homology, but a specificity of mechanism and modality. Lastly, they are not univocal; they define innumerable points of confrontation, focuses of instability, each of which has its own risks of conflict, of struggles, and of an at least temporary inversion of these power relations (Foucault, 1977: 26-27).

The notion of discourse, as developed by various philosophers, from Michel Foucault, Jacques Lacan, Jurgen Habermas to Pierre Bordieu, range across various disciplines from psychoanalysis (Lacan) to communicative ethics (Habermas); the notion of discourse in these abstract traditions relies on a conceptualization of power that is relational, dialectical, and situational, without having examined its actual situated practices, the way power is really exercised on a moment to moment basis by those who are encumbered in an institutional setting (see Conley and O'Barr, 1998). Thus, as much as Foucault rigidly maintains that power is dialectical, exercised not possessed, resisted, and contested by the subjects who are most affected by its operation, there is a noticeable gap in what he superficially calls 'discourse'. As I have demonstrated in this section, exercises of power, by those who are legitimately conferred the right to use it (police) and by those who have the least of it, can and do subvert power in the lexical, clausal, sentential, intonational, and prosodic moments of production of discourse—discourse-in-interaction (Conley and O'Barr, 1998).

By using actual acts (language) of police officers and citizens in interaction it is possible not only to locate such instances of 'discourse', but to also witness, freeze, and analyze strategic interplays of power by those who dominate and are ostensibly dominated. As I have shown, domination can be "extended"—subverted—by tactically manipulating conversational devices such as repair, repetition, and turn inversion. I have shown how apparently "powerless" citizens who are at the mercy of the bureaucratic Leviathan use ordinary conversational mechanisms to temporarily, at least for a fleeting turn, realign the asymmetrical distribution of power, thereby reconfiguring their statically ascribed roles. What is more methodologically and analytically alluring for micro-sociological endeavors such as the present one is that those points of contestation, resistance, and "focuses of instability" are not left to impression and philosophical pondering. Those points are observable, verifiable, and analyzable in the sequential organization of talk, for that is where concepts such as power reside, are enacted, resisted, and recontextualized (Molotch and Boden, 1985).

The Role of Presuppositions on the Function of Silences between Turns

Silences during talk can be interpreted in a variety of ways, as trouble in comprehension to the prior turn (Sacks et al., 1974), prior referent (Schegloff, 1984a), trouble in recognizing the caller in telephone calls (Schegloff, 1968), or as a way of being polite (Tannen, 1985). Consider the following data:

Sacks et al. (1974: 714)
        J: Oh I could drive if you want me to
        C: Well no I'll drive (I don't m//in')
        J: hhh
            (1.0)
        J: I meant to offah
→   (16.0)
        J: Those shoes look nice when you keep on putting stuff on em

As Sacks et al. (1974) note, the meaning of silence is contingent upon its sequential placement; silences within a turn is a pause, hence, other speaker's entrance into current turn talk is dispreffered; however, Sacks et al. (1974: 715) also observe that silences after possible turn completion points should be "minimized." Post transition relevant place silences should be minimized because silence is interwoven with morality and truth-value (Saville-Troike, 1985). The implicature between truth, morality, and silence is most saliently illustrated in courtroom interactions.

In the courtroom, silence works as a stylistic device; that is, attorneys do not have multiple opportunities to create and maintain impressions of victims and witnesses on the witness stand; they have one shot; hence, defense attorneys may "load or build pauses into utterances to reduce the chances of embarrassing errors, disfluencies, or repairs which might spoil a competent performance or disrupt the rhythm of questioning or both" (Matoesian, 1993: 140). Silence also works as a way of "squeezing" the maximum utility out of turns. Consider the following example:

Excerpt 38 (*COPS* Data: "Games")
118   PO1:   So where exactly did they dump it?
119   (.6)
120   BM: Okay you see where he's at right now?
121   (.)
122   PO1:   Yup
123   (.4)
124   BM: Okay
125 →   (1.1) now watch
126 →   (.8) right there
127 →   (.6) where he goes to that lot right there
128 →   (.4) right there on the corner

As already mentioned in earlier chapters and sections, the BM (suspected burglar) in excerpt 38 uses several strategies to delay answering the questions the police officer poses to him: repetition, turn inversion, repair. An interrelated component that binds the aforementioned components with moral impression management is the elapsed time between turns and utterances. The BM gains— creates—extra time to answer by using discourse markers and fillers in conjunction with silence. In excerpt 38, there are four distinct pauses within a single turn; although the lengths of silence within that single turn (lines 124-128) are potential places for turn transition, the speaker is able to prolong his turn by framing his utterances as contiguous utterances (e.g., okay, now, right there).

The nexus of truth-value and morality come to an apex in the moral inferences that are generated by silence. Silence not only "conveys impressions about testimony and credibility" (Matoesian, 1993: 144), but it generates moral inferences about the content of talk and the speaker, such as deception, uncertainty, lying, and concealment (Matoesian, 1993; Walker, 1985). As Walker (1985) notes, pauses before answers create not only negative evaluations about the speaker but implants doubts about the veracity of the answer. As one lawyer observes: "If a person is being honest, the time to respond is going to be slower than it is if they are going to be dishonest. If you're dishonest, you have a mental construct which does not equate to reality, so if you're being dishonest, you have to refer back to that construct and see where this question fits in" (in Walker, 1985: 66). The moral inferences that are generated as an effect of silence, however, work both ways. In other words, there is no inherent connection between silence and deception; that is a function of prior assumptions made about the speaker. Thus, as Walker (1985: 73) writes, "what appears as a pause for thought in the friendly witness is suspect as a pause for concealment in a witness for the other side."

Excerpt 39 (*COPS* data: "Naked enough")
55   PO: What's his name?
56   →   (.7)
57   W: U::h
58   →   (1.3) Kevin

Excerpt 40 (*COPS* data: "Naked enough")
65   PO: How long you known him?
66   →   (2.3)
67   W: U::h (.3) bout a month

Excerpt 41 (*COPS* data: "Naked enough")
82   PO: Did he tell you his name was Kevin?
83   →   (1.5)
84   W: Yeah

Excerpts 39-41 come from an episode of *COPS* in which an officer witnesses movements in the backseat of a car in the parking lot of a nightclub.
When he goes near the car he finds a couple engaged in sexual activity; he re-
moves both occupants and questions them. The officer tells the woman that he
wants to make sure that she is not being held against her will. The speaker (W),
then, is already situated in a possible role as a 'victim' and the male as a possible 'rapist'. Hence, although the W's responses are filled with long pauses (line
58, 66, 83) and hesitation markers (uh), those features are not interpreted as
signs of deception. The woman is questioned and released. Consider the following cases where the opposite occurs:

Excerpt 42 (*COPS* data: "Naked enough")
122   PO: Why does she call you Kevin?
123 →   (1.2)
124   M: A lot of people call me Kevin
125   (.3)
126   PO: Why do a lot of people call you Kevin?
127 →   (1.8)
128   M: I have basically a (brother) (.8)

Excerpt 43 (*COPS* Data: "Games")
129   PO1:   What was the last address you lived at?
130 →   (.8)
131   BM: My last address?
132 →   (1.0)
134   PO1:   Where do you get mail?
135 →   (.8)
136   BM: I don't really get mail I haven't had mail in

In excerpt 42 and 43, when officers ask a WH question to the male subjects,
there is a measurable micro-interval delay in the suspect's responses. In excerpt
42, after the woman in excerpts in 39-41 is questioned, the officer questions the
male; the officer begins with the assumption that the male citizen might be a
possible 'rapist'. In excerpt 43, the officer begins with the assumption that the
guy pushing a water heater is, in fact, a burglar (see chapter 3). In the two episodes concerning the possible rapist and burglar, both are arrested. Why does the
same type of silences between turns effect such divergent interpretations?
       The police, like attorneys, judge the truth validity of a verbal response first
and foremost by its temporal demarcations; untruthful responses are: mumbled,
delayed, evasive, apologetic, qualified (Inbau et al., 1986: 49-50).[13] Moreover,
denials are restricted to specific aspects of the crime, replete with requests for
"repetition of interrogator's questions even though they were clearly, directly,
and audibly stated" (Inbau et al., 1986: 50). With this assumption already in
place, then, the measurable and noticeable pauses in the question/answer sequence can be interpreted *by the police* as evidence of deception, not trouble in
comprehension. The most rational interpretation of guilt or innocence lies not in

the features of talk but in the assumptions that are made about the speaker (Hilton, 1995).

The Interactional Function of Address Terms

The terms that participants use to address one another is "one of the most simplest techniques available for depicting another participant" (Goodwin, 1990: 84); whether the address term is a formal title, last name, or first name, it is an indication of inequality in power (Wardaugh, 1984). In other languages, there are marked forms of the language to indicate a difference in status of the speaker. The well-known distinction between French 'Tu' and 'Vous' is a good example of overt deferential forms in language. Honorifics—deferential forms of language such as 'sir', ma'am'—are sometimes built into the morphological and syntactic structure of utterances. For example, in Korean, separate lexical choices exist to indicate deference to an elder; honorifics are also morphologically appended at utterance final positions to indicate respect.[14]

There are numerous social variables that determine the type of address terms that will be used: one's place in the social and occupational hierarchy, age, sex, race, and distance (Wardaugh, 1984). Hence, students do not usually address their teachers by their first names, nor patients their doctors, children their parents. Wardaugh (1984) also adds that in societies claiming to be egalitarian, there may be doubt as to the choice of appropriate address term. One of the examples he uses is that of a police officer and a young male offender. When there are doubts as to how to address the other participant, Wardaugh states that the optimal strategy is to avoid using any address terms at all.

Consider a classic sociolinguistic conversational data of the traffic stop of Dr. Poussaint by a white police officer in Mississippi:

(Wardaugh, 1984: 273)
1   PO: What's your name boy?
2   Dr.: Dr. Poussaint. I'm a physician...
3   PO: What's your first name boy?...
4   Dr.: Alvin

In the southern part of US, whites have historically used 'boy' to address grown black men in order to denigrate them (Kennedy, 2002). The officer's first line then is already an indication that the officer considers the interaction a hierarchical politeness system since the address term is asymmetrical in status. The Dr. responds to the question by stating his title first, then last name, and finally, his occupation (line 2). The Dr.'s response is an attempt to realign the asymmetrical relationship the officer displays in the first turn. In the social hierarchy a physician is deemed to possess greater social prestige (power) than a police officer. However, the police officer again uses the derogatory address term in the third turn while asking his first name, another indication of power differential, despite the introduction of new information about the doctor's social status. As Wardaugh states this practice has been used to "put blacks in their place."

Contrast the Dr. Poussaint example with the following. A police officer initiates a traffic stop after he realizes that the plates are stolen. And after the driver has been successfully detained and cuffed, the officer asks the driver where he got the car:

Excerpt 44 (*COPS* data: "Driving a baby")
034 → PO1:   Where'd you get the car mae::ng?

The officer in this excerpt articulates a common address term (man) in an interesting way: the alveolar nasal changes to a velar nasal (hence, the "nasal" and vowel lengthening). In addition, the vowel undergoes a significant elongation process resulting in a diphthong-like sound. In this episode of *COPS*, the police officers use 'man' a total of seven times throughout the five minute encounter. As Goodwin (1990: 87-88) notes, that term by itself is semantically neutral; however, she notes that it is possible to "color" the address term with disrespect depending on the structure of the talk that surrounds it.

There are two interpretations that could explain the officer's usage of 'man': (1) he is using a solidarity politeness system by addressing the subject as his equal, thereby involving the other speaker as a strategic way of showing camaraderie and solidarity or (2) he is using a hierarchical politeness system, hence, talking "down" to someone inferior. Of course, if the first option is used to explain the choice of address term, then the address term employed by the white police officer to Dr. Poussaint could also be argued in a similar fashion. Consider the following address terms that citizens use toward police officers:

Excerpt 45 (Midwest City Police Traffic Stop #3)
17   PO: You know why I stopped you?
18   → D: Why sir?

Excerpt 46 (*COPS* data: "Naked enough")
38   PO: You in the military?
39   → M: No sir

In excerpt 45, a motorist is pulled over for speeding. After the officer asks to see the driver's license and proof of insurance and receives them from the motorist, the officer asks the motorist if he knows the reason for the stop. The motorist replies with an inquiry appended with an overtly marked deferential address term (sir).

In excerpt 46, a police officer self initiates a suspicious activity call; he asks a male citizen who wears a short "military style" haircut if he is in the military. The officer's question is a yes/no interrogative that requires a yes/no answer; and in the next turn, the male occupant answers the question with a no, followed also by an overtly marked deferential address term (no sir). Citizens who talk to police officers, however, are not the only ones who use polite address terms. Consider the following data:

Excerpt 47 (*COPS* data: "Jimmy Dean sausage")

12   →   PO: You the involved ma'am?

162 →   PO: Put your hands behind your back sir

In excerpt 47, the officer uses overtly marked deferential address terms of both gender. The officer is dispatched to the scene of a domestic disturbance; he utters line 12 in the initial moments of the call when he arrives on the scene and a woman runs up to him. The officer also uses the polite address term even as he is arresting the male disputant (line 162). The exchanges between cops and citizens, however, are not always polite and respectful. Consider the following:

Excerpt 48 (*COPS* data: "Naked enough")
155   PO: What's this?
156 → M: What's that? My wallet man

In a prior spate of talk the officer had asked M (male occupant) if he had any identification on him, and M replied that he had not. In excerpt 48, when the officer searches the man's pants, he finds a wallet in the back pocket. He then asks, "what's this?" referring to the wallet. M repeats the officer's question and gives a response with the address term shown in the excerpt. M is here confronted with an inconsistency and later arrested for lying to the police. In the "Naked enough" episode, after M is caught in a lie, he uses 'man' in a defiant manner for the next few turns as he is struggling to fight free from the officer (Goodwin, 1990); however later in the encounter (after he has been cuffed and other officers show up on the scene), he switches back to a polite address term.

Earlier I suggested the possibility that officers could use 'man' as an involvement strategy, using a solidarity politeness system by addressing the subject as their equal, thus showing camaraderie and solidarity or as a way of "talking down." Another explanation is that certain address terms are characteristic of a certain group of people or region. Consider the following examples:

Excerpt 49 (Midwest City Police Traffic Stop #2)
25   PO: I clocked you doing 44 in a 25
26   (1.0)
27   D: I'm sorry about that officer I'm just
28 →   trying to get home from Glen Ellen ma:n
29   PO: heh heh ((laughter)) well it doesn't matter
30   you're doing 44 in a 25

Excerpt 50 (*COPS* data: "Games")
39   PO: Don't give me no pr[oblems
40 → S: [ain't no problem dawg
41   PO: All right? (.8) Let's go

In excerpt 49 a young male is pulled over for speeding. The officer in his turn announces the problem and in the next turn, the young motorist attempts to apologize and tries to give an excuse—with 'man' appended at the utterance final slot. The officer, in the next turn, laughs and informs the driver that his excuse has no relevance to the encounter. In excerpt 50, the officer cuffs the man suspected of burglary before he questions him further, and the officer utters line 39 as he is doing so. The suspect addresses the officer as 'dawg'.

In excerpts 49 and 50 both participants use address terms other than a crisp 'sir' or 'ma'am' when they talk to the officer. The officer's conversationalist in excerpt 49 is a young male, in excerpt 50 a black male. In both excerpts an attempt by the officer to realign the asymmetrical relationship created by the address terms is absent. That is, unlike Dr. Poussaint who attempts to repair the address term the officer uses toward him, the officers in excerpt 49 and 50 attempt no such repair sequences. The absent deferential address term is not deemed problematic, as demonstrable in the next turn, because the absence is not what the officers orient to.

'Man' is an address term that "young people" commonly use in ordinary conversation; 'dawg' is an address term, amongst other more controversial terms, that young African-American males commonly use. Whether 'man' or 'dawg' is a component of a non-standard linguistic system, such as the Black English Vernacular (BEV) or slang used by young people, when used by members of that group—egalitarian—they work as a way of establishing and showing solidarity and camaraderie (see Kennedy, 2002). A problem could arise when members of a group use a member specific address term outside of membership, but that problem has to be oriented to and demonstrated empirically in the next turn by the next speaker.

The address term "man" can be used in different ways to do different things. As Goodwin (1990: 87-88) notes, it can be used as a way of affectively commenting on an addressee. A related way in which "man" works to convey affect is in its role as a discourse marker, rather than as an address term. For instance, in utterances such as "Man, I'm going nuts," "Man, she driving me crazy," or "This is some tall bullshit man," "man" functions less as an address term than as a discourse marker of sorts. One empirical observation that supports this interpretation is the fact that man is used toward and with female speakers present. As a hypothetical example:

Kelly: What kind of dreams you been having Pete?
Pete: Man, some really funky ones
Kelly: Oh really?

When Pete prefaces his utterance with "man" in response to the question posed in the prior turn, obviously, it is not being used as an address term toward Kelly, a female. Rather it marks some sort of affective/epistemological stance. Discourse markers such as "you know," "okay," "well," "oh" etc. work to create coherence and "index an utterance to the local context in which utterances are produced and in which they are to be interpreted" (Schiffrin, 1987: 326). For example, in Kelly's third turn response "oh" is used as a discourse marker to indicate a change of state or receipt of new information (see Heritage, 1998b; Schiffrin, 1987). According to Schiffrin (1987: 328) four conditions have to be met in order for a term to be counted as a discourse marker: (1) it has to be syntactically detachable from a sentence (2) it has to be commonly used in initial position of an utterance (3) it has to have a range of prosodic contours (4) it has to operate at both local and global levels of discourse, and on different planes of discourse.

In the examples I have used to illustrate "man" as a discourse marker (man, some really funky ones; man, she's driving me crazy; man, I'm going nuts) the term "man" (1) is detachable from the sentence without affecting the semantic content of the utterance (2) does occur in utterance initial position (3) does show prosodic variation (vowel elongation, slightly stressed at the utterance final place of articulation) (4) can be used both globally and locally. Utterances like "this is some tall bullshit man" however would not meet the second condition stipulated by Schiffrin. Would "man" in this case still be counted as a discourse marker? It has been suggested that "man" in this case is a type of footing shift (Goffman, 1981) in which speakers display their affective or epistemological stance towards some object/issue/state of affairs, etc.[15] Consider the following data from *COPS*:

Excerpt 51 (*COPS* data: "Naked enough")
166   PO: Get in the car you're you are under arrest
167   M: Man oh man

In excerpt 51 the term that is used predominantly as an address term is not used that way at all; it is more appropriate to call its usage as a type of a "response cry" (Goffman, 1981). Thus, the male suspect, after he is told that he is being arrested, a type of bad news delivery, utters "man oh man," similar to the way we would normally react upon sustaining a slight physical injury (e.g., hitting our elbows against the door) or being told bad news (see Maynard, 1996). Simply put, it is an interjection of sorts and not an address term at all. Consider a similar case in which 'man' is used as an affective interjection marker:

Excerpt 52 (*COPS* data: "Jimmy Dean sausage")
176   PO: Okay I'll explain something here in a minute okay?
177   ((PO puts one handcuff on the BM))
178   → BM: Man come on with this (shit)
179   PO: Put your other hand behind your back
180   BM: I got my daughter over there
181   ((PO puts other hand in cuffs))
182   PO: Uh okay we're gonna make arrangements
183   → BM: Ma::n this is some bull(shit)
184   PO: Right now you're being placed under arrest for assault
185   and for possession of marijuana with the intent to distribute
186   BM: No no no no no

In excerpt 52 an officer is dispatched to a domestic disturbance. During the course of the investigation, the female disputant tells the officer that the male disputant has marijuana stashed in his truck. After the responding officer listens to both stories, he goes over and checks the male disputant's truck and finds drugs and drug paraphernalia. Before he actually arrests the male disputant, the officer delays the telling of the bad news (line 176). When the officer actually handcuffs one of the BM's hands, the BM interjects with "man come on with this shit" (line 178). "Man" appears again after the other hand is placed in cuffs (line 183).

In this excerpt the BM displays his affective stance towards the receipt of bad news in an incremental and intensified way. First, when one of his hands is handcuffed, thus marking the beginning of his temporary loss of freedom (objectionable state of affairs), he lets out the interjection "man," along with a metaphorically synchronous summary of his new state of affairs: 'shit' (line 178). When the other hand is handcuffed, thus completing the temporary loss of freedom initiated in the prior sequence, the BM interjects with the same term as in line 178. However, two modifications occur: (1) the vowel in 'man' is noticeably lengthened, thus prosodically marking the disagreeable change in state; (2) the "shit" which had described a prior state of affairs is intensified to "bullshit." Finally, when he is told of the official bad news, that he is being arrested for assault and intent to distribute (a much more serious charge), the BM's affective stance toward his change of fortune intensifies and is openly protested (line 186).

The address term "man" illustrates the problem of coding I have extensively mentioned in prior chapters. In the excerpts I have used, that address term is used three ways: (1) as a way of disrespecting police authority (2) as a way of showing solidarity (when generously defined) and non-disrespect (when parsimoniously defined) (3) as a way of encoding negative affect upon the delivery of unpleasant news (arrest). And to show such nuances of meaning and intention in coding, the observers would have to interpret the utterance not on its formal grammatical features but on its interactional features—what work does the address term do? In other words, researchers who code demeanor on its mere categorical usage (did the subject use 'man' when addressing the police officer?) have no way of differentiating the polite, impolite, and affective meaning that was intended and understood; if researchers, however, do discriminate between the three uses in their coding, then what they have done is not coding in the interpretive sense but in an analytical sense. If analyzing meaning and intention (language use) is what the observers are doing, then they are doing discourse analysis, not coding.[16]

Conclusion

In this chapter, I have examined the discursive interactions that occur between police officers and citizens. I have outlined some of the conversational features of the prototypical police-citizen encounter, the traffic stop. I have argued that the opening sequences of a traffic stop can be viewed as a five-part sequence that socializes motorists into acceptance of police power.

By examining the sequence by sequence organization of talk in police-citizen encounters, I have shown that the coercive power the police possess is not exercised in an all or none fashion, but that it is enacted micro-sociologically, organized on a turn by turn and sequence by sequence basis. This point, as it relates to the study of citizens' demeanor, demonstrates that the police give numerous sequential opportunities for citizens to conform to the institutional framework of talk, and to effect a favorable impression management.

Notes

1. I should qualify that by police-citizen encounters I mean uniformed officers riding in marked police vehicles, with lights and sirens. In Chicago, patrol officers are instructed in the training academy to pull the vehicle over, walk up to the vehicle, and initiate traffic stops with a self- introduction such as "Hi, how you doing tonight. My name is Officer X of the Chicago Police Department. May I see your driver's license and proof of insurance please?" Once motorists provide the officer with necessary documents, officers are taught to ask, "Do you know why I stopped you?" The rationale, according to the instructors at the training academy, is that the question "opens communication between citizens and the police." As one patrol officer related to me, "some people have a good reason for breaking traffic laws." What is noteworthy is that police officers I have interviewed or encountered in actual stops or on *COPS* rarely make such formal self-introductions. As one patrol officer snidely remarked to me "What, they can't see the flashing lights and my badge and my gun and tell who I am? I'm the police."

If I may conjecture here, the absence of formal and categorical self-introductions may be more related to geography and modernization than anything else. For instance, most of the traffic stop data for this study were collected near Chicago. And as I already mentioned in this note, Chicago officers are trained to open the traffic stop that way, but the ones I've interviewed or talked to rely on the semiotic nature of the uniform to convey their institutional affiliation. This conjecture can be further strengthened from the following traffic stop data from *COPS*:

```
3    PO1: Turn it off
4    D:   Huh?
5    PO1: TURN IT OFF
6         Can I see yo hands ( ) who's car?
7    D:   Mine
8    PO1: Step on out
9         Hands on the car
10        You have a license or ID?
11   D:   Yea I got ID
12   PO1: Slide back back back of the car right here
13   D:   (mumble) Hey uhh
14   PO2: Hey what's up? That's what up ah-ight? first of all you don't have
15        a driver's license so you're not supposed to be driving a car
16        that's the first thing. I don't care whether you bought the car or
17        not the law says for you to operate this car you have to
18        have a valid driver's license. Now you have an attitude
19        you got a taillight out
```

This episode of *COPS* takes place in Philadelphia; two patrol officers make a traffic stop after witnessing a car driving at a high rate of speed; in addition, the car does not have visible license plates. After they activate the sirens and pull the car over, both officers approach the car and open the encounter with line 3.

Now, there is a lot of action that is taking place here (directives, safety, repair, opening, covert topic initiation), and some of these phenomena will be addressed in greater detail. However, for now, I just want to note that the Philadelphia officers, much like Chicago officers, do not make formal self-introductions. That is, they do not say, "Good evening. My name is Officer X of Philadelphia Police Department. May I see your driver's license and registration please?" Moreover, that the directives are routinely phrased as bald imperatives rather than in a "polite" way may be another defining feature of big city police. Contrast the way the big city traffic stops is opened with a police department in a much smaller city:

PO: Hello. Can I see your driver's license please? Good evening ma'am, my name is officer X with the Southern City Police Department. The reason I'm stopping you is you are doing 42 in a 30. Is there any medical emergency you're in a hurry for?
D: (shakes her head)

In this traffic stop the officer does begin the interaction in a way that is characteristic of bureaucratic institutions (see Zimmerman, 1992): he introduces himself (my name is officer X) and categorically identifies his institutional affiliation (with the Southern City Police Department). This officer from the Southern City Police Department was assigned to the Traffic Division: his entire shift was spent making traffic stops for speeding. When I spent time riding with other beat officers, most of them did not open the encounter (self-identification) in this way, although some did. There are numerous possibilities as to why this particular officer does begin the encounter the way he does (small city police, traffic specialist, polite manner); but the key point is that it *is* markedly different from the ones I have shown. Also, all of the Chicago patrol officers and Southern City police officers I spoke with said that the first thing they did after they approached the car was to greet the motorist. And using actual data, I will demonstrate how this "police articulation" of greetings can be manipulated to perform a bureaucratic and a social function in a later section. I am indebted to Beau Comeaux and Officer Hebert of the Southern City Police Department for their generous donation of the verbal data.

2. Of course, this is not to say that motorists who are generally pulled over have no idea as to why they are being stopped. This is not true of motorists who have been pulled over, especially, for speeding. Thus, I should clarify that the manner in which the accusation is made is direct, but the accusation itself is indirect because it has yet to be announced and ratified.

3. Some readers have suggested that I provide an example of this type of behavior that other researchers have noted; however, I find this difficult to do since there is a paucity of instances where citizens do not say anything at all. Pauses and silences between turns are common but I have not run across such cases. If an example of such a hypothetical encounter could be formulated, it would probably look something like this:
Police Officer (PO): How you doing may I see your driver's license and proof of insurance please?
Motorist (M): (silence)

If motorists continue to remain silent and not say a word, officers would repeat the question/request several times; moreover, they would probably say it in a different way (see Mastrofski et al., 2000; 1996). The effects of such continuous silence however would be disastrous for the motorist.

4. In Schegloff's article (1988b), the original example is "Do you know where Leo is?" For my example, I have merely changed the name from Leo to Waldo.

5. That the officers display a preference for other speakers' articulation of the official announcement suggests that the announcement (speeding) can be conceptualized as a bad-news delivery sequence (see Maynard, 1996; Schegloff, 1988b). Being pulled over for speeding and receiving a citation is, in not so many ways, bad news since motorists incur financial punishment. As Maynard (1996) and Schegloff (1988b) note, those who bring bad news forecast them vocally and nonvocally, that is provide clues and signals about the news to come; furthermore, bad news deliverers equivocally construct their talk in such a way that the bad news itself is articulated by the recipient.

In the data I've presented the motorists' next turn responses to the "do you know" question offer empirical support to the "do you know" question as a forecasting strategy in a bad news delivery sequence: the motorists reject the guesses at bad news as the preferred response (Schegloff, 1988b). However, it must be kept in mind that the "do you know" question is not used solely as a way of delivering bad news; this way of covertly and equivocally raising a topic occurs in the third sequence in the overall structural organization of traffic stops; that is it occurs after the legal summons, and the request. And as already mentioned, the first two sequences work as a "perspectival display" of moral character (see Maynard, 1992,1991), in addition to its other bureaucratic functions. That I have conceptualized CPI with an accusatorial tincture, rather than as a general bad news delivery sequence, is related to what the motorists do after the bad news announcement and the role of the speaker.

6. Of course, what counts as an offensive act should not be assumed a priori, even speeding. And Antaki (1994) warns against using merely the physical context of a setting to impute an offensive act as an accusation; that attribution must be made based on an accusation and exoneration's placement in the sequence of talk. In the data I've discussed thus far, we can see how the two emerge from the talk. When the motorists are given a opportunity to give an account through CPI, it is rejected; when the problem is stated to them— accused—then the account follows.

7. Again, if the yes/no question is viewed in an ordinary and social way, the motorists' responses display an absence of dispreferred features (mitigations, accounts, excuses). If, however, the question is seen as a way of initializing a "pre-blame" then their responses bear structural resemblance to denials, the preferred responses to accusations and blames.

8. What the motorist may be surprised at is the officer's apparent inflexibility. That is, the officer has already defined the parameters of acceptability of excuses—medical emergencies only. However, that the officer again asks the same question even after the motorist's rather passionate telling surprises the motorist. This officer, in fact, had a reputation amongst the Southern City Police officers as one who was "no-non-sense" and "very good." One of the linguistic strategies that made this officer's reputation may be that he minimizes the potential escalation of talk into arguments. Of course, he accomplishes that by collapsing several sequences into one turn; he gives no opportunity for motorists to respond to the various speech acts in his turn. And when he gives the motorists chances

to answer the questions he poses, he topically constrains the next turn answers thereby semantically limiting the motorists' contributions.

9. Of course, this doesn't necessarily mean that the motorists do not give excuses; they do, as the Chinese food delivery guy example shows. However, in order for motorists to do so, they have to first negatively answer the question, and then go on to provide an account. Grammatically, this is tactical because it minimizes potential conflict talk.

10. In a courtroom, the model legal institution where its entire business is conducted with language, attorneys (prosecution and defense) possess the power to dominate victims and witnesses through language use (Conley and O'Barr, 1998; Atkinson and Drew, 1979; Hirsch, 1998; Matoesian, 1993). For example, in a cross-examination, the defense attorney (DA) has the power to alter the participation structure through objections, silences, and manipulation of the syntax of questions. The result of having such power is that the sequential and topical structure of talk remains under the control of the attorney. For example, by manipulating the syntactic structure of the question, the attorney is able to constrain the turn size of the defendant by limiting the response type: the defendant's answer may be constrained to a terse yes/no answer if the question format is a simple yes/no interrogative. Although the defendant is able to exercise a bit more freedom to a WH question, the attorney is able, nevertheless, to decontextualize the question and align the defendant toward a strategically desirable impression management. In addition, the selection of topic is also at the mercy of the questioning lawyer. According to Matoesian (1993: 165), although the defendant (victim) does manage some control over the topic selection, the "defense attorney's control mechanisms to manipulate talk far exceeds the complementary capabilities of the victims."

11. In a felony traffic stop, officers approach the car with their weapons drawn instead of walking up to the car. Officers usually open the encounter with imperatives and commands, and make the occupants prostrate on the ground.

12. For now, I just want to mention in this section that "what's going on?" is a fact-seeking interrogative designed to elicit accounts. How the WM constructs his account is an entirely different type of action and analysis. In chapter 5, I analyze how disputants in a domestic dispute tell their stories to minimize their own culpability and maximize the other party's blameworthy actions.

13. There exists quite a literature on the "science" (the more appropriate term is art) of detecting truth and deception in police interrogations. In all of these studies, however, the police begin with certain presuppositions in place (guilt vs. innocence). Again, there is no natural connection between hesitation markers and interturn silence; that connection is artificial, a function of prior assumptions prior to any talk. In general see Adams (1996), Brougham (1992), Clare and Gudjonsson (1993), Fisher, Geiselman, and Raymond (1987), Gudjonsson (1992), Inbau, Reid, and Buckley (1986), Kassin (1997), Kassin and McNall (1991), McConville (1992), McConville and Baldwin (1982), McIlwane (1994), Moston, Stephenson, and Williams (1992), Napier and Adams (1998), Pinizzotto and Deshazor (1997), Rabon (1996), Royall and Schutt (1976), Vessel (1998), Waltman (1983).

14. Consider the following way deference is morpholologically woven into utterances in a greeting in Korean:
1) ahn nyoung
    (hello)

2) ahn nyoung   ha seo   yo
    (hello)   (particle) (honorific)

The lexical root of the greeting is 'ahn nyoung'. This type of greetings would be exchanged by those equal in status, such as age. It would be a grave sociocultural norm violation if a younger person or a subordinate were to utter such greetings to an elder, such as parent, employer, and teacher. The latter would be more felicitous.

15. I am indebted to Prof. Matoesian for this insight.

16. This does not mean that language use could not be studied using the principles of statistics; but it's just that the first interpretive move would be analytical in a linguistic sense, not statistical.

CHAPTER 5
"WHAT I LOOK LIKE FIGHTIN' HIM?":
WHAT DOMESTIC DISPUTANTS TELL THE POLICE

This chapter examines the police response to a domestic dispute, and the way "family beefs" is discursively and sequentially organized. What would a "live" view of the police response to a domestic dispute reveal about the way domestic disputes are interactionally managed by the officers and disputants? What goes on in a domestic dispute? What do the disputants say and how do they say it? How do they allocate blame, attribute motives, and accomplish their respective interactional goals?

This chapter describes how disputants negotiate, resist, and contest their claims during their interaction with the police and one another (Spencer, 1987). It attempts to unpack the conversational details of incipient disputes, its progression, and resolution, along with the "out of the blue" character of domestic assaults. In addition, this chapter describes how identities such as "violent batterer" and "blameless victim" emerge from the talk itself. The analysis presented in this chapter rests on six minutes and forty-three seconds of microlinguistic conversational data.

There are abundant anecdotal and ethnographic accounts of police response to domestic disputes; and there is consensus in prior police literature that domestic disputes are "chaotic" and "disorderly," that there is no order to the occasion (Black, 1980). This chapter challenges such findings by demonstrating how the disputants use language in a sophisticated way to impeach another's credibility and "authorize" their own version of events. While it could be argued that such single case analysis is unrepresentative of domestic disputes in general, the goal of this chapter is to show the "constitutive order" (Schegloff, 1987: 102) of a dispute: how the disputants make accusations, impute and deflect blame to give form and substance (meaning) to the dispute as a socially organized activity.

The "Beef" in Family Beefs

Police officers generally do not like to handle domestic disputes, the "family beef" (Black, 1980). There are two principal reasons for this: first, the work that the police do is formally conceptualized as a law enforcement activity (fighting crime). Hence, resolving family disputes is seen as a "waste of time" since it is not related to their official mandate; furthermore, domestic disturbance arrests are not organizationally valued as other "serious" (felony) arrests (Sherman and Berk, 1984; Buzawa and Buzawa, 1993: 339). Second, police officers do not like to handle domestic disputes because they are often *thought* to be unpredictable and fraught with danger (Muir, 1977: 84). Consider the following recollection of a domestic dispute that a Chicago police officer candidly relates:

Excerpt #1 (Fletcher, 1990: 32-33)
The landlord of the building told me as we went up, 'these people have a gun in there. Be careful.' So when we walked in, this woman was yelling; she's going off on us and she's getting up and down and stuff. All of a sudden, she sat down real fast on this couch. She has her hand down by her crotch, so I grab her arm. My partner grabs the guy. I turn to see her and she's a big woman—she pulls out this big six-inch barrel revolver, a .22, and it's staring me right in the pus. The only thing I could think of to do was to grab it by the cylinder...Okay, so I grab it—she's trying to pull that trigger, right?—I got it by the cylinder. I give her a whack in the puss with my other hand and pull the gun away. I was lucky she didn't have a bad gun. If you get one of those and grab the cylinder, you're out. You lost. You're dead.

Excerpt #1 poignantly illustrates the unpredictability and danger that police officers face when attempting to resolve a dispute between intimates. When the police arrive, both participants turn against the police and direct their anger toward them.[1] The only reason the police are able to safely resolve the quoted dispute without sustaining injury to themselves and without fatally wounding the disputants is through luck: the gun that the woman uses against one of the officers is a "good" one.

In domestic disputes, police officers can choose from a wide range of courses of action. They can: (1) "listen passively to the disputant(s) (2) verbally restrain disputant(s) (3) threaten physical restraint (4) apply physical restraint (5) request separation of disputants (6) impose separation on disputants (7) physically force separation (8) divert attention of disputants (9) question to elicit the nature of the problem" (Bayley and Bittner, 1984: 45). Some officers have an uncanny ability to diffuse tension and potential violence from materializing (e.g., the professional) while others inflame the dispute (e.g., the enforcer), or avoid them altogether (e.g., the avoider). Consider Officer Tubman's response to a domestic dispute:

Excerpt #2 (Muir, 1977: 32-33)
It was a day watch, and I got a 975, stand by and preserve the peace. It was on the third floor of this big apartment building. I was alone and had no transreceiver. I went in, and things had quieted down. She wanted to get her stuff. So anyways in the course of the deal, I found a marijuana joint. I found a little more grass around. Anyway I found it. It was the man's anyway. He was there, and she was there. I saw it, and she had showed it to me and wanted him to go to jail. I was alone and had no transreceiver. He was a real big guy, and he had some friends around the apartment. I didn't arrest him. I was just out of recruit school. I might have done the same thing now. I would have tried to get a cover unit, and if I had waited for it, he might have still been around. I just let it slide. She took off with all her clothes. The decision was whether to arrest him or not. He got a little upset about it. I told her to hurry and get her stuff out. I didn't want to make anything of it.

Muir describes the way Officer Tubman handled the above family beef as a "bumbling quality" of police work. He critiqued Tubman for his lack of prudence: the assignment originated as a radio call, not as a self-initiated activity, hence, Muir argued, Tubman would have had ample time to formulate a strategy as to how he should deal with the call. Moreover, Officer Tubman forgets his portable radio and his cover (back up unit); most importantly, Muir attributes Tubman's "bumbling quality" to his incapacity to anticipate what was likely to happen. Consequently, Tubman was unpleasantly surprised and humiliated during calls. And notice how a police officer's inability to anticipate events leads to embarrassment and the acquisition of an unflattering reputation among other officers: Tubman sees illegal narcotics but decides not to do anything; or more correctly, he can't do anything about it because the male disputant is bigger than him, and has several friends in his home; he has no back up, hence, he has no way of contacting for assistance should he need it because he forgot his radio—bumbling.

While accounts of police response to domestic disputes abound in anecdotal literature (Baker, 1985; Fletcher, 1990; Middleton, 2000), there are three main theoretical approaches to the study of domestic disputes: psychological, feminist, and sociological. In psychologically-oriented research, scholars attempt to explain men's intimate violence as a function of their maladaptive personality traits (e.g., anti-social, psychopathic) (see O'Leary, 1993; Walker, 1993, 1979). That is, men who suffer from violence prone personalities commit physical and psychological violence against their intimate partners. When applied to women, they are thought to be responsible for their victimization due to "masochistic" personalities. This theory, essentially, blames women for possessing a trait that unconsciously or consciously enjoys the pain the abusive men inflict on them— a myth that has been thoroughly debunked (see Browne, 1987; Walker, 2000; Yllo, 1993).

A notable psychological concept that has buttressed the trait perspective is Lenore Walker's (1979) theory of the battered woman. According to Walker, women in abusive relationships learn to become "helpless" since they lose the ability to control and predict future outcomes (e.g., when their next beating will occur). Consequently, Walker (1979) states that some women actively participate in the battering incident by precipitating the "inevitable explosion so as to control where and when it [battering] occurs, allowing her to take better precautions to minimize her injuries and pain" (Walker, 2000: 126). For Walker, domestic disputes/assaults occur in cycles: they begin with a (1) tension building process that leads to an (2) acute battering incident, which culminates in the abusive men's (3) loving and contrite behavior (for Walker's Cycle Theory of Violence see Walker, 2000: 126-138).

Feminist researchers explain domestic assaults not as a function of personality deficiencies, but on the patriarchal structures that permit men to dominate, control, and abuse women in the first place. Thus, feminists, along with critics of psychologically oriented research, tend to view the economic and social inequality between men and women and cultural prescriptions of sex roles as central factors that lead to violence (Bowker, 1993; Browne, 1987; Dobash and Dobash, 1979; Yllo, 1993).

Sociologists who study domestic disputes tend to be outcome and policy oriented. Rather than using the dispute process itself as a resource for inquiry, they have focused on their outcomes. As a result, their findings have been primarily used to shape law enforcement policies, dictating what police officers in domestic disputes should do. This type of prescriptive research is best illustrated in the paradigmatic study of domestic disputes.

Sherman and Berk (1984: 265) randomly assigned three experimental conditions to the calls for service in Minneapolis. Police officers who responded to misdemeanor domestic assaults were instructed to (1) arrest (2) offer advice or mediate or (3) separate the disputants by ordering the suspect out of the home for a period of eight hours. Sherman and Berk (1984: 270) concluded that arrest alone achieved the purpose of deterring future violence: "arrests make an independent contribution to the deterrence potential of the criminal justice system. Therefore, in jurisdictions that process domestic assaults offenders in a manner similar to that employed in Minneapolis, we favor a presumption of arrest: an arrest should be made unless there are good clear reasons why an arrest would be counterproductive" (see also Berk, 1993).

The Minneapolis study generated replication studies in six other cities; when it was replicated in Milwaukee, WI Sherman, Smith, Schmidt, and Rogan (1992) found that arrest did not uniformly deter future offences by suspects. They found that arrest is a deterrent for those who already have a "stake in conformity," such as employment and marriage. For those who were unemployed and not married (just living together) Sherman et al. (1992) asserted that arrest increases the likelihood of repeat violence. Pate and Hamilton (1992) found that only employment and not marriage, achieved a deterrent effect in Metro-Dade County, FL.

The Minneapolis study conducted by Sherman and Berk (1984) and the replication studies in other cities have altered the way police officers respond to domestic assaults, favoring mandatory arrests over officers' exercise of discretion (Berk, 1993; Gelles, 1993; Strauss, 1993). Critics, however, have argued that arrest, and sometimes, mediation, may not be the best police response. For example, Walker (2000, 1979) notes that police officers are inadequately trained to deal with domestic assault cases and "if a woman is thought to have played a role in causing her abuse, the officer may decide that she is not a good enough battered woman and fail to make an arrest" (Walker, 2000: 195). Buzawa and Buzawa's (1993) criticisms of mandatory arrest policies are more complex. They find methodological flaws with the original Minneapolis study, stating that a small sample of officers were responsible for a disproportionate number of cases. Furthermore, they argue that the study focused exclusively on the poor and unemployed, thus not representative of the Minneapolis population.

In most prior works on domestic disputes, there is a neglected and overlooked component. When the police are contacted to intervene in family beefs, they have to negotiate and "work through" the call before an arrest is made. That is, before cops arrest, mediate, or separate, they have to listen to the claims each disputant makes, untangle the accusations they hurl at one another, discern the validity of those claims, detect inconsistencies, and then attribute blame. It is this microsociological and discursive element of blaming, making claims and counter-claims in Lenore Walker's Phase II (battering incident) that has been absent in the literature on domestic conflicts (Vuchinich, 1984; see also Briggs, 1996a,b).

This deficiency is particularly noticeable since the role of language in domestic disputes/assaults is already well noted. Walker (2000: 33) reports that verbal abuse and confrontations precede eighty-percent of battering incidents (see also Browne, 1987; O'Leary, 1993). These verbal confrontations and minor battering incidents constitute the meat and potatoes of Walker's Phase I, the tension building cycle. Bowker (1993: 155) also notes that most of the battered women tried to talk the men out of beating them; in addition, they tried to "extract" promises from the men to not batter them again and to avoid certain topics of talk. Generally, violent encounters between intimates are preceded by "verbal confrontations" of some sort: "The events [assaults] described to us were almost preceded by a verbal confrontation relating to ongoing aspects of the marital relationship, with the husband or wife making demands on their partner or complaining about various transgressions. The majority of these arguments were not trivial but conferred on long-standing contentious issues" (Dobash and Dobash, 1979: 98). Some of the "contentious" issues involve money, husband's jealousy, and a man's unfulfilled expectations concerning "traditional" woman's roles (Browne, 1987; Dobash and Dobash, 1979). In the following accounts we get a fleeting glimpse of how such assaults and disputes begin:

Excerpt #3 (Walker, 1979: 86)

While I was fixing dinner for us, Ira and his mother were sitting at the table, and the three of us were talking about the movie we just saw. I didn't like what his mother said about one of the characters. I didn't agree with her, and I told her I thought she was wrong. Her interpretation of what had happened was dif-

ferent from mine. Ira became enraged. He threw the glass of water he was
drinking at me. He then went to wipe me off, as I was dripping wet. As he was
wiping me with a towel, he started slapping my face.

Excerpt #4 (Dobash and Dobash, 1979: 100)

'There's never anything but bloody cheese, cheese, cheese, cheese all the time.'
So you'd get it, and then I might just answer back; and I'd say, "well if it's good
enough for me, cheese, and it's good enough for the children, what's wrong
with a cheese sandwich...it might be the way your face just looked for a second
at him, or something; and then he'd just give you one across the face, always
across the face.

We get a better understanding of how disputes initially begin by glossing
the accounts the abused women offer. The men blatantly and directly accuse the
women about money problems, fidelity, and food preparation, and hurl insults
pointing out enduring personality flaws in them. And when the accusations and
insults are verbally responded to—canonically in the form of a disagreement
with the man's position—that counter move catapults a violent act (Browne,
1987), thus transforming a conflict talk sequence (Dersley and Wootton, 2001;
Goodwin, 1990; Grimshaw, 1990; Vuchinich, 1990) into a battering sequence.
The abusive men see these types of verbal responses to accusations as a challenge not only to the content of the preceding turn, but also as a challenge to
their authority. It is misleading, however, to only think of a woman's verbal
reply as a challenge to authority. Sometimes, the men interpret women's attempt
at physical withdrawal from the argument, mere silence, and other paralinguistic
cues as a challenge to their authority (Vuchinich, 1990, 1984): "if she answers
his verbal harangue, he becomes angrier at what she says. If she remains quiet,
her withdrawal engages him" (Walker, 1979: 61). Consequently, the husband
gives the wife a beating "out of the blue" (Browne, 1987: 48; Walker, 2000).

In this type of post-battering incident interview data, verbal disputes prior to
the physical assault are anecdotally acknowledged as a noteworthy precedent;
however, the social and linguistic processes that constitute the verbal disputes as
a socially organized activity are never addressed. The actual sequencing of verbal disputes is left unexplored since the accounts are offered after the incident:
talk is never treated as an object and topic of inquiry, as a process in itself
(Goodwin, 1982; Grimshaw, 1990; Vuchinich, 1984); instead, they are used as a
vehicle for representing the contents of the disputes (see Antaki, 1994; Briggs,
1996a). Thus in excerpt 3, the woman disagrees with her mother-in-law's assessment of the movie, treating her formulation as an opposition or an "argu-
able" (Eisenberg and Garvey, 1981; Maynard, 1985a) and paves the foundation
for an argument or conflict talk (Grimshaw, 1990). The mother-in-law however,
is not able to materialize the argument because before she has a chance to escalate or deescalate her daughter-in-law's opposition, the batterer enters the talk
and treats his wife's initial disagreement with his mother as a highly offensive—
oppositional—act (Goodwin, 1982; Vuchinich, 1984); this in turn initializes the
incipient use of physical force (throws the glass of water), one of several reac-

tions that is available in response to an opposition (Eisenberg and Garvey, 1981).

In excerpt 4, the husband's use of the word "cheese" might be used by interview and survey researchers as a way of coding the context of the dispute as having its origin in poor food preparation. But there is much more in the given account: the abused woman directly quotes the batterer's words through reported speech, thus not only transplanting herself in the past moment of enunciation but also animating the angry husband's words, thereby replaying the past event in a highly affective "frame" in the context of a narrative performance in the present (Goffman, 1981, 1974; Hirsch, 1998). According to Hirsch (1998: 195) "reported speech adds excitement to a narrative, audibly displaying the perpetrators of blameworthy or mitigating acts, and thus contributes to disputant's attempts to address the task of disputing." Moreover, reported speech constitutes a powerful poetic device for conveying social and cultural norms (Briggs, 1996a, b). But one of the most strategic benefits of reported speech is that speakers can inject their affective components such as prosody, intonation, pitch, and other meta-communicative commentary into the quoted speech (Besnier, 1990). And although we do not exactly know how the abused woman might have actually articulated the husband's words, we get a hint of the husband's affective state in the past speaking moment.

Cheese is uttered three times, and after the third repetition, cheese is combined with a universal quantifier to temporally mark the "extreme" frequency—habitual character—of its presence (Pomerantz, 1986). Hence, lexical repetition is used as a way of reiterating the message ("cheese, cheese, cheese"), but it is also poetically inscribed on to the form and structure of the batterer's message (see Jakobson, 1960). We might even speculate that the escalation of the dispute can be seen and heard in the paralinguistic moments of the husband's complaint: beginning with the first utterance of cheese, each subsequent repetition may have been accompanied by an increase in volume, pitch, and intonation, his anger reaching a climax in his lexical final utterance ("all the time") (Goodwin, 1990; Vuchinich, 1990). Furthermore, to convey the habitual presence of cheese on the dinner table, the vowels may have been lengthened as a way of suprasegmentally signaling the extremeness of such actions (Hirsch, 1998).

The mere coding of disputes as having their origin in poor food preparation, then, overlooks the way the message (cheese as the source of conflict) itself is encoded in its form—as a form of social action, with each discrete element marking escalation and rise in the dispute itself (Briggs, 1996b). If the batterer's complaint about cheese which initiates his assault is portrayed as something illogical and crazy, notice the way the battered woman favorably portrays herself in the reporting context (interview) by marking her actions with a diminutive, thus minimizing and mitigating her own antagonistic and hostile stance (Hirsch, 1998; Vuchinich, 1984). That is, she does not frame her response as an overt challenge to his authority; instead, she "just" answers back, lexically downplaying her oppositional stance while highlighting her husband's aggravated complaint (Eisenberg and Garvey, 1981; Goodwin, 1983). Another technique the woman uses is a hierarchically ordered category of familial consumers: if cheese is good enough for me and the children, why not you?

By preliminarily examining the abused woman's interview data, we can see the complex ways that blame is performed and deflected in the account as a socially organized activity (Antaki, 1994; Goodwin, 1990; Grimshaw, 1990). To mine merely for content (coding) would miss all of the rich interactional details of the dispute itself, such as the fact that cheese is not only reportable as a representation of foodstuff, but that it is also used as a resource in the dispute as a way of initializing and escalating the verbal conflict prior to the physical one. In other words, "cheese, cheese, cheese, cheese all the time" is a linguistic pre-performance of the physical violence to follow. But in addition to the linguistic features, poetic, paralinguistic, and metalinguistic cues add a dramatic and emotional flair to the message itself while simultaneously creating the antagonistic relations in the context of performance rather than in a description of it (Bauman, 1986; Matoesian, 2001).

There is an obvious interplay of power in domestic disputes: one disputant physically dominates another. Language scholars, however, have noted another way that power is enacted, embodied, and contested in the interactional moments of conflict processes—recontextualization (Bauman and Briggs, 1990). Thus, not only is the content of verbal exchanges in disputes between intimates held to be important, but how such verbal disputes arise, get managed, and framed is crucial to understanding the conflict talk as an occasioned performance (Antaki, 1994; Brennis, 1996, 1988; Goodwin and Goodwin, 1990). This point is especially noteworthy since verbal interaction constitutes the bulk (two-thirds) of Walker's (2000) cyclical theory violence. For instance, the tension building cycle is marked by verbal conflicts that precede the actual battering sequence; in this phase, we might see the brewing conflict in the blunt accusations, direct insults, and unmitigated disagreements the male batterer hurls at the woman. Put another way, tension building is embodied in the form of the language as oppositional stance the batterer assumes. Furthermore, there is more to "loving and contrite" behavior than buying expensive gifts. It entails verbal promises to desist ("I swear I'll never hit you again"); it may be accompanied by a generous dose of apologies peppered into the contrite behavior ("I'm so sorry I knocked out all your teeth"); we might even find excuses and justifications that creep their way into the batterer's talk ("You know I do it because I love you so much"). Put bluntly, language is the "bread and butter" of domestic disputes; we might even assert that the troubled relationship is mirrored and constituted in and through the talk. Consequently, the language used in domestic disputes is not just an "epiphenomenal reflex of other relations" but a dynamic construction of those relations (Briggs, 1996a).

Disputes have received much attention in the literature, most notably in the areas of children's arguments (Boggs, 1978; Boggs and Lein, 1978; Brennis and Lein, 1977; Corsaro and Rizzo, 1990; Eisenberg and Garvey, 1981; Lein and Brennis, 1978), their social organization (Goodwin, 1990, 1982), their origins (Maynard, 1985b), and their social functions (Maynard, 1985a) and in family arguments (Vuchinich, 1990, 1984). In legal contexts, disputes have been examined in courts (Conley and O'Barr, 1990) and mediation hearings (Garcia, 1991; Greatbatch and Dingwall, 1997). In the latter, analysts are able to gather their data only after the disputants have sought the assistance of public institutions whose business concerns resolving the disputes (Garcia, 1991). Consequently, "such a procedure glosses over much of the original interactional detail, and it thus comes to disregard the potential significance of this detail" (Dersley and Wootton: 2001: 612). To remedy this deficiency Dersley and Wootton offer a moment by moment look at dispute sequences, prior to institutional involvement, that end up with one party's physical departure. They conclude that one party leaves the dispute when another identifies "deleterious and generic personal deficiencies"—offensive personal deficiencies that the one who remains refuses to change. According to Dersley and Wootton (2001: 633) this refusal "forms a warrantable basis for the leaver's departure."

The "Disorderly" Order of the Pre-Narrative

In excerpt 1, a Chicago police officer recalled that as he and his partner walked into the disputants' home, "this woman was yelling; she's going off on us." Although we do not know the exact content of what the woman was yelling about or how she said it and what "going off" entails, perhaps it is the performance of such verbal acts that lead to the characterization of domestic disputes as being "disorderly." From where does this impression arise? This section unpacks the details of yelling, screaming, and "going off" to see if domestic disputes really are "disorderly" as prior police scholars have suggested. In the following data, the host cop receives an assignment and he tells the viewing audience the following framing narrative:

Excerpt 5 (*COPS* data: "Jimmy Dean")
```
1 PO:   We're responding to a ss uh party of two suspicious it
2       actually sounds like a domestic assault ( ) um basically
3       ex-boyfriend ( ) uh hit his ex-girlfriend in the
4       face with ( ) an some sort an object while he
5       was moving out ( ) uh apparently she's bleeding
6       and he's supposed to be leaving the scene
7       and we may be running into him here
8       in a minute ( )
```

The call that the host officer receives is initially encoded as a suspicious fight in progress (man and woman fighting), but the officer transforms the sketchy and uncertain call into a predictable and routine assignment ("actually sounds like a domestic assault") from the information that the dispatcher provides (Manning, 1988). And as the framing narrative it provides the viewing audience with a metapragmatic template of interpretation (see chapter 3). Hence, in the beginning moments of the episode, prior to any substantive contact with the disputants (lines 3-5), the officer succinctly summarizes what is about to occur in the interaction phase: "um basically ex-boyfriend uh hit his ex-girlfriend in the face with an some sort an object while he was moving out." And as the officer arrives on the scene, parks his car and gets out, a woman rapidly walks toward him. Line 12 is the beginning of the verbal contact between the police and the alleged disputants:

Excerpt 6 (*COPS* data: "Jimmy Dean")
12 PO: You the involved ma'am?
13 BW: (Yes [he came into mah house)
14 PO: [You involved?
15 BW: (came into mah house)
16 PO: Okay calm down I'll hear both stories
17 BW: He came into mah house tresspassed
18   [after I told him to get out
19 PO: [All right okay just relax
20 BM: STOP LYING
21 BW: And then then ([af af after I)
22 BM: ([ )
23 PO: Sir sir sir ma'am Out here do me a favor
24   stand right there okay?
25   ((to both parties))
26   You got some ID You got some ID?
27 BW: I got mines upstairs
28 PO: Okay you have some ID?
29 BM: [Mine's over there in my (van)
30 BW: [Go check his truck cuz he's got weed in it
31 BM: What? ((raised pitch))
32 PO: Do me a favor go ahead and turn off your
33   vehicle for me I'll do it do you mind if I
34   turn it off?
35 BM: I'ma park it right there
36 PO: No no we'll leave it right here for now
37   Where's your ID at sir?
38 BM: I don't have it on me right now
39 PO: Do me a favor don't reach into there
40   for anything okay?
41 BM: Okay
42 PO: What happened here today sir?

Police officers who show up to domestic disputes face a different constraint on the interaction from other institutional discourses. In legal settings such as courts and mediation hearings speakers' roles are institutionally ascribed prior to the interaction (e.g., as plaintiffs and defendants, victims and witnesses).[2] That is, a judge or a mediator usually opens the encounter, explains procedures, and then elicits an account/narrative (Atkinson and Drew, 1979; Garcia, 1991; Briggs, 1996b; Conley and O'Barr, 1990; Hirsch, 1998; see also Antaki, 1994). In this encounter, the "official" request for a story, an account, occurs in line 42 ("what happened here today sir?"); the delay is attributable to the fact that the officer must first clarify and establish the identities of the involved parties. As Balyey and Bittner (1984:45) state, one of the first things the officers on scene must do is establish control of the situation, to "shift the axis of interaction from the disputants to the officers." The noteworthy point is that officers must find out who the disputants are before they can elicit the nature of the problem (line 42). Moreover, in all of the possible responses to domestic disputes, officers have to use language to get their actions accomplished.

In this encounter the dispatcher tells the responding cop that the male disputant (BM) may be leaving the scene and may run into him while en route. When the officer arrives on scene, he sees a woman walking towards him; he also stops a green truck leaving the area. In line 12 the officer makes verbal contact with the female disputant (BW). The officer's first question that is addressed to the BW is an interrogative that seeks to establish the identity of the woman as one of the disputants. The officer's intended addressee is lexically (and gender) marked with a polite address term (line 12: ma'am). After the BW affirmatively answers, she states her complaint/accusation that the BM came into her house. The officer then asks the BM who has exited the green truck if he is involved (line 14). In line 15 the BW repeats her complaint.

In lines 12 and 14 the officer attempts to discern the identities of both parties; this projected action can be supported in two ways. First, when the officer addresses the BW, he lexically marks her as the ratified—direct—recipient of his talk (you the involved ma'am?). When the officer asks a clipped form of the same question in line 14, no address terms are present.[3] Second, the officer asks the second yes/no question in line 14 only after the BW fulfills the grammatical and semantic constraints projected in the prior turn. That is, the officer asks the second question only after receiving a satisfactory answer to his question in line 12. By doing so, however, the officer's turn (line 14) overlaps with the BW's complaint and accusation (line 13). The BM has no turn space to answer because before he can do so the BW "usurps" the on-going participation framework (Goodwin, 1990). She intercepts the question addressed to the BM and uses that turn to repeat her complaint—a complaint not "heard" as such in the prior turn (line 13). Consequently, the BW's usurpation of the participation framework invokes a stern warning from the officer in line 16: he tells her to calm down, that he will listen to both stories.

That the officer is orienting to the establishment of relevant identities, and not eliciting a narrative, is also demonstrable in the following way. Grammatically, the officer's question in line 12 merely asks the BW if she is the involved person. The BW's turn in line 13, however, goes beyond the relevancy requirements of the preceding turn; she provides a complaint, an accusation—an account. The BW treats the yes/no question as an indirect request and an invitation for an account. However, the officer does not treat it as such because he begins his turn (line 14) concurrently as the BW begins her narrative. In other words, the officer's yes/no question in line 12 is not an indirect invitation for a story but an identity establishing, fact seeking, yes/no interrogative. Notice that after the officer receives a satisfactory answer to his question in line 12 (BW's 'yes' in line 13) he changes the recipient status of his talk, addressing the BM as the direct recipient of his talk. That the officer is concerned with establishing identities, and not with stories and accounts, can first be seen in the officer's interruption (line 14) of the BW's turn in progress (line 13) and again in line 16. When the BW offers an unsolicited account in line 15 (after usurping BM's turn), the officer lays down the contextual footing (definition) of the situation, explicitly prescribes the turn taking order, thus socializing the female disputant into the interactional order of the P-C encounter.

Even after such failed attempts to tell a story (line 13, line 15), and after receiving a stern chastisement (line 16), the BW again begins to formulate an account (line 17); this time she upgrades the complaint against the BM by using the word "trespassed" and adds a temporal adverbial marker, highlighting the BM's flagrant infraction of the law and her directive. This time, however, the officer does not even wait for the BW to complete her turn: he interrupts her turn in progress (line 17-18) to berate her for telling an unsolicited and out of turn complaint, and repairs the turn order (line 19)—"out of turn repair" ("all right okay just relax").

If the officer does not hear the BW's complaint and accusation as such, she receives a sympathetic ear from the BM. He responds to her complaint in a direct manner and enters into a direct speaker-listener framework with the BW as a ratified participant. Recall that the BW's "he came into mah house" is addressed to the officer, and phrased in the third person, thus bearing sequential resemblance to a mediation hearing since accusations are directed to a neutral third party, not the disputants themselves (Garcia, 1991). In line 20 the BM utters a directive to the BW to "stop lying." There are two noteworthy features (paralinguistic, participation framework) of the BM's turn in line 20: first, there is a noticeable increase in volume, thus marking escalation into an argument (Brennis and Lein, 1977; Goodwin, 1990; Vuchinich, 1984); second, it is not addressed to the officer but to the BW. "STOP LYING" (line 20) as the second pair part to a "You involved?" (line 14) makes no sense; it only makes sense if it is seen as a response to an accusation—"actions which describe the addressee as the agent of an offensive act" (Goodwin, 1982: 78) ("he came into mah house").

The BW continues to tell her story as contiguous action despite two "impediments" to her sequential flow: (1) from the police officer who admonishes her for attempting to tell a story when no such invitation was extended (2) from the BM's denial. What is noteworthy here is that the BW continues to address her talk, as an account, to the officer while the BM addresses his talk as a response to the BW's accusations. This type of bifurcated participation framework is not without consequences. In mediation hearings, the disputants address their talk to the mediators rather than to their co-disputants; consequently, the interactional organization (i.e., participation framework) of mediation hearings minimizes arguments since accusations and denials are addressed to the mediators rather to each other (Garcia, 1991). When the participants depart from the speech exchange system of mediation hearings and use ordinary rules of turn taking, Garcia notes, the talk resembles the character of an argument. And in excerpt 6, there appears to be three different yet concurrent contexts of talk: the

BW's attempted turns to tell an account demonstrates her orientation to the officer's (1) information seeking questions as an (2) elicitation of a narrative. The BM's adjacently placed denials to the BW's accusations impede the progression of her on-going narrative, but it also perpetuates—escalates—the sequential organization of talk, and serve as the fodder for (3) argumentative/conflict talk (Garcia, 1991; Grimshaw, 1990; Hutchby, 1998; Maynard, 1985a).

After the BM adjacently places his turn to the BW's account (line 22), the host cop self selects himself as the next speaker and breaks the adjacently placed exchanges. Consequently, he breaks the rhythmic cycle of accusations, denials, and counter-accusations of an emergent argument by first reconfiguring the sequential organization of talk, and then by physically separating the disputants. He tells one to come "out here" (proximal deixis) while ordering another to go "over there" (distal deixis).[4] The officer employs a powerful rhetorical strategy to get this done. He "softens" or mitigates the directive by embedding a request ("do me a favor") in the midst of a command, thus placing himself at the discretion of the disputant, facing the possibility of rejection; he appends a tag question ("okay?") at the end of the directive to project a preference for compliance, facilitating conformity to coercive police power (see Ervin-Tripp, 1978).

I use the words "admonish," "berate," and "reprimand" to describe what the officer does when the disputants break frame from the mediation-like format in the initial moments of the encounter because what the officer says (line 23: "sir sir sir, ma'am") bears a striking relation to the way a parent—Rorschach-father in uniform—mediates a dispute between two fighting children. There are three noticeable features that buttress this comparison, repetition, linguistic simplification, and the degree of social control that is embedded in the form of the directive (Ervin-Tripp, 1978; see also Ervin Tripp, 1982, 1976). The officer uses the address terms (sir and ma'am) as a polite way of attempting to get the disputants to address their talk towards him, not each other, thus hindering the emerging argument from escalating. When the multiple address terms fail to do so, the officer switches from a summons to a directive. Moreover, "out here" and "stand right there" are rather grammatically simplified, forceful, and baldly formulated directives in an attempt to get an action accomplished—separating the disputants (Corsaro, 1979, 1977; Dore, 1978, 1977; Ervin-Tripp, 1978). And these features support the observation that in a domestic dispute, the police officer looks more like a mediator, a social worker, and a parental figure sanctioning lesser competent individuals—children, disputants—rather than a law enforcer since he spends more time trying to control the disputants' turn taking, maintaining peace on the conversational floor (Corsaro, 1977; Ervin-Tripp, 1982, 1978; Dore, 1978; Blum-Kulka et al., 1985). Finally, in line 26 we get a sense of what the officer has been trying to accomplish in the preceding lines. After asking the BW if she is involved and getting an account the officer at last asks for identification, completing the action projected in earlier turns.

Before the officer finally orders the subjects to produce official identification, the participants spend several turns orienting to and creating new context of talk. The officer's questions in the beginning of the encounter have simply asked if the persons on the scene are the involved parties; the questions the officer asks are not open ended. I wish to elaborate on the BW's turns since they far out-number the BM's turns. In line 13 she states that he came into her house; in line 15 she repeats the complaint; finally in line 17-18 she repeats the complaint for the third time, followed by "trespassed," and "after I told him to get out." Her turns are more relevant to a WH question—story elicitor—than a yes/no inter-rogative. What does the BW gain through such repeated accusations?

"He came into my house" does not denote overt criminal behavior. The BW uses the singular genitive referential to describe her residence: it is her house, not "our" house; and by establishing her ownership, hence property rights, she invokes the discourse of rights, contracts, and law. The motion verb she uses to characterize the male disputant's actions does not connote an explicit violation of criminal law. Only when her complaint is not treated as one does she "usurp" the participant framework and repeat her complaint in line 15. In response to the BW's repeated complaints, the officer says that he will hear both stories.

The BW repeats her complaint again in line 17; but this time it is not her rights that are emphasized but the BM's infraction of the law. In addition, an official charge is used to formulate his wrongdoing. Whereas "came into my house" minimally connotes criminal intentions, "trespassed" denotes encroach-ment on her space and property. Furthermore, "trespass" is formulated in a more bureaucratic register than "came into." That is, she punctuates his guilt by em-phasizing his culpability in disobeying the law, despite her warnings to "get out," to leave the premises to which he has no claims or rights. So why does she formulate her charges in such a fashion? Why does she forego a legally justifi-able sequential opportunity to sanction the offender using the most punitive complaint against her "assailant?"

I have stated that the BW's complaints are not heard as complaints because the contextual footing operative in the initial moments (lines 12-26) is establish-ing identities, not account giving. The BW upgrades the seriousness of the BM's offense when the two turns involving "came into mah house" (lines 13, 15) have no consequences; that is, the officer does not respond to the complaint: there is an escalation of charges in the BW's third complaint (line 17-18).

In line 26 when the officer asks both disputants for IDs—the action pro-jected in the cop's initial "are you involved?"—the BW replies that she has hers upstairs (line 27); the BM replies that he has it in his car (line 29). In line 30, after the BM mentions his car, the BW tells the officer that the BM has drugs in his car, a more serious allegation. In the next turn (line 31), the BM responds to the accusation by uttering a "response cry" (Goffman, 1981).[5] There is a notable difference in the officer's orientation to the BW's complaints in lines 13, 15, 17 and line 30. The officer pays no attention to the BW's first three complaints. When she intensifies the charges against the BM (he's got weed in his car) the officer does not ignore her but shows that he has heard the "complaint" and does something about it.[6] And unlike her prior turns, the introduction of this topic (weed) is "procedurally consequential" for the next turn. After the BW makes this complaint, the officer orients his turn to her prior one; he does not tell her to calm down, to just relax and wait her turn; instead he commands the male disputant to turn off the ignition to his car, where the alleged drugs are located.[7] Simply put the trajectory of the encounter changes.

To revert back to the question posed earlier ("why does she formulate her charges in such a fashion?"), the following must be considered: (1) the main narrative has yet to be told (2) female disputant has invoked her discourse of law three times, all with little or no sequential import (3) the charges she has made against the male disputant has been incrementally upgraded in seriousness, from "came into mah house," "trespassed," to "he's got weed."

This pre-narrative—attempt at narrative before the officially requested one—sequence is a strategic and tactical place in the encounter (and talk) to metapragmatically impeach the opposing disputant's moral character. Since the main stories have yet to be told, if one of the parties could impeach the credibility of the other disputant, it works to his/her advantage. By framing the male disputant first as an intruder, a trespasser, and a drug possessor, the BW impeaches the man's moral character by categorizing him as a certain type of person (criminal) before any substantive talk.

Furthermore, the BW's repeated complaints force a change in the parameters of the sequential organization of talk and the encounter itself. With her repetitions of "he came into mah house" the BW creates both the story telling and dispute context in the midst of a fact seeking interrogative context (Goodwin and Duranti, 1992). Her accusations escalate the talk and generate denials from the BM, thus moving out of the ID establishment and story telling context into a conflict talk sequence. And it is only when the BM treats the BW's accusations as an opposable action that the conflict is mutually and collaboratively brought to existence. In this encounter, the trespassing charge is not only invoked as a source of dispute but it is also used as a resource to launch the dispute. However, the accusations that the BW makes do not bear the brunt of responsibility; to initialize and sustain the argument, the male disputant has to bring the accusation to life through a denial. Only then does conflict talk emerge as the byproduct of the interaction. And when the BW makes the accusation about illegal drugs in the BM's car, the dispute call is transformed into a possible narcotics encounter—another escalation in the organization of the call itself.

Perhaps the "disorderly" character of domestic disputes arises from the fact that events that transpire within them are unpredictable, as excerpts 1 and 2 vividly illustrate, and as prior police scholars have noted. However, there is another face to the "disorderly" impression of domestic disputes that prior police researchers have taken for granted. As a speech activity, a domestic dispute is not just a single event, with one overriding context. As I have shown there are numerous contexts within a domestic dispute, those that are locally constructed by the disputants in the sequential moments of talk. There are other possible features of disputes that give the "disorderly" characterization: the disputants speak rapidly (rapid tempo), loudly (increase in volume), repeat the same message, and talk out of turn (deviations in the sequencing pattern).[8]

In excerpt 6 the BW usurps the participation framework when the officer doesn't respond to her complaint; the BM does the same when the BW intensifies the accusations against him (line 20, 31). In a way, this exchange can be impressionistically coded as being "disorderly" since the two disputants usurp each other's turns, taking hostages of intended recipient's answer slots, "formulating utterances which constrain the talk of others, differentiating himself by flaunting his ability to defy conversational practices" (Goodwin, 1990: 97). And this forces the officer to act like a parental mediator sanctioning two argumentative children. However, as a verbal performance, their actions are orderly in that they are used to accomplish a valuable interactional goal (e.g., impeach credibility). Moreover, their identities as disputants are not only ascribed because they are the participants in a domestic dispute and enact them, but because they also actively create the hostile and antagonistic relationship in and through their talk.

Through her repeated and intensified accusations, the BW portrays the BM as a deviant male. Consequently, the subsequent activity he engages in (story he tells) is cast amiss. That is, listeners will interpret whatever story he tells as originating from a trespasser and a drug possessor. In this sense, the BW's incremental blames serve a valuable metapragmatic function since they instruct how his forthcoming story is to be interpreted prior to the actual utterances themselves. Furthermore, the repeated accusations structure a constraint in the BM's turn design: he has to somehow respond to the accusations as a part of his narrative. The pre-narrative—metapragmatic display of morality—then does not provide the listener (officer, audience) with proof or evidence of the man's culpability in a conventional after-the-fact sense, but supplies the listener with a moral presupposition about the speaker. It offers a tactical framework for moral assessment, and casts the moral template of interpretation (see Mehan, 1990). In this pre-narrative sequence, the woman damages the man's credibility by constructing him as a particular type of deviant male for the police. How does the male disputant repudiate the claims she has already made while launching counter assertions of his own?

He Said: Impeaching the Source

After the host officer finally establishes that the woman who walked up to him and the man in the green pick up truck are the involved parties, he asks for identification; then he physically separates both disputants, and asks the male disputant (BM) for a narrative:

Excerpt 7 (*COPS* data: "Jimmy Dean")
42 PO: What happened here today sir?
43 BM :   I came back to move my stuff (though)
44   we talked about it last night
45   I told her I was moving [she
46 PO: [how long ya
47   been living together?
48 BM: Well I just moved in like probably about a week
49   two weeks maybe I told her "I'll need to move"
50   you know what I'm saying "by the end of the
51   week" I mean end of the month cuz I need to

52   get a place right? so she said "Okay" you know
53   "you could move in for awhile" I said "Okay no
54   problem" so last night we talked about it ( ) and I
55   was moving today she's mad because I took my
56   Jimmy Dean sausage that I bought you know I'm
57   taking my food with me and stuff like that right
58   so ( )bit me in the hand tore up my shoulders
59   scratched me up

The BM begins his narrative by setting the scene as his temporary residence. Hence, the deictic particle "back" spatially marks his knowledge claims
of territorial familiarity and legitimate presence. Simply put, he is not an intruder and a trespasser as the BW alleges. He comes *back* to his temporary
home—to move what rightfully belongs to him. In his first line (43), in addition
to establishing the descriptive structure of his narrative, the BM provides a
counter-claim against the BW's repeated complaint that he came into her house.
By doing so he reframes her accusation as an unjustifiable one and turns it on its
head. The BM provides a powerful legitimacy claim to his presence, and recon-
textualizes the BW's repeated attempts to impeach his moral character and legal
identity (trespasser).

In the initial moments of his narrative, the BM sets the descriptive (opening) scene and offers a counter-claim to the BW's accusations. However, we can
see evidence that the shape of the BM's turn design in his narrative has been
affected by the BW's repeated—unsolicited—accusations in the pre-narrative.
The host cop makes the official request for a narrative in line 42, first, to the
male disputant. In studies of courtroom narratives of domestic disputes, it has
been found that second narratives usually "respond" to the first by "taking up
the tasks at hand presented by the first account" (Hirsch, 1998: 152); that is, they
shoulder the burden of responding to the first narrative in addition to telling their
own stories. In the "Jimmy Dean" episode, this sequencing pattern is inverted
because the BM (first turn narrator) spends the first opening line responding to
the accusations the BW makes in the identity-establishing context; his first line
is used to refute the dispute-creating and storytelling context of the BW's talk.
For the female disputant her repeated accusations in the prenarrative have a
valuable interactional effect, despite the officer's stern warnings: she constrains
the yet to come account of the first turn narrator (BM) by compelling his account to redress hers: she effectuates a recontexualization of footing in an upcoming turn. By doing so, she relegates the first narrator's turn to that of the
second turn narrator.

The officer interrupts the BM's narrative to ask, "how long ya been living
together?" in line 47. His short stay is lexically marked with the diminutive
"just"; he has no long-term plans to stay. The fact that he told her he was moving is reported in line 45 as indirectly quoted speech, placed in a quotative frame
using the past tense verb of saying, before the officer interrupts. Contrast line 45
with line 49, after the BM has fulfilled the relevancy requirements of the officer's question in line 46-47. He uses the same quotative frame, but this time he

directly quotes his own voice from the past dialogue with the female disputant. In the indirect quote, his relocation is constructed in the past progressive, implying that his decision has already been made (line 45). In line 49 the same action is projected onto the future and stated in a future tense. He switches from "was moving" to "will need to move."

The BM not only reports his own voice but reports the BW's voice as well. He recreates the dispute prior to police intervention using reported speech. Reported speech is concerned with both representing discursive action as well as reflexive commentary on that action (Besnier, 1992). According to Matoesian (1999b), reported speech serves both an evidentiary and affective function: it permits the experiencer to "re-live" the past moment in time as if it were occurring in the present. This is strategically accomplished by reducing the intertextual gap between the reporting and reported context using direct quotations in which the reported words are repeated verbatim. However, direct quotes are not just representations of reported speech since the speaker in the reporting context is able to inject prosodic, suprasegmental, and other expressive features of language into his utterances (Besnier, 1990). In essence, the speaker's affective stance "leaks" into the speech being reported.[9] Therefore, when the BM directly quotes the female disputant's words, he interweaves his affective stance into her utterance. The BM claims that she acceded to his relocation (in other words, rationally, after debating about the matter). However, when he ascribes her motive to the officer, her "rationality" in the reported event (dispute prior to police intervention) is syntactically constructed in a contrastive format with the "fickleness" and "irrationality" in the current story telling context.

The BM states that they both engaged in a dialogue concerning his upcoming relocation (in line 44). In describing the past conversation, he uses "we" to refer to the BW and himself. That is, both parties agreed to the current living arrangement. Moreover, he sets up his action as something that has been planned, deliberated, and rational, not a spontaneously and impulsively conceived event. Nowhere is this "rationality" more evident than the metalinguistic emphasis on talk. Rational individuals talk about problems and settle problems through words, not physical violence. Hence, by portraying himself as a rational speaker, one who not only thinks about the consequences of acts, but one who gives careful consideration to what is being said, he orients to rationality as the locus of his authority as a speaker (Chafe, 1992; Irvine, 1992; Shuman, 1992).

The authority behind the male disputant's claims is encoded into his story in the following way. His narrative is filled with statements that do not summarize or make a point about events in the story.[10] The BM includes several metalinguistic evaluations in the midst of his story as a poetic enactment of his rationality. These types of evaluatives are produced at "critical moments in the testimony such as when describing events or actions that are central to their perspectives on the conflict" (Hirsch, 1998: 146). And the BM's perspective on the dispute is described in the first clause and commented on in the immediately following clause. For example, in his first line of the narrative (line 43), he describes an action (line 43: I came back to move my stuff), while implicitly providing commentary on his mental state at the time of the utterance (line 44: we talked about it last night). He tells the officer that he has been temporarily living with the BW for one to two weeks (describes past action), only to comment on why he needs to move (I need to get a place right?).

As an evaluative device that encodes his perspective and emotional state in the past event, his rationale for moving works as a way of commenting on and "pronouncing" his commitment to the conventional social and moral order: he is trying to attain independence and financial freedom. Put differently, he is not a freeloader, one who "piggybacks" off the labor and riches of his woman, but one who is committed to being an adult and "doing the adult thing" (moving out on his own). The male disputant's pronouncement has a double effect: first, it implicitly and historically comments on the moral character of the female disputant. It should be recalled that piggybacking—"hitching a free ride on both the action initiated by the prior turn speaker and its sequential implicativeness" (Goodwin and Goodwin, 1990: 105)—is precisely what the BW does in the initial identity establishing context when she violates the sequencing pattern and repeatedly accuses the BM of coming into her house when it is not her turn to speak. Second, his pronouncement comments on his own moral character: it shows that he is not a freeloader; to do so, however, he has to tacitly "piggyback"—use it as a resource—off the BW's piggybacking. When the BM describes the current event (his moving, the dispute itself), notice how he switches the object of the commentary: instead of his prior rational actions, he emphasizes her "irrational" behavior.

By describing past action and simultaneously commenting on his past emotional state, the BM amplifies his rationality vis-à-vis the BW's talk. That is, he deliberates before acting and speaking; moreover, his rationality is paralinguistically embodied in his talk: he does not speak rapidly; nor does he raise his voice or tone; he speaks in a deliberate and calm manner—like grown up adults are supposed to do. Not only is the BM's projected rationality demonstrable in the content of his talk (e.g., we talked about it last night), but it is also enacted in the forms of talk (post description commentary).

If the BM's rationality is sequentially inscribed in the slot after the descriptive action clause, it is concurrently mobilized with another tactic that he uses to get that very message across. When the officer asks how long they have been living together, his answers are replete with vagueness. For instance, when the BM begins his turn in line 48, he uses uncertainty markers and hedges such as "like," "probably," "about," and "maybe." And when he continues his story, after the officer's interruption in line 46-47, the time frame of his temporary stay is again "imprecise." He says at first that he'll be moving by "end of the week" then repairs it to "end of the month" (lines 50-51).

In line 54, he again repeats his earlier claims (that they talked about it) before attributing explicitly formulated blame onto her. In his narrative the focus is on talk—talk becomes the key action that the male disputant uses to assert the authority of his claims. It is after the second metalinguistic commentary within his narrative that he imputes a motive: "she's mad because I'm taking my Jimmy Dean sausage that I bought."

The BM claims that the female disputant became violent because he took his food. The overwhelming feature of his turn design is the ascription of sheer "triviality" (childishness) of her actions. In other words, to be mad enough to attack someone for taking a piece of sausage is extremely irrational. Contrast this imputation with how he has negotiated his identity so far: he has characterized himself as someone who engages in a dialogue before acting; he informs her of his intention to move before actually doing so: he is rational. He magnifies her "irrationality" by syntactically placing irrationality immediately following the embodied ideal of rationality. The contrast structure of his turn design creates a powerful poetic effect: it foregrounds his rationality while magnifying her irrationality.[11]

The BM's earlier turns that describe the time frame of his upcoming relocation are very imprecise and contain several hedges, hesitation, and uncertainty markers; toward the end of his narrative, however, those hedges disappear. Before he concludes his story (lines 58-59), he inserts his perspective on her motivation, which is done in an uncharacteristically meticulous fashion. He doesn't just mention generic brand sausages but a specific brand.

Speakers often use universal quantifiers such as "everybody," "everything," "all," and "all the time" to add credibility and weight to their claims (Pomerantz, 1986). In these cases, "extremeness" is used as evidential justification of one's beliefs and claims—general, unspecific, and external claims. There is a caveat to extreme case formulations (ECF) however. As a universal and extreme description, ECFs are logically fragile since they can be readily refuted through limited counter-examples (Edwards, 2000). Thus, an alternative function of ECFs may be to highlight and emphasize a point, to "signal a speaker's investment in that point" rather than a literal and accurate description (Edwards, 2000: 364).

Recall that the BM's imputation of the BW's motive is summarized in his causal statement "she's mad cuz I'm taking my Jimmy Dean sausage," a specific, restricted, and particular description of a type of breakfast pork sausage. As noted, this attribution is the paradigmatic example of triviality and irrationality: to be mad at someone for taking a piece of meat is laughable and borders on the absurd. However, as a way of emphasizing and highlighting the essentially absurd female disputant's character, the precise case formulation does more than merely describe the BW's motive. As a way of highlighting the BW's irrational behavior, the meticulous characterization of the purported source of the dispute adds a dramatic effect: he magnifies her "irrationality" by (1) syntactically placing irrationality (pork sausage) immediately following the embodied ideal of rationality (discourse of talk). (2) The precise characterization (Jimmy Dean sausage) followed by a trail of vague and uncertain descriptions creates a noticeable contrast from its background.[12] The precise case formulation inscribes the BW into a particular moral category (irrational woman) onto the talk itself and demonstrates the BM's commitment and "investment" in his claim (Edwards, 2000; Pomerantz, 1986).

She Said: What I Look Like Fightin' Him?

After the host officer listens to the BM's narrative (lines 43-59), he orders the male disputant away from the immediate location; he then asks the woman to tell her side of the story[13]:

Excerpt 8 (*COPS* data: Jimmy Dean)
```
88   PO: Okay Ma'am tell me what happened here tonight
89   BW:    Okay >he say he told me he was gonna be at mah
90        house at five o'clock (to get his stuff out) cuz I was lettin
91        him hold my stuff (in there he slept over) mah house< so
92        he he came into the house immature >actin like
93        so I was helpin him get his stuff out of the house<
94   PO:    Do yawl have any kids in common?
95   BW:    Ye::s my son no my (friend) no we don't
96   PO: Do you live together?=
97        =uh huh I had my son >What I look like attackin him?<
98        >When I had my own child in the house I wouldn't do
99        nothing like that he got a daughter gonna bring her over
100       here she playin in the toilet (sew) a::ll over the tub
101       he just standing there< I was tryin to open up the
102       door to put...
103       [radio call ]
104       >I was trying to open up the door to help put his
105       stuff out for his daughter fell I don't need to make
106       up I wouldn't hurt nobody else's child< hhh ((draws breath))
107       >He gonna tell me "why you gonna make my daughter
108       fall" and started punchin me in my face< and I was
109       swingin back and he kept hittin me what I look like
110       fightin him?
```

The female disputant (BW) begins her narrative by setting the scene and the time of the dispute. She states that the BM was going to be at her place at five o'clock because she was letting him hold her stuff (lines 89-90). Then she repeats her accusation that he came into her house. This time when she makes a complaint, notice that the officer does not silence her but listens. He hears the complaint as such because it is produced after he elicits it, in the context of a storytelling sequence (line 88) (Antaki, 1994; Jefferson, 1978). There is also a noteworthy difference between the BW's and BM's opening lines. The BM spends the opening lines of his narrative refuting (line 43: I came back to move my stuff) the unsolicited accusations that the BW makes in the identity- establishing context (line 13, 15, 17). In the BW's opening first lines, she does not (yet) justify her blameworthy actions and respond to any of the BM's claims. She just begins to tell her story. Although the female disputant is the second turn narrator, the opening lines (lines: 89-92) of her narrative display features of a first turn story.

There is one noteworthy aspect of the BW's characterization in line 92 that I want to elaborate on. She states that the BM came into her house acting "immature." This type of referencing represents culturally organized ways in which behavior of persons is classified into preset categories. And as Jayyusi (1984) notes, such categorization work is imbued with moral and evaluative assessments. In the "Jimmy Dean" episode, the BW has thus far classified the BM as a law-violator (trespasser, drug dealer/user); the term she uses to describe this category is inconsistent with what is commonly expected. For instance, when someone comes into our house, the words we would associate with such an event is "frightening, shocking, helpless, scary" etc. The words used to describe the agent of such acts would also be metonymically related. She uses the word "immature."

The BW's use of the word "immature" contradicts and simultaneously creates a new category. Immaturity contrasts with maturity: being an adult is categorically linked to the latter while being a child is linked to the former. In line 92, then, she provides a grossly inconsistent grammatical correspondence between one category (trespasser) and its incumbent description (immature). As a way of invoking—creating—the "adult" category, however, "immature" does just that. The main point of the BM's narrative is that he's moving out because it is the adult thing to do (not freeloading). And by describing the adult male's behavior as being "immature," she *responds* to the pragmatic force of the BM's first turn narrative, molding her turn and story in response to his, displaying the "double burden" of her narrative that is characteristic of second turn narratives (Hirsch, 1998).

The main contention of the BM's narrative was the BW's irrational (trivial, childish) behavior. And by referring to her opponent as "immature," (1) she counters the BM's implication that she acted irrationally and (2) she defends and tacitly aligns her self-image in antithetical relation to his: she constructs her membership in the "adult" category and classifies the BM into the "child"/non-adult category. Consequently, she effectuates a recalibration in the ascription of blame. Notice how her adultness is subsequently transferred into action: she cooperates in his decision to relocate; instead of disagreeing, opposing, and arguing about his purported departure, as needy and argumentative women are wont to do, and as the BM alleges, she helps him move (line 93). By providing evidence of her calmness, thoughtfulness, and capacity to exercise rational thought, she provides a powerful counter-claim against the BM's ascription of blame.

In accounts, disputants often state their claims in such a way that they are seen as innocuous victims rather than precipitators of their own victimization (see Antaki, 1994).[14] To accomplish this, several linguistic devices are routinely employed in narratives: sequential placement of topic, lexical repetition, expressive phonology, and poetically structured sequences (Hirsch, 1998; Matoesian, 2001). In the beginning of her narrative, the BW aligns herself as a mature adult. After the officer interrupts to ask about their living arrangement (line 96), she answers that question (line 97: uh huh I had my son) and then provides an explicit self-evaluative (line 97). Although this type of utterance makes no contribution to a story's internal progression and coherence, it does comment on the moral character of the storyteller (rather than the story), and it is used as a metapragmatic device for projecting her perceptions on the fray in a strategic and poetic manner.

In the BW's narrative, "What I look like fightin him?" does not stand alone; it is tossed into the narrative mix, and poetically enacted through its sequential placement and manner of articulation.[15] "What I look like fightin him?" is uttered rapidly, as one unit, in a rising high-pitch tone. In its content and style, the non-narrative statement displays the inapposite character of the BM's accusation (line 58-59: "bit me in the hand, tore up my shoulders, scratched me up"); moreover her response not only signals the accusation's inappositeness, but also provides an implicit and reflexive commentary on her emotional stance through the prosodic contours of her talk. And if this statement (line 97) portrays the speaker in a particular light, as one who is emotionally committed to her stance in the fray, the next two clauses elaborate on that point. That is, she isn't the type of person who would attack another person (lines 98-99: "I wouldn't do nothing like that"), especially when her child is in the house also (line 98). She lays the structure of her self-assessed moral character in the first clause, and adds layers of support to her moral foundation in the subsequent two clauses. These are encoded in the message through speed, intensity, and tone of speech delivery, which simultaneously responds to the BM's imputation of blame and comments on her commitment in and to her narrative.

After the third clause evaluative (line 97-98) she begins to narrate the incidents that led to the fight: (1) he got a daughter (2) gonna bring her over here (3) she playing in the toilet (4) all over the tub. Although lines 98-101 are articulated in a very rapid way, almost in one long breath, there is a noticeable rhythmic quality to the BW's narration. She begins to relate the past event by first formulating a syntactically simple sentence that introduces the agent and the patient/theme (he got a daughter); the very next clause describes what the agent does to the patient (gonna bring her over here). This relationship between the agent, patient, and action is established in a contiguous way through the elision of the subject (he). In the next clause, the patient of the prior two clauses becomes the agent: the daughter now is the one playing in the toilet, and in the clause immediately after, she expands on the prior action (playing in the toilet) with an adverbial clause that compounds the extreme impropriety of such acts (all over the tub). And after the BW constructs the descriptive scene in two proximal couplets (i.e., "playing in the toilet" and "all over the tub") she proffers the resulting state: "he just standing there" (line 101).

"He just standing there" underscores the BM's flagrantly negligent behavior as a caretaker and attributes blame in two ways. First, as a resultant state, it stands in juxtaposition against the action oriented and grossly inappropriate sense of the preceding clauses; but not only that, the descriptive couplet (she playin' in the toilet, all over the tub) sets up an expectation that the parent will— should—do something about the grossly inapposite state (playin in the toilet) and the neglected child in the clauses to follow. The next clause only mentions what the father fails to do, and alludes to his impotence as an adequate caretaker.

That is, his daughter is playing in the toilet, but he does nothing—he just standing there (line 101).

Second, the blame is grammatically inscribed in the present and in the past in conjunction with the degree adverbial "just." "He just standing there" constructs the BW's experience as a progressive, which suggests that the BM's activity has not yet been completed but is still ongoing. That is to say, although the BM is standing there at that moment in time, he is also not finished "standing there." As a way of relating past action, it dramatically and vividly illustrates what the BM neglects to do in the BW's narrative despite witnessing action that warrants parental intervention (see Wolfson, 1978). Moreover, the "ongoingness" of the past progressive implicitly suggests that the BW's experience of the BM "standing there" is tactically proffered to emphasize its elongated duration.

That the male disputant is continuing to incompetently stand there suggests another way the blame is grammatically crafted in the BW's narrative. Standing, much like kicking and talking, describes an action, action that is dynamic; however, this otherwise dynamic verb has a contrastive effect in the BW's narrative: rather than indexing action, it punctuates the BM's inaction, his passivity. And notice how the BW maximizes the BM's inaction through a minimization of the verb: she prefaces the dynamic verb with the diminutive "just" thus preemptively counteracting the semantic and pragmatic force of "stand."

When the BW starts to explain why the BM attacked her, she attributes his motive to the fact that she dropped his child on the floor as she was opening the door (line 104). This telling is performed in a "lively" manner by directly quoting the BM's speech. And before she justifies her self-defensive actions, she sets up her utterances in a contrastive format. Indeed, all competent parents would be outraged if someone harmed their child. However when she reports his words, the quote is entirely devoid of affect: there is no pitch or tone variation; there is no emotion—life—in his words. This contrasts markedly with the way her narrative is replete with pitch variation, intensity, and speed. By removing the affective features of the male's speech in her reported speech, she eliminates the BM's anger and emotion in his talk. In a sense, the speaker and the speaker's words (line 107-108: "why you gonna make my daughter fall?") are "lost" in the reporting context. Ironically, it is his "voice" that is denied through the woman's reporting of his speech.

The BW's use of reported speech (line 107: "why you gonna make my daughter fall") as an evidential marker and the subsequent violent behavior that follows (line 108: "started punchin me in my face") is placed adjacent to one another in a contrastive way. This time, it is not the anticipatable expectation that is absent which is noteworthy, but its unexpected action that creates the dramatic flair. The tight coordination between the effect (BM's violent reaction) and the cause (dropping the child) articulated within the in-progress turn connects two disparate acts in an immediate fashion, and sequentially creates the male disputant's violent character disposition.[16] That is, the lack of turn space (and time) between the BM's accusation (why you gonna make my daughter fall?) and the assault (started punchin me in my face) sequentially marks the BM's potency—anger, motive, and the capacity to engage in violent behavior.

In a way, the "out of the blue" character of battering incidents that abused women often recount can be empirically "seen" in the fine-grained details of talk here. The BM's blows come without augur, as if out of nowhere; this impetuousness and out of "no-where-ness" does not, however, exist as a pregiven state; instead, they are locally and contextually forged, negotiated, and accomplished in the moments of talk through adjacently placed contrastive utterances. It is the contrast between the beating (effect) and the proffered justification (cause), and the interweaving of action (what does happen) and expectation (what should happen)—through reported speech—into a snugly compressed sequential relation that discursively constructs the blameless victim and the violent batterer (see Hirsch, 1998).

When the BW states that he "started punching me in my face," the indifferent tone of the utterance and the violent action creates a powerful disjuncture between speech and action. To go from calm and monotone speech to sudden aggressive action bespeaks a violent character disposition. And in the next clause (line 109) when she constructs her self-defense in a passive voice ("was swinging back"), her agency is minimized and mitigated (Komter, 1994).

The BW downplays her part in the dispute and assault principally through two interactional moves: (1) she foregrounds the male disputant's aggressive character (2) she frames her actions as self-defense, through a prototypical "not at fault" denial (Dersley and Wootton, 2000). First, there is a qualitative difference between the action verbs 'standing' and 'hitting'. The former is passive while the latter is active. Hence, the BW lexically marks the difference between the two and punctuates the BM's aggressiveness. Second, the male disputant's penchant for aggressiveness is grammaticalized as contiguous action. Throughout lines 107-109 four distinctly separate acts are causally connected in time through the coordinating conjunction "and." The first conjunction in line 108 solders the reported speech ("why you gonna make my daughter fall?") and the initial assault ("started punchin me in my face") to build a powerful contrastive effect. Next, she links his assault and her counter-assault together, thus framing her aggression as a response to his. He starts punching her; she swings back; hence, the transpiring events are beyond her control—it's not her fault (Dersley and Wootton, 2000). The BW relates that when she starts to swing back, the BM keeps hitting her (line 109).

In addition to binding the internal events of the story, the repeated conjunctions also add another perspective to the fray. Women who are battered often relate feelings of helplessness; researchers report that battered women feel as though the events that occur in their lives are beyond their control and ken (Browne, 1987; Walker, 1979). Now, notice how this impression manifests itself in the current narrative. The conjunctions fasten together the reason for the assault (why you gonna make my daughter fall), the assault itself (started punchin me), her reaction to the assault (I was swinging back), and the persistent assault (kept hittin me) as being connected in time (lines 107-109). Moreover, she implicitly signals to the listeners that the events she is describing are occurring in a rather intensified way, one right after the next, with little time to think about them; the repetition of "and" and the rapidity of her delivery further compounds this impression. In effect, the rapidly delivered talk, along with the serially linked actions, serves as a mirror of the battering incident itself: the blows come out of nowhere, in a flurry-like manner. In the content of her narrative and through her performance, the BW iconically displays her "helpless" state in real time talk: there is a flurry of accusations and then blows that arrive unexpectedly; and in its midst, she reacts as any reasonable victim would (she swings back). She portrays herself as one who merely defends against a violent and angry man, a victim who has been caught in a world of events that have spiraled out of control. Simply put, she does nothing to cause her own victimization.[17]

Cop Says: Entextualization

The stories told by the disputants are primarily entextualized by the responding officers. The narrative that the host officer tells the TV audience is principally forged from the disputants' talk, from the troubles they experience, endure, and tell. And when the officer listens to both disputants' stories, weighs their claims, and formulates his/her own version of events, the officer extracts— "lifts"—discourse from one interactional context (storytelling), and embeds it in another one, entextualization (Bauman and Briggs, 1990). Entextualization essentially involves taking an utterance out of one interactional context and inserting it in another. Extracting a discourse from one moment of utterance to the next involves decontexualization, the capacity to remove a text from one "social context" and recontextualize it in another—the ability to exercise control, "social power" (Bauman and Briggs, 1990: 74-76).

The entextualization of narratives on *COPS* is inextricably bound to the operative participation framework at the moment of speaking. As noted in a prior chapter, there are multiple participation frameworks in effect at any given moment on *COPS*. First, there is the ever-present TV audience that looms in the background. Second, there are fellow patrol officers and supervisors on scene, in addition to the host officer, who may enter as speaker and listener in the talk. Third, there are the citizens who become participants in the P-C encounter, those who end up telling their stories to the police, the cameraperson—anyone who will listen. And telling—performing—a story, a narrative, "intensifies" the entextualization process (Hirsch, 1998). As already noted, the main narratives of the disputants have a functional purpose (i.e., attribute and deflect blame). The officer's narrative, however, is not guided by such personal concerns. Its textual authority arises not from metadiscursive practices, but from the officer's situational, contextual, and bureaucratic exigencies (e.g., accountability to the patrol supervisor, fellow officers, the viewing audience).[18]

After both disputants have told their stories, the officer must "process" both stories: ascribe credibility, detect inconsistencies, and determine an appropriate course of action. In the present case, the male disputant has sustained visible wounds on his hands. One of the main points of dispute lies in his claim that she attacked him out of jealousy and anger (she's mad cuz I'm taking my Jimmy Dean sausage) while she contends that she bit him in the course of defending herself. The officer is only able to infer this after inquiring about how the male disputant sustained his wounds and catching the female in a lie (see note #17). And it is after the initial identity-establishing sequence (the pre-narrative), two main narratives, and the brief clarification sequence (see note #17) that the officer discusses the case with another officer on scene:

Excerpt 9 (*COPS* data: Jimmy Dean)
122 PO: Looks like we have a domestic assault um possibly
123　　　provoked by him but looks like right now mutual
124　　　combat and it looks like there's a little uh marijuana
125　　　involved also from the description she gave me
126　　　I saw the possible bag in the car in his truck
127　　　also apparently he attacked her for him moving his stuff
128　　　out that apparently belonged to her and uh she her
129　　　statement was that she bit him to get him off of her
130　　　okay that's what we have right now

So how has the officer understood the dispute thus far? How have the stories of the two disputants affected the officer's decision to manage the course of action? How is the officer's story fashioned—entextualized—out of the two main narratives? One feature of the officer's narrative that is noteworthy is the presence and absence of text. What is present in the officer's text? What is left out? How does the officer allocate blame, ascribe motive, and assign culpability?

First, culpability. The male disputant states that she attacked him; the female disputant states that he attacked her. This is a classic case of the he-said/she-said, accusation/counter-accusation format of an argument. The presence of teeth marks, however, demonstrates the female disputant's active involvement (regardless of whether it was aggression or self-defense); this point is especially highlighted by the fact that she tried to lie about it to the officer in line 111-118 (see note #17). Hence, rather than assigning greater responsibility to one participant, or imputing the role of 'victim' the officer distributes culpability in equal proportions: he characterizes the dispute and the ensuing physical altercation as "mutual combat" rather than as an assault.

Epistemological cautiousness and uncertainty are common features of institutional talk (Heritage, 1998a); and in the host officer's narrative, his stance toward the status of his knowledge is marked with uncertainty. The phrase "looks like" is used in lines 122, 123, and 124 to indicate the dubious state of his knowledge. In lines 127 and 128 his uncertainty is lexically marked with "apparently"; other indicators of epistemological uncertainty include the use of hedges ("um") and derivative of the modal verb "possible" (lines 122, 126). Another tactic the officer uses to mark his uncertainty while authorizing his knowledge is to attribute the author of the knowledge to another source (Hill and Irvine, 1992). For example, the author need not be a person; it can be an inanimate object (identification card, driver's license, bureaucratic document). In this episode, the officer's discovery of marijuana is attributable only to what the female disputant tells him; her statement authorizes his knowledge and evidential authority. Stance markers then serve a bureaucratic function of "covering one's ass" since the source of his knowledge is imputed to someone else.

In addition to the presence of several uncertainty markers, there are other differences between the disputants' narratives and the officer's. For instance, excerpt 9 contains only present time-sequence markers (line 123: right now); the BM's and the BW's narratives begin with a clear setting and timeline (i.e., BM: I came back to move my stuff; we talked about it last night. BW: He say he was gonna be at mah house at 5 o'clock). However, the officer's narrative is not centered around the dispute and its surrounding events. The disputants' narratives on the other hand transpire in the context of concrete life activities, such as thinking, talking, moving, playing, etc. (see Briggs, 1996b). The officer's tale is not situated as a part of any recognizable (social) life; it is without attachments and history. And rather than entextualizing the story through a vivid narrative performance or through metalinguistic statements, the officer animates and authorizes the bureaucratic version of events through an absence—absence of poetic and dramatic narration.

Notice that the account the officer gives to fellow patrol officers (and to the TV audience) is done in a language characteristic of bureaucratic organizations. That is, the officer does not use the HP to animate and enliven what he is telling; nor does he use explicit evaluatives such as, "I'm the police, what I'm telling you is the truth" as a marker of his credibility. He just relates his findings in a matter of fact fashion, without anger, passion, and emotion that is characteristic of modernization, rationalization, and bureaucracy (Weber, 1978).[19] Discursively, this routinized, passionless, and organizational discursive signature is entextualized onto his talk through negation: the officer's story is noticeably slower in tempo when compared to the disputants' narratives; it also lacks the intensity and the poetic qualities of performance, such as reported speech, pitch and tone variation, and repetition. Compared to the disputants' narratives, the officer's story is dull, without life and emotion. However, it is precisely its "lifelessness" which gives it epistemological authority and import, and animates it as a bureaucratic narrative—the iconic embodiment of objectivity.

In this episode, there are several violations of the criminal code. In the "prenarrative" and main narrative the female disputant (BW) states that the male disputant (BM) is guilty of (1) trespassing, (2) possession of illegal narcotics, (3) assault and battery and (4) parental negligence. According to the male disputant, she is guilty of assault. In the officer's narrative, assault and narcotics are factored in; others are left out. As for "nailing down" a motive, both the male and female disputant's understanding is conspicuously absent ("she's mad cuz I'm taking my Jimmy Dean sausage" vs. "I was trying to open up the door to help put his stuff out for his daughter fell"). Her story that she bit him in self-defense is included in his story ("cuz he had me"). When the officer decides to verify the woman's allegations concerning the contraband substance, the officer walks over to the man's car and as the officer searches the car he states the following:

Excerpt 10 (*COPS* data: Jimmy Dean)
147 The scales digital scale the baggies (the weed) uh right now

148 right now looks like we got packaging material digital scales
149 in there looks like he's been selling uh dime bag
150 marijuana from here there's enough marijuana here
151 to charge him with felony possession with intent
152 they put it on there weight it out cut it up separate
153 it then bag it and they'll sell ten dollar increments
154 what he looks like he has right now

The primary recipient of the preceding narrative is the TV audience, the ratified participant; it is not uttered for fellow officers or supervisors. Other officers do not accompany the host cop when he searches the car, only the cameraman stands nearby recording his actions. The recipient design of his narrative is implicative in the post lexical item expansion. For example, police jargon is initially used in the narrative, only to be repaired and expanded in the subsequent turns. Reference to "the scales" is further repaired and qualified by an adjective phrase; "the baggies" in line 147 is reformulated as "packaging material"; "weed" in line 147 becomes "dime bag marijuana" in lines 149-150; "dime bag marijuana" is restated as marijuana that is the resulting product of various states of processing which are sold in ten dollar quantities.

The first part formulation is more appropriate for fellow officers who share the same bureaucratic sociolinguistic competence; that the officer has to explain the significance of the present items to the lay audience impels the officer to restate it in a different language. Hence, mentioning a scale (bureaucratic, technical jargon) to fellow officers may be adequate, but the presence of a diverse audience compels qualification and a change in footing (Goffman, 1981): the scale becomes a digital scale that is used to weigh the drugs. And for those who are not familiar with the functional purpose of "baggies," the officer explains and instructs the TV audience that baggies are used as packaging material for the drugs. A similar topic repair-expansion sequence is used to explain the meaning of "dime bag marijuana."

As the officer searches the male disputant's (BM) car, the BM's categorial identity shifts. This transformation in categorial incumbency is signified in the officer's narrative through a switch in pronominal reference and adjective phrase modifying the contraband noun. In the officer's narrative to other officers, before the allegation of possession of marijuana is verified, the adjective that precedes marijuana is the diminutive "little": [adjective phrase] marijuana. When he searches the car the same item (marijuana) is referred to in several different ways. In line 147, it is referred to as "weed." Two lines later it is referred to as "dime bag" marijuana. In the next line it is referred to as "enough" marijuana.

What is noteworthy is that with the discovery of other category bound activity related items such as baggies and scales, the referential term increases in seriousness: it begins with "little" and culminates with "enough"—enough to charge him with intent to distribute. By distribute, the officer is presumably referring to the fact that the drugs will be sold on the illegal market for a profit. Whereas the male disputant was categorized as someone who possessed marijuana in earlier turns, in line 149, his categorial identity is changed to one of a dealer, one who sells drugs. As a type of person with membership in a larger set, the male's inclusion in the set is lexically marked in the pronominal switch. Thus, in line 152, the officer does not refer the male disputant in the singular but accusative-plural "they"—a class of persons who engage in the type of category bound activities stated by the officer. In other words, they—the drug dealers— put the drugs on digital scales, weigh it out, cut it up, separate it, then bag it, and sell it in ten dollar increments. By orienting to the officer's lexical switch in pronominal reference, then, we get a glimpse into how the officer understands not only the male disputant, but also another class of law violators who have not been involved in the case.

I have thus far shown how recipient design affects lexical choice and repair. More broadly, the implicativeness of recipient design is intimately related to another facet of the officer's narrative, topicalization. The topic of the officer's narrative concerns drugs; the usage of technical vocabulary relates to drugs, as well as the membership categories he uses to inscribe an identity to the male disputant. Despite the fact that the call originates as a domestic dispute, the entire frame of the episode changes to that of drugs. How is this variation to be accounted?

It has been argued that reality based TV programs about crime "cultivate" or shape how the consumers view the "real world" portrayed in the program (Oliver and Armstrong, 1994). The viewers who see these programs are likely to believe that crime is rampant, report higher levels of fear, and thus push for tougher crime policy legislation (Dobash et al., 1998; Doyle, 1998). Furthermore, its counter view acknowledges the reflexive and "circular" nature of media and culture: what is seen not only affects "reality," but "reality" affects what is chosen to be seen. In other words, viewer's cinematic, popular, and moral tastes, desires, and beliefs frame the contours of what the media elects to show (see Oliver and Armstrong, 1994, 1996; Doyle, 1998). But the occurrences in the contents of the program have been found to be disproportionate in comparison to official government statistics: "crime on this show [*COPS*] is...shaped more by organizational demands of television than by carefully documented representations of reality. The bizarre and sensational take place over the typical and ordinary" (Kooistra et al., 1988: 153). But what scholars who focus exclusively on representations of crime in popular culture and mass media overlook, while excluding prior police research, is that domestic disputes and narcotics arrests are the "typical and ordinary" events in a class of atypical and not-so-ordinary events in the lives of frontline police officers. That one "ordinary" event is opted for another in my example hints toward an alternative explanation that is not mutually exclusive from the research findings from discussed media and culture studies.

Policing is imbued with an unmistakable tincture of morality. Police officers conceptualize themselves as representatives of the moral order, and view their work as the site of battle between forces of good and evil (see Herbert, 1996a). Officers not only dislike handling domestic disputes because it is "unpredictable," but more significantly, because they are considered trivial and unworthy—"bullshit"—calls. Indeed, police officers routinely express frustration regarding "domestics" because they are seen more as a "private" matter than a public one (Sherman and Berk, 1984). And precisely because calls are hierarchically graded in the police occupational culture and ideology, domestic dispute calls do not fit into a binary moral template. Narcotics arrests, as an offense category, however, receive a higher valuation; more significantly, narcotics creates a readily identifiable categorial incumbency: as the most visible representatives of the immoral order, those who sell drugs are evil; and police officers realize their occupational ideology in the surveillance, pursuit, and arrest of those who embody the face of evil.

In a way, what the police do in this episode is no different from what the disputants (the "bad guys") do: the female disputant initially "piggybacks" off the utterance that the officer addresses toward the male disputant (Goodwin and Goodwin, 1990). The male disputant in his narrative claims that he is not a person who does such things (freeload, piggyback), but that is precisely what he ends up doing: he benefits from the BW's piggybacking and shapes his turn around it. And the topicalization of drugs also shows how the police "piggyback" from a domestic dispute about "Jimmy Dean sausage": rather than showing a routine call for service in a family dispute, finding and "pinching" a drug dealer epitomizes the essence of the ideological nature of their profession: fighting crime.

And this piggybacked activity is the face that is shown and highlighted to the public for their consumption, not only because it is what the police officers (along with producers and editors) believe what the public desires to see, but how they themselves want to see and be seen. Although called on as peacekeepers to maintain order, the officer's narrative is imprinted on his talk to reflect the ideology of justice, law and order—as "men and women of law enforcement" battling forces of evil. But as I have shown this evil does not exist in the context of the original call for service, but has its genesis in a class of law violators who have not even been present on the scene or involved in the case.

Conclusion

Domestic disputes are often said to be unpredictable and chaotic; consequently, police officers do not like to handle them. Police officers also dislike making arrests in domestic disputes since it shames the man of the house. But more significantly, arrests are hierarchically ranked according to their organizational worth: arrests provide a glimpse into the organizational logic and ideology. For instance, while the police respond to a domestic dispute, the trajectory of the encounter I have used as my data steers away from domestic violence and instead focuses on narcotics. Moreover, the language used to classify the male into a deviant category shows what has been absent from the legally justified reason for their presence.

The unpredictable and chaotic aspects of the "family beef" are manifest in this example. While the police officially respond to a routine dispute between two intimate partners, they stumble onto a drug case. Moreover, there are several places in the encounter where the encounter has the potential to escalate. In prior works on the police, scholars have posited that domestic disputes are disorderly, chaotic, and disorganized (see Black, 1980). However, as I have shown here, the chaotic impression of domestic disputes that prior police researchers have assumed emerges from the orderly interactional details, from the fact that disputants yell and scream at each other, at the officer, and talk out of sequence. However, as I have shown here, language use in domestic disputes is orderly, strategic, and tactical, and serve a valuable interactional goal: they metapragmatically impeach moral character and attribute blame.

The disputants—ordinary members of the social world—use conventional methods of storytelling to attribute blame, put themselves forward, and discredit the moral character of their interactional foes. If disputants vary sequential placement of topic, use repetition to emphasize a key point, talk out of sequence to tactically and strategically plan their moves, make claims and counter those claims using metapragmatics, then there is nothing chaotic, disorderly, and disorganized about family beefs as a communicative activity. Perhaps prior researchers have erroneously inferred their conclusion precisely because they have not been able to hear or see what the disputants do and how they do it. That is, they have never actually looked at what the disputants say—empirically, sequentially—in their own words.

Notes

1. There is a consensus amongst the officers that this type of occurrence is quite common (see Baker, 1985; Fletcher, 1990). Police officers seem genuinely baffled as to why the apparent victims of abuse turn against them, who have been summoned to help them. According to Lenore Walker (2000) there is a plausible explanation for this: battered women report that men escalate their level of violence after the police leave, as a way of "punishing" the woman for calling the police. Walker argues that if women attack the police, the men see them as "siding" with them, thus showing solidarity with the abusive husbands and lessening the likelihood of retaliation.

2. This does not mean that roles such as victim and defendant are statically produced. What I mean is that in institutional settings such as the court, the judge already has available to him/her an official speaker designation (as plaintiff and defendant), and it is this speaker identity that is not "obviously" available to cops who show up to domestic disputes. Of course, identities such as victim and plaintiff must also be negotiated locally, on a moment to moment basis, during the interaction through language use; but I just want to point out that the police officers face a constraint that is different from courts in that they first have to locate and discern the identities of relevant parties. The interactional constraint is evident in the sequentially delayed request for a narrative, which in institutional setting like courts, would be found more up front.

3. It could be argued that the "you involved?" in line 14 is a repair sequence; however, I cannot find evidence in the data to support that claim. Line 12-14 is an action sequence

designed to establish the identities of the relevant parties—both of them. When the BW answers the "you involved?" question in line 14, the officer does not acknowledge her response, but he sanctions her, stating that he'll listen to both stories. And precisely because the officer has not heard both stories and, more importantly, the BM's answer to the yes/no question, he gives her a stern warning.

4. It would have been interesting to see how the proximal and distal deictics were interwoven with the officer's gestures; however, such information was not available.

5. On the surface, "what?" looks like an open class repair initiator, designed to clarify mishearings and miscommunications (Drew, 1997). However, the manner in which the term is articulated (rise in intonation and pitch) suggests that the BM is reacting to the incredulity of the BW's claim, as a way of encoding his affect. Hence, although "what?" wears the grammatical cloak of a clarification question, it does the work of utterances such as "you gotta be kidding me, I don't believe this, you're joking"—a sort of a response cry (Goffman, 1981).

6. It should be noted that possession of drugs is more serious than trespassing. Also, in the former complaint, she is not (perhaps) directly affected by it, as she is by the BM's trespassing. And by raising this new and more serious complaint, the BW effectuates a possible shift in the frame of the domestic dispute. Ultimately, this is what ends up happening in the encounter. The BM is arrested for drug charges and assault.

7. The officer accomplishes this directive in a sophisticated way. I call it sophisticated because the officer prefaces the command (turn off your vehicle) with a request, thus, again, disguising his power, and encapsulates its supplicant flavor by personalizing it (for me). Then after realizing that the BM can drive away from the scene while in the car, the officer bluntly states that he'll do it, only to repair the bald directive to a more polite request (do you mind if I turn it off?). The officer gives the BM face saving options rather than pure face threatening ones. Should the BM not oblige the request the officer makes, its interrogative form makes mitigated and extended answers possible; however, should the officer formulate his directive as a bald command, the only options available to the BM are compliance or disobedience (Vuchinich, 1990, 1984). Although the officer has every legal right to make such bald directives, the officer hides that coercive aspect of his power by softening his directives.

8. I do not mean to say that such features are disorderly, but that they merely give the impression of being such. As I will demonstrate in the upcoming sections of the chapter, there is nothing disorderly about the repeated accusations, escalation in charges and paralinguistics.

9. For a discussion on reported speech see (Bauman and Briggs, 1990; Besnier, 1990, 1992; Briggs, 1992a, b, 1993; Hamilton, 1996; Hickmann, 1992; Lucy, 1993; Waugh, 1995)

10. These types of statements that do not contribute to the storyline is what Hirsch (1998) refers to as "non-narrative" statements.

11. For a historical overview of the relationship between law and poetics see (Tiersma, 1999). For a concrete example of how poetics is used in real time moments of trial testimony see (Matoesian, 2001, 1997)

12. In an earlier data I've discussed, there is another example of this. In the suspicious person stop, the WW (young white woman), cannot give the host cop her partner's full name; moreover, when the officer questions the source of her knowledge, he at first uses "extreme case" formulations to first give credibility and weight to her epistemological claims. She begins with "everybody" then reduces the course to "a lot of people," the finally, to herself, the phenomenological "I." In this encounter, there is also a gradual shift from the general (everybody) to the precise (I).

13. Before the officer asks the BW for her narrative (line 88), the following sequence takes place. The officer first asks the BM to tell his story (line 42); the BM tells the main points of his story in lines 43-60; in line 60, as the BM concludes his story, he also accuses the BW of physical assault (bit me in the hand, tore up my shoulders, scratched me up). Notice what happens next: she denies the accusation, accusation that is addressed to the officer as a part of his story. Consequently, the BW is sanctioned again by the officer for talking out of sequence, and telling her side of the story when it isn't her turn (line 62).

```
42   PO: What happened here today sir?
43   BM: I came back to move my stuff (though)
44        we talked about it last night
45        I told her I was moving
46        [she
47   PO: [How long ya been living together?
48   BM: Well I just moved in like probably about a week
49        two weeks maybe I told her "I'll need to move"
50        you know what I'm saying "by the end of the
51        week" I mean end of the month cuz I need to
52        get a place right? so she said "okay" you know
53        "you could move in for a while" I said "okay no
54        problem" so last night we talked about it ( ) and I
55        was moving today she's mad because I took my
56        Jimmy Dean sausage (( slight laughter)) that I bought you know I'm
57        taking     my food with me and stuff like that right?
58        so [(        )
59        [(radio call)
60        [bit me in the hand tore up my shoulders scratched me up
61   BW: [I didn't scratch you up
62   PO: [Okay maam I'll hear your side relax
63        Do you need rescue sir?
64   BM: I don't know she[
65   PO:                  [Let me see your hands
66   BM: She's gonna bit me here put a hole in it
67        right theuh [( ) call yaw cuz nobody round
68   PO:             [three two four dispatch ((to dispatcher))
69   BM: here wanna let me use they phoneright quick
70        I'm like "this is crazy" you know how she just
```

```
71        jumped [on me got=
72  PO:        [ten four we've got a subject here with a
73        bite on his hands ((address dispatcher))
74  BM: I ain't gonna worry about it cuz I'm bleeding
75  PO: Is there any weapons in your car sir?
76  BM: Oh naw
77  PO: Before I before I walk over there you mind if I take a
78        quick check make sure there's no weapons
79        I'm gonna have you sit right there on the curb
80  BM: Okay this is wait a minute now this is my man's
81        [truck
82  PO:    [Okay go have a seat right there
83  (radio call)
84  PO: All right Imonna leave the door shut just sit
85        right there
86  BM: I understand ( )
87  BW:      It's in a white yellow white n' yellow bag
88  PO: Okay Ma'am tell me what happened here tonight
```

After the officer berates the BW for talking out of sequence, the officer continues to question the BM regarding his injuries. As an aside, the host officer's "let me see your hands" in line 65 initiates another action and creates another context within the current story telling context. Later when the officer utters the same utterance, he uses the contextual footing in line 65 to get another action (arrest) accomplished.

What is noteworthy about this transition from the elicitation of BM's story (line 42) to the BW's story (line 88) is that the BW "jumps" her turn twice, once to deny an accusation (line 61) and once to accuse the BM again of a far more serious narcotics charge. The female disputant first makes the narcotics accusation during the "pre-narrative" sequence in line 30 (go check his truck cuz he's got weed in it), and does so again in line 87 (it's in a white n' yellow bag) immediately before the officer asks for her "official" story (line 88). The referent of "it" of course is historically related to the weed in line 30. What is noteworthy is how the BM and the officer react to that piece of news.

As already stated, when the BW first mentions this topic, the BM utters what could be described as a "response cry" (Goffman, 1981) to signal his incredulity and the outrageousness of her accusation. The BW, it should be recalled, topicalizes the drug charge precisely because the officer does not "listen" to what she has to say. After she mentions the drugs, the cop tells the BM to turn off the ignition to his car, asks for his ID—simply put, the officer orients his turn to what the BW says. In this excerpt, after the BW repeats her prior accusation, the officer does not go immediately over to the BM's truck and search the car, but elicits her narrative, a rather extended turn at talk.

The value of such an invitation is that it creates the impression of fairness. He has already listened to the male disputant's story; now he listens to the woman. He listens to both sides of the dispute. This way, the officer doesn't appear to be solely interested in making a narcotics pinch to the viewers at home. Furthermore, the officer presents himself as one who is detached and impartial, concerned with hearing all sides of the dispute. In other words, he is not just favorably aligned with the female disputant for giving him the narcotics information. Moreover, in addition to the viewing audience, there is still the male disputant who is in proximity, within overhearing distance. And to "jump" to the narcotics investigation would jeopardize his safety since the officer has not checked the truck for weapons yet.

14. Recall from excerpt 4 how the battered woman "just" answers back to the husband's repeated complaint about the enduring presence of cheese on the dinner table. As mentioned earlier, the word "just" plays an important role in her account: she lexically downplays her role in the event, minimizing her role as a precipitator in the ensuing battering incident.

15. As Hirsch (1998) notes, this type of self-assessment does not deflect or attribute blame. However, it contrasts with the BM's narrative since he produces no such statements; his statements are factive.

16. Before the BW articulates lines 107-108, she noticeably draws in breath, thus physically getting ready to speak. And when she actually says "why you gonna make my daughter fall and started punchin me in my face" it is delivered in a very rapid fashion.

17. Excerpt 8
```
107 BW:>He gonna tell me "why you gonna make my daughter
108     fall" and started punchin me in my face< and I was
109     swingin back and he kept hittin me what I look like
110     fightin him?
111 PO: Mkay How'd his hand get cut?
112 BW: Probably from my earring cuz my earring be
113 PO: No that's because teeth marks on there=
114 BW:=Cuz I bit him cuz he had me I had not I (swear)
115 PO: Let's see your face
116     Anybody see this?
117 BW: No in my house my children (that's when) he was
118     and punching me in my face
119 PO: Okay do me a favor just sit right by your door
120     right there okay? We'll be back in a second
```

After the BW finishes telling her narrative, the officer acknowledges the end of her turn (line 111: Mkay) and attempts to clarify a slight discrepancy in her story. It should be recalled that the BM had stated that she had bit him during their fight; in the BW's narrative, she does not account for that bite on the male disputant's hand. When the officer does ask the BW about it, she first—hesitantly—answers that her earrings might have caused the cut; the officer disagrees—catches her in an inconsistency, a lie—with that version and offers the cause based on physical evidence (the BM's cut on his hands). Only then she changes her answer to one of self-defense, and "fesses up" to the biting in line 114. The officer examines her face to validate her story, and when there are no physical marks, he asks for witnesses. When she cannot do so, he goes to confer with fellow officers.

18. A noteworthy situational contingency that arises during routine patrol work is order-maintenance (Bittner, 1967a, b). Another that routinely arises in the course of routine patrol work is the necessity to "cover one's ass" (van Maanen, 1978a). Hence, in officer's narratives, a more pressing bureaucratic relevance may be to minimize his/her potential culpability while maximizing a citizen's. Although this example of "covering one's ass" is not illustrated here, in other data, there are instances of such. In a separate paper, I plan to pursue the topic further. For now, I just want to mention this possibility.

19. The most well known embodiment of bureaucratic language in the context of law enforcement would probably be Sgt. Joe Friday from *Dragnet*. Hence, in a way, Sgt. Friday's "just the facts ma'am" substantively represents the professional policing model of a dispassionate and mechanical service that is LAPD. However, that bureaucratic tincture is simultaneously encoded in the monotone and lifeless form of the message in Sgt. Friday's delivery.

CHAPTER 6
CONCLUSION: COERCION, RHETORIC, AND LANGUAGE IN A TIME OF CHANGE

As William K. Muir (1977) noted long ago, possessing the ability to educate and build rapport with citizens through the "sophisticated" use of language defines the consummate professional; and the attempts of police officers to verbally control the actions of citizens through directives represent the discursive embodiment of that ideological and practical mandate of modern policing (Mastrofski et al., 2000, 1996; Reiss, 1971; Whitaker, 1982). In prior police research, however, there has been an empirical gap in explaining how police officers go about doing such things. Mastrofski and Parks (1990: 476) once remarked that dominant methods of research, quantitative behavioral studies, informed little about "what police say and how they say it and why they say it." That is to say directives such as requesting, advising, warning, or threatening are first and foremost speech acts; as such, merely coding and describing such speech acts overlooks how those types of discursive acts operate in actual—sequential—detail. Consequently, readers have been treated to the researchers' and coders' interpretive judgments about speech acts—their descriptions—rather than how they work (Schegloff, 1992a).

This tendency to overlook social action for its mere description can be more expansively formulated as a duel between objectivism and constructionism (Maynard, 1988). The former treats language as a referential medium of communication—a mirror of reality—while the latter assumes language to be the very sites and facilitators of production of struggles, power, identity, social order, and conflict. In this paradigm, language is seen as a way of discursively—

hence, socially—constructing reality. Hence, police and citizens constitute the interactional fabric of the institutional-social interaction collaboratively by using language to negotiate social and moral identities, blame implicativeness, and power, while simultaneously reproducing that social order. The logic of the pre-supposition behind this is thoroughly dialectical and dialogical. An example of this type of assumption embodied in the analysis can be seen in the work of Manning (1982: 124), who conceptualizes the police as processors of signs con-taining a "structural system for encoding incoming data"; in this way "the envi-ronment is created and enacted and then rationalized and cast into organizational rhetoric." Manning's work provides a way in which the police invoke rules and practices through a semiotic and cognitive filter with which they organize and interpret the vicissitudes of police work.

   Language and Demeanor in Police-Citizen Encounters, rather than being a radical point of departure from the past and current literature on the police, is merely a logical extension of those assumptions and premises that have been presupposed but unexplored. As already stated, the analytical points I have made throughout the chapters are implicitly—and sometimes explicitly—portended in the seminal, as well as existing, works. For instance, that language lies at the cornerstone of professional policing is already well established in the work of William K. Muir (1977), and implicitly embedded in the work of David Bayley (1974: 47-49); and recently, the salience of speech acts in the routine activities of patrol officers has been fruitfully explored in the work of Stephen Mastrofski and colleagues. Furthermore, the main problems I have set out to examine in this work—the talk between the police and the public—have already been antici-pated. For instance, Black's (1980) *Manners and Customs of the Police* presup-posed the import of talk in P-C encounters; hence, he perspicuously noted that certain encounters between the police and the public posed a recurring analytical dilemma for prior researchers, but not treated as units of analysis due to the limi-tations of dominant methods of analysis. Consequently, Donald Black noted that observers were prone to coding errors when they were observing and categoriz-ing the demeanor of communicatively sophisticated citizens (Black, 1980; Bayley, 1986). Communicatively sophisticated citizens pose a coding problem because they say one thing to mean another, and animate the voice of deferential citizens as an occasioned performance in situ—do disrespect. That is to say, such verbally sophisticated citizens usurp the polyphonic voices of deference in a single voice.

   If the communicative process between the police and certain segments of the public is so "slippery" that it eludes the methods of existing paradigms—that is if there is no formal link between language form and function—then why don't researchers who study P-C encounters use a method of analysis that does justice to the processes that occur within them? Mastrofski et al. (1996) have an answer:

   The interaction approach is also far more demanding, for it requires a detailed accounting of the decision making processes of both police and the citizens they encounter. Empirical research in the interactionist mode typically is based on laboratory observations, surveys, and ex post facto accounts of events by participants. Our explorations of either [psychological, sociological] approach is limited by our data. The observations lack indicators of citizen attitudes and cognitions; we lack a detailed coding of the interplay of actions taken by parties during the compliance encounters (Mastrofski et al., 1996: 273).

In the preceding excerpt, Mastrofski et al. provide a succinct summary of the limitations quantitative police researchers face and their rationale for not choosing the interactionist approach. Mastrofski et al., however, make two notable flaws. First, Mastrofski et al. (1996) are right to observe that "empirical research in the interactionist mode typically is based on laboratory observations, surveys, and ex post facto accounts of events by participants," but they *forget* that there is a branch of sociology and interactional linguistics that uses the verbal "interplay of actions taken by parties" during social encounters as data and for analysis—empirically, in context, in their own right. In the fields of interactional sociolinguistics, conversation analysis (CA), discourse analysis, pragmatics, and linguistic anthropology, the whole business involves uncovering the interplay of verbal actions—accounting of the decision making—between participants. CA in particular, uses actual instances of social encounters, video-audio recorded and transcribed, to demonstrate line by line, turn by turn, utterance by utterance the intentions and understandings of those intentions of speakers in social and institutional settings (for a general review, see Maynard and Clayman 1991).

Mastrofski et al. make the second mistake by assuming that a "detailed *coding* of the interplay of actions taken by parties during the compliance encounters" (my emphasis) is what will overcome prior limitations. The problem of coding has been extensively addressed in the previous chapters as well as elsewhere (Maynard, 1989). Essentially, the coding process involves a fantastic illustration of reductionism at work. Rather than using the actual behaviors— behaviors that are justifiable and warrantable topic in their own right—of subjects as primary units of analysis, coding schemes utilize the researchers' observations of those behaviors as the primary units of analysis; it is this fundamentally preinterpretive move that acts as an epistemological prophylactic, desensitizing researchers to the rich and nuanced character of social intercourse, adding an additional filter between reality, its representation, and analysis.

To remedy this gap in the literature, I have borrowed heavily from interactional sociolinguistics, conversation analysis, and, in particular, Goffman's notion of footing to provide an analytical framework with which to understand and elucidate how citizens adopt the voice of deferential ones to perform, as well as hide, their moral identities. The analytical observations made in *Language and Demeanor in Police-Citizen Encounters* have been possible because I have used a "method" other than the primarily accepted ones in criminology and criminal justice, one that is more consistent with the analysis of language in general. These observations have been made possible because the set of assumptions I have presupposed about the nature of data collection and analysis and epistemology in general have been structured by a different (not better) analytical vision. That is, rather than asking questions that are categorical (e.g., was a request made? was the request fulfilled, partially fulfilled, or not fulfilled at all) and numerical (if so how many times, and under which conditions?), I have aimed my analytical sights in a phenomenological direction.

This type of question is not concerned with 'did or did not the phenomenon occur?' or its frequency of occurrence, but how the phenomenon occurs. And to explain how a phenomenon works and its constitutive order, as experienced and articulated by themselves, I have looked to the subjects' actual—verbatim—words and accounts in their sequential context. The goal of a 'how' analysis is to uncover the members' methods, practices, procedures, assumptions, and logic—interplay of actions taken by all parties—as demonstrated by the subjects themselves in their action (talk) (Merleau-Ponty, 1962; Schutz, 1962; Garfinkel, 1967; Maynard, 1996; for police, see Bittner, 1967a, b). The how question is fundamentally different in its logic, assumption, and method from the how many and did it occur question. As I have argued here and elsewhere, that how question is not something that is alien to P-C encounter research because it is implicitly embedded in the questions that police researchers already ask—a logical extension of prior and current work (Shon, 2003).

In *Language and Demeanor in Police-Citizen Encounters* I have sought to learn about the police and their exercise of coercive power through the way they talk. Rather than observing the police and the public, and the interactions that ensue as units of analysis, I have assumed a linguistic (and Goffmanesque) stance and examined the utterances rather than the "utterers." To put it another way, the unit of analysis in *Language and Demeanor* has principally been the language (utterances) that the police and citizens exchange rather than the police officers and the citizens themselves ("utterers"). *Language and Demeanor* thus represents the linguistic turn—"conversationalization"—in police studies, one that is, again, anticipatable and expectable from the prior works and made possible by a "method" that is more consistent with its expatiation (Shon, 2003).

Demeanor without Trial

The dramaturgic metaphor has often been a favored conceptual tool to untangle the complex web that is police work, patrol work compared to a "social stage with an unknown cast of characters" (Reiss, 1971). Manning (1997: 5) echoes a similar sentiment when he writes that policing is a "masterful costume drama, a presentation of ordering and mannered civility that was also dirty work...policing is a job...where immorality, venality, violence, and lies are routine." While both scholars astutely note that police work entails a situational and contextual assessment of citizens' veiled morality in their contacts with the police, their exegesis implies the emergence of citizens' "true" identities once their roles are uncovered; and yet, as much as the dramaturgic metaphor permeates the theoretical currents of policing, how the police and public go about actually enacting such roles in the quotidian details of social interaction has been assumed prima facie.

Again, a citizen who uses honorific address terms towards the police obviously conforms to the normative rituals of politeness, and enacts the role of a deferential citizen; similarly, a person who dons the blue uniform, pins a shield/badge, and carries the "tools" of his/her trade visibly enacts the role of a police officer. However, it is neither theoretically fruitful nor interesting to conceptualize demeanor and identity (role) in such static fashion. Whether actors play a part on the "front stage" or the "back stage" of street encounters, Goffman (1959) has definitively shown that they are capable of assuming at least two distinct roles. Simply put, a role is fluid and contingently accomplished. In *Forms of Talk*, Goffman (1981) relocates his dramaturgic metaphor to the scene of communication, and introduces the notion of *footing* to illustrate how discursive identities (roles) are constructed in real time moments of verbal interaction. Goffman introduces a malleable way of understanding 'role'/'identity' that is embodied in talk: (1) *animator* refers to the enunciator or one who physically produces the spoken words (2) *author* refers to the one who composes the spoken words and (3) *principal* refers to the person actually responsible for the enunciation and composition of the utterances. And as Matoesian (2001: 166) notes, footing can be shifted by manipulating discourse features such as intonation, topic switch, lexical choice, and "paralinguistic behavior" such as laughing and grinning. The next direction in police-citizen encounter research entails the expatiation of how such social, legal, and moral identities are forged in the microlinguistic details of face-to-face interaction.

This book illustrates what prior police researchers using coding schemes and ethnographies have often assumed into their works: the discursively emergent nature of demeanor, and the sophisticated ways that the police and citizens use language during their encounters. In this book, I have attempted to show how that power and office is enacted and created through talk, in the words that police officers use (lexical choice), their turns at talk (turn order), and the constraints they embed into their turns (turn design). Furthermore, *Language and Demeanor in Police-Citizen Encounters* has added an empirical bite to Black's (1980) key analytical dilemma: being communicatively sophisticated and subtle involves shifting *footing*; I have shown how citizens use politeness markers, honorific address terms, and agreement markers to challenge the police and "perform" disrespect; they use pauses, silences, and invert turn order to wrest the axis of control from the police for a fleeting turn to temporarily subvert the interactional order of P-C encounters. Communicatively sophisticated citizens merely adopt or *animate* the voice of deferential citizens to present a deferential self. Overtly hostile citizens simply merge the *animator*, *author*, and *principal* into a solitary voice. Goffman's notion of footing allows a reconfiguration of citizens' demeanor in a way that is not structurally determinative; and using such an analytical framework, this book has offered a processual and endogenous view of how demeanor and socio-legal identities of citizens emerge from the turn by turn organization of the talk itself, using language to hide behind the voices of others, shifting footing, and strategically manipulating discursive identities to effectuate favorable impression management (Goffman, 1959).

This lack of correspondence between the form (what police officers and citizens actually say) and meaning (what police officers and citizens actually mean) of utterances suggests a shortcoming in the way prior researchers have conceptualized the nature of demeanor. Again, it would be patently misleading to believe that more sophisticated coding schemes and statistical analyses would remedy such gaps in the literature. Capturing spoken words into coding sheets merely reduces speech acts to descriptions of them, in effect, trading ends for means. Again, that's because the form of a language bears no logical or necessary relation to its function. As I have shown in this book, a citizen who swiftly answers an officer's questions with a crisp "yes/no sir" is not necessarily conveying deference. In order to understand what the participants in P-C encounters are doing—displaying demeanor—the actual interactional (conversational) details must be examined in their own right (end), not as conduits to something else (means). To impose a category of demeanor without having examined the actual sequences of interaction is akin to pronouncing a defendant's guilt without the procedural rigor of a trial.

The discourse analytic approach that has been used in this study adds a new perspective on the micro-sociological details routine police work. In prior research, the absolute capacity of the police to "coerce others to refrain from using illegitimate coercion...to kill, hurt, confine, and otherwise victimize non-policemen who would illegally kill, hurt, confine, or victimize others" (Muir, 1977: 44) has been regarded as a theoretical foundation of modern policing (Bittner, 1978; Manning, 1997; Weber, 1978). Although the police seldom resort to this absolute power, how officers morally respond to the possession of that coercive authority has been regarded as the measure of professionalism (Muir, 1977). When that theory of coercion has been ethnographically pursued, it has been shown that there is a noticeable gap between their official and practical mandate (Banton, 1964; Bittner, 1967a, b; Meehan, 1992). In this book, I have shown how the police actually go about exercising that awesome power they possess by examining their language use.

I have shown how coercive authority of the police and citizens' demeanor both emerge from the sequential and interactional organization of talk-in-interaction. When the structures and forms of talk are examined, it reveals that the police cloak their power under the guise of a veil, and they exercise it in a sequential manner. The police routinely disguise their coercive authority by phrasing their directives under the veil of politeness; they formulate utterances in grammatically simplified ways to facilitate conformity. In other words, the police mitigate or "soften" raw and brute authority. Furthermore, the police give numerous opportunities to citizens to present a deferential self, and conform to the bureaucratic order of the encounter: they make requests, greet citizens, indirectly initiate a problem, and allow citizens to give accounts and excuses before and after they are informed of a legal violation. That the speakers are legal and institutional representatives also constrains the interaction in a way that is different from ordinary social encounters. Citizens "react" to the uniform (institutionality) in a defensive way, as if they have been accused of an infraction, thus giving concrete and discursive form to the psychoanalytic interpretation of police that other researchers have impressionistically alluded to (e.g., Niederhoffer, 1967).

In addition to its physically coercive nature, *Language and Demeanor in Police-Citizen Encounters* illustrates another facet to police power—the power to set agendas, the power to control the flow of talk, and the power to control definitional contexts, frames, and footings of talk (Molotch and Boden, 1985; Goffman, 1981, 1974). Simply put, the police possess the capacity to define an interaction on their own terms. Hence, police officers can articulate greetings in a way that is socially lubricative, or they can utter them in a way that imprints their "bureaucraticness"; their ability to be equivocal provides them much leeway to frame and authorize an interaction on their interactional footing rather than the citizens'—the police "definition of the situation" (van Maanen, 1978a). Of course, what a situation is and how it unfolds depends on its articulation, and the kinds of constraints that are imposed in the questions that the police ask. Police power means having the ability to determine what gets to count as a relevant next turn answer, but it also means having the power to ask and frame questions that delineate the relevant next turn answer— the "footing" of talk. In this way, we can see the contextual and sequential ways that police power is practically embodied in the minute details of talk-in-interaction.

A warrantable question that scholars who have not been persuaded by the arguments made in *Language and Demeanor in Police-Citizen Encounters* could ask is: how can a researcher know what the participants mean? In other words, how can someone's intention—an unobservable, internal, psychological state— be accessible to analysts for inspection? Rather than toiling needlessly in a philosophical sort of way about the ontology and epistemology of consciousness, the key is to be sociological: let the subjects speak for themselves (Moerman, 1988; Schegloff, 1991). That is to say, analysis would be crafted and empirically verified from the actual utterances of participants who are mired in the social world rather than in a theoretical armchair. For instance, as demonstrated in chapter 4, interlocked requests open up binary interpretive possibilities. As Muir (1977) observed, those types of questions work as "attitude tests" that police officers routinely give citizens. It could also just be that the officer wants to check the motorist's license; the officer could be rightly suspicious about something and may be using the traffic stop as a justification for a car search. The speculations are limitless.

What is not limitless, from an analytical point of view, is how citizens respond to that interlocked turn. If a citizen responds with a greeting, then, we can, for the moment, rule out that the citizen has understood the utterance as a bureaucratic request. Therefore, knowing the sequential position of utterances within a stream of talk delimits the interpretive conditions; we can infer the intentions and meanings of utterances based on the way speakers orient to turns (Atkinson and Heritage, 1984; Sacks et al., 1974). Thus, beginning the analysis of demeanor from the participants' own behavior need not be psychological, reductionistic, or speculative: it can be done rigorously and empirically without turning the analysts into mind readers. However, this type of approach entails that police scholars conceptualize and operationalize language as a form of social behavior in its own right, not as conduits to and reflection of demeanor. And it is only through the adoption of such a presupposition that the orderly and rule-driven encounters between the police and the public can be further explored. Moreover, *Language and Demeanor in Police-Citizen Encounters* has demonstrated that those rules have to be sustained by both parties in an intersubjective way. Of course, these methodological and theoretical points are ones that conversation analysts and ethnomethodologists such as Harold Garfinkel, Harvey Sacks, and Emanuel Schegloff have already made. In this study, I have merely pointed the "method" at P-C encounters.

Language in a Time of Change

Policing has been and is suffused with a fundamental paradox that is inherently built into the conditions of the work, as numerous others have noted; one of those paradoxes concerns the fact that no other occupation encodes the capacity to hurt and kill the clients of the service who bestow that right in the first place. It is this coercive face of policing in a democratic and free society that is fraught with tension and creates uneasiness in the public since the very existence and definition of the police are inconsistent and antithetical to the ideals that legitimate and offer structural support to them (Goldstein, 1990). The ideals of democracy presuppose equality, egalitarianism, and reciprocity in the subjecthood of its citizens; policing necessarily entails the use of coercion by intruding into the private affairs of citizens and impeding their free movement (Chevigny, 1969). Democratic policing entails respecting the dignity, autonomy, and constitutional rights of citizens, not only in the way they are abstractly conceived, but in the palpable ways that they are treated in public spheres. Thus, policing the street requires a balancing of the aforementioned with the exercise of an intrinsically face threatening and coercive act.

It is this campaign toward equality and reciprocity and the reduction of coercion—along with a poignant realization of the failure of the professional model—that has been the impetus for the shift in the philosophy of policing. This emergent trend in policing differs from the two principal ones in that the citizens who are most affected by police power and its exercise are no longer relegated to the backseat in the policymaking decisions. That is, unlike the citizens of political era policing where they existed as mere benefactors of the patronage system in exchange for their vote, or the passive recipients whose only access to the police required a simple and anonymous act of picking up a phone and awaiting the rapid response of officers in squad cars in the professional era, the most recent shift in the policing paradigm conceptualizes citizens as implicative partners in the fight against and discourse about crime (Meares and Kahan, 1999; Trajanowicz, 1994). Simply put, citizens are no longer idle consumers of professional police services, but active and responsible agents who set the agenda of the police, and determine priorities that are significant for them in their respective communities.

This type of redefining of the police, the public and their respective roles, it has been argued, represents a radical reconfiguration of the assumptions behind policing, one that diminishes the ideological, epistemological, and communicative asymmetry between the police and the public; the community-oriented model of policing, unlike the previous models, has embraced and presupposed the principle of egalitarianism in its mission and mandate, thus proactively attempting to lessen the schism between the police and the public through a recontextualization of their footing in the community (Skogan, 2004). In essence, community policing involves a reinvigoration of the ethos of voluntarism, from the rank and file officers in police organizations to the average citizen, empowering the cultivation of civic-mindedness and personal agency in the pursuit of communal efficacy (Putnam, 2000; Greenberg, 2005). To achieve that end, activists, researchers, and police executives have forged an artificial space to foster a "dialogue" between the public and the police. Such a move has been hailed by researchers, practitioners, and citizens alike, with community policing being proclaimed as the embodiment of democratic policing in the midst of pluralism (Skogan and Roth, 2004; Roth et al., 2004).

Conceptualizing police-community relations in accordance with a discourse model attempts to mirror the advancements made in other disciplines (e.g., political theory, ethical theory), and by doing so, it is hoped that the talk between the police and the public will result in the enlistment, engagement, and help from the community, that they will forge a real partnership against crime and disorder—through talk. This communicative metaphor represents an alternative role for the police, as well as the public, since most of the discourse about crime and justice has been one-sided. In the traditional model of policing, the police have postured themselves as experts and wielders of bureaucratic knowledge (thus dictating public policy), and citizens have always been the audience to such monologues. Community-oriented policing represents an inversion of that process in that it "facilitates" the police in listening to the public, about what is important to them, on their own terms, in their turf, in their language. As researchers have shown, the "listening" and the ensuing "dialogue" have been artificially manufactured in the local churches, school cafeterias and gymnasiums across communities, in a grassroots sort of way, the voices of participants reverberating like an audible metronomic beat of the very democratic ideals that gird the emergent policing paradigm.

By relying on a discourse theory of institutions, the vested participants hang their hope that the fundamental recalibration of roles, from service providers and consumers to partners, mediated by a neutral conversational space that encourages the exchange of ideas and discourse, along with policies that are consistent with the expressed needs and desires of communities, will produce a style of policing that is less coercive, one that is qualitatively different from the previous decades, in a way that is built on mutual trust, cooperation, and respect, much like an ideal conversation in an ideal speech context, rather than distrust, cynicism, and racial strife. In a way, these assumptions are theoretically consistent with a communicative model of social theory since a genuine dialogue entails an environment free of coercion, intimidation, and fear; in such a hypothetical setting, turn order, turn size, and topic selection are not scarce commodities since the possession of those goods are not affected by accessibility, class, gender, and race; the very possession of a generic, metaphysical identity, qua subject, secures one's place in the debate table (i.e., Rawls, 1971, 1993; Habermas, 1996). In such idyllic *Mayberrys*, everybody gets to talk. The rhetoric of community policing, with its cacophonous repetition of the word "dialogue" in its definition, mission statements, and press releases, assumes this philosophical baggage, with or without their knowledge.

It is this type of convoluted rhetoric of community policing that has been the subject of critical scholarship in the criminal justice sciences. Recent work on the rhetoric of community policing, despite its discourse of partnership, egalitarianism, and access, suggests a much more invidious form of social inter-calation into the lives of citizens. For instance, a deconstructive analysis of community policing indicates a set of hidden assumptions based on fixed repre-sentations of intersectionality of race, class, and gender. Furthermore, it has been argued that the police function more as the "foot soldiers" in the reproduc-tion of social order through a daily practice of proffering of master significations rather than as disinterested agents of social control (Williams, 1999). In other words, there appears to be a disjuncture between the theoretically conceived model of community policing, and in its empirical form. Rather than empower-ing the public, it has been shown that the language of "problem solving" merely moves the state's coercive power "further into unregulated space and the daily lives of citizens" (Kappeler and Kraska 1999:194). The sparse critical works on community policing thus iterate the observation that the enforcement tools of the policing trade have merely shifted from night sticks and pepper sprays to sym-bolic forms of social control silhouetted with thinly worn veil of benevolent invasion.

The work of Kappeler and Kraska (1999) and Williams (1999) has been mainly a textual deconstruction of the rhetoric and language of community po-licing, while the work of Websdale (2001) represents an ethnographic foray into the lives of the very people who have been most affected by the tactics of com-munity-oriented policing. The conclusions are not encouraging. For instance, Websdale (2001) draws parallels between community policing in Nashville to slave patrols of the antebellum South since policing functions as a codified and formalized mechanism for the social regulation of the poor in a way that is le-gitimized and authorized under the benevolent auspices of "problem solving." Websdale also exposes the way policing is intimately bound to the pyrrhic pro-duction and perpetuation of a "dangerous underclass" in a way that enhances the state's economic interests, as an integral component of the "criminal justice jug-gernaut," while doing little to address the criminogenic conditions (e.g., unem-ployment and underemployment) that breed such illegalities (see Reiman, 1995). Websdale's (2001) work on community policing thus forcefully argues that the very institution of the police and their activities cannot be cogently discussed without an examination of the role of the political economy and labor markets that shape them. Websdale (2001: 219) summarizes the effects of community policing thus, echoing the conclusions of Kappeler and Kraska (1999): "com-munity policing is the law enforcement equivalent of growing employer surveil-lance in the workplace, extending the ever-increasing presence and gaze of au-thorities into the lives of workers. At another level, community policing initiatives, all their talk of consensus building and caring about community feedback, may constitute yet another example of the disingenuous language so characteristic of postindustrial America."

To illustrate the symbolic and intrusive character of policing in the poor, marginalized sections of Nashville, Websdale titillates the readers with an excerpt of an interview in which the subject (Byron) recalls his experience with community policing:

> **Byron**: "Well, in my opinion, I feel like I'm harassed for no reason at all. You know, it's like...you walk down the street, uh, you could be trying to visit a friend from the housing projects, and I get off the city bus on one side of the street and the police is on the other side. I'm coming across the street. But before I get to where I'm going, you know, they, like, asking me questions. 'Let me see your ID'. 'Why?' I'm askin', 'Why?' He says, 'Cause I want to. Is you on the lease?' I say, 'No, but I'm visiting my mother, my sister, some of them, they on the lease. They got their car and their own project house and I'm a family member. Why can't I come see 'em without being questioned?'"
>
> **Websdale**: So they're stopping you for no reason?
>
> **Byron**: "For no reason. I mean, I get off one bus and come across the street and I got jewelry on or if I got a beeper on, and they say, 'you doin' something.' They think everybody's dealing drugs...whatcha you doin? Whatcha been up to? Where you work at? Do you work? Why you over here? Just questioning me all the time."

In this excerpt readers are treated to a glimpse of Byron's world, a resident who feels that he is unfairly targeted by the police for harassment. Byron recounts that the police are constantly vigilant of his movements and whereabouts, that the police "stop him for no reason." This type of self-generated P-C encounters and aggressive policing tactics (traffic stops, "stop and frisks") usually involve the minority (Lundman and Kaufman, 2003; Spitzer, 1999; Walker, 2001), and are inextricably tied to claims of racial profiling, police brutality, and civil rights violations, which in turn engender a hostile attitude toward the police and create further gaps between the minority and the police (Anderson, 1999; Radelet, 1977; Skolnick, 1973). These types of policing tactics, along with the tragic shooting of an unarmed civilian, can strain already tense police-community relations, and serve as the impetus for a violent, mass social protest (Bimstein, 1973).

Now, notice that the "let me see your ID" is similar to the "May I see your driver's license" in that both work as a way of conversationalizing and "opening" the encounter; but the former is syntactically and grammatically different from the canonic request articulated by police officers during traffic stops since the utterance is formulated as an imperative. This difference illustrates the fact that directives—speech acts that are designed to influence the actions of another—are not born equal, and that they can be hierarchically classified according to the degree of force that is embedded within them, and the amount of social control the speaker wishes to exert over another speaker (Ervin-Tripp, 1976: 29). Hence, imperatives (e.g., Let me see your ID) represent a far more socially controlling and "brute" form of a directive than imbedded imperatives (e.g., Could I see your ID) and question directives (e.g., Do you have an ID?).

In the excerpt above, that initial directive elicits as the next turn response a response that challenges the relevancy of the previous turn, its contents, its felicity, and in a nutshell, disrespects police authority (why?); and as a result, the police officer, in his turn, in not so many words, socializes Byron into the fundamental asymmetry between the public and the police, and demonstrates his ability to define the footing of talk. It is Byron's challenge to a preliminary action embedded in the first utterance—"post-pre"—that initially offends the police. This move, as I have argued in this book, snatches the locus and sequential control of the interaction from the police to the citizens; and as a result of Byron's 'why' the police role is now reversed: rather than doing the questioning and interrogating, the officer, for a fleeting turn, is put in the position of the "powerless" since he has to conform to the sequential contours of talk the citizen has created. Thus, rather than giving the officer a chance to articulate his reason for the stop, Byron "jumps" the normative interactional—sequential—order of P-C encounters and attempts to preemptively move to the reason for the stop, much like the way impatient drivers emulate the demeanor of six-year-olds who repeatedly ask "What did I do? What did I do?" Consequently, he is categorized as a particular type of a citizen and treated accordingly. Either Byron doesn't understand the fundamental differences between institutional interactions and treats the encounter in a social way, or Byron is challenging the very legitimacy of the institution—legitimacy that has been eroded by the frequency of such contacts—precisely through such monosyllabic interrogatives (see Lundman and Kaufman, 2003).

In addition to the preemptive move toward the reason for the stop which has been implicative, there is one noteworthy sequence that, either as a result of forgetfulness or non-occurrence, has not been mentioned at all in the excerpt: how the police officer initially "approached" Byron. Just as squad cars summon motorists to interact using sirens and flashing lights, police officers who stop and interrogate pedestrians must communicatively signal that intention and desire to interact; and the way this is accomplished reveals how ideology of policing interpellates socio-legal-moral identities of citizens, and the way linguistic ideologies sustain the ideological infrastructure of police work. Consider the following recollection from a Los Angeles police officer serving as a Field Training Officer (FTO) (Middleton, 2001: 80):

> On one particular evening, I had a young officer from Kentucky. He really wanted to do a good job because he loved this new business called police work. On East sixth Street we stopped a heroin addict obviously under the influence of the drug. I let my partner approach him.
>   "Hey, nigger, get over here." The man stopped and turned around. My partner barked at him again, "That's right—you, nigger."

It appears that identities of subjects in intrusive police work are negotiated during the encounter itself, free of the historical and linguistic encumbrances that usually seep their way into discourse. But this assumption would neglect the ideologies—about people, language—that facilitate the linguistic production in the first place. Consequently, it may be possible to argue that "subjectivization" process begins before the subjects of policing are assigned a subjective space as policed subjects. For a detailed elaboration, I supplement the above with one of the most famous cases of P-C encounters in philosophy.

Althusser (1971: 170) states that "ideology interpellates individuals as subjects" when the subjects themselves ratify the calling. Hence, if someone knocks on a door and is asked "Who's there?" and that person answers "It's me," and opens the door, it is the familiarity of that person's voice as someone already known that leads to recognition. Althusser would state that recognition is achieved because "All ideology hails or interpellates concrete individuals as concrete subjects, by the functioning of the category of the subjects" (Althusser, 1971: 173) and because individuals are "always already subjects and as such constantly practice the rituals of ideological recognition" (p. 172). To illustrate this intersubjective process, Althusser uses the example of a police officer hailing a citizen: "Hey you there!" Althusser (1971: 174) writes that the citizen becomes a subject "by this mere one-hundred-and eighty-degree physical conversion" upon the officer's verbal summons to interact, much like the way the black male in Los Angeles stops and turns around in response to the LAPD officer's "Hey, nigger, get over here." For Althusser, interpellation of subjects qua sub-·jects is constituted when subjects give recognition to such hailing.

If ideology finds embodiment in the recognition of the police summons by turning around, thereby delineating an interpellative identity, then for theorists such as Butler (1997: 31) "the subject need not always turn around in order to be constituted as a subject, and the discourse that inaugurates the subject need not take the form of a voice at all." That's because the act of naming itself is performatively sufficient to unilaterally inscribe an identity. The interpellative act is unilateral since power appears as a name, through "nominalization." That is, the performativity of naming creates—constructs—the effect. Thus, when a police officer yells "Hey you there!" it is not radically different from a divine performative since the very act of beckoning signifies and materializes coercive power of the police, and consequently, inscribes an identity. Hence, Althusser (1971: 176) is right when he says that "individuals are always-already subjects," but "subjectivization" does not begin with the individual's turning around. It has already taken place. Subjectivization is embedded within the ideological apparatus that facilitate such linguistic productions in the first place, and the subject need not participate in the subjectivization. And while subjectivization is usually understood as a reflexively—mutually—experienced state of recognition embedded in a symbolic network, giving meaning and "totality" to the subject, the space occupied by the subject need not be prepared by the subject him/herself. Thus, Zizek (1991: 186) states that subjectivization designates "recognizing oneself as a socially defined somebody"; but the divine-like performative of the police imperative delineates the subject's positionality without his designation or recognition: there is hardly anything reflexive and intersubjective about such unilateral action.

If the arguments made in the preceding paragraphs seem unrealistic and fantastic, then consider what would have happened (and usually do) to Byron and the unnamed black Los Angeles male had they not ratified the summons and chose not to turn around. In effect, then, we can say that race, or color of one's skin, subjectifies an individual as a certain somebody, and in essence, functions as a name: giving an identity, being (re)created—the name (skin) forcing "itself upon you, to delineate the space you occupy, to construct a social positionality" (Butler, 1997: 33). This force of interpellation works oblivious to the subject's protests, inclination, and awareness; the violence of the name rests on its "inaugurative" rather than its "descriptive" function.

Ideological structures are also implicative in that the semantic and pragmatic force of utterances such as *"Hey, nigger, get over here"* or *"What's your name, boy?"* derives power through reiteration and citation: social structures that are already in place for their articulation and meaningfulness (Butler, 1993, 1997). The Kentucky-born LAPD officer is able to talk down to the unwitting pedestrian precisely because the structural, cultural, organizational, and sociolinguistic system for "talking down" to blacks is already in place (Kennedy, 2002; Independent Commission, 1992). Without such structural support, the utterance would crumble under the weight of its own force and farce, much like the way that the N-word would crumble when uttered by a professor in reference to an African-American student in a faculty meeting at a college in the Northeast. That the utterance is spoken and attains its performative effect illustrates the racist social structures that give such utterances linguistic (hence social) frames of meaning. That is why how Byron was summoned to interact is significant for ideological analysis, and why actual words used by the police and citizens alike can't be just glossed over through a coding sheet. A coding sheet would simply have reduced such titillating moments into oblivion.

This type of inaugurative and interpellative violence of language is not that different from symbolic murder, for it names the others for what they are not, and "freezes" (to use Butler's vocabulary) the other while reducing the complexity of existence to the "simple and the singular." To "freeze" the other necessitates symbolic murder because unilateral hailing hails not only the wrong person, but it must first discursively "murder" the right person to do so. Interpellative violence works by fundamentally negating and repressing reality and subjectivity. Thus, the unnamed black Los Angeles male is constructed as being something he is not; he loses his descriptive and historical specificity and embodies the homogeneity of linguistic sameness by being summoned in such a fashion. Do police officers in community policing programs talk to citizens in a way that is qualitatively different from their counterparts? How do the community-based police officers talk with their "co-partners?" Would this type of discourse analytic approach support the conclusion drawn by Kappeler and Kraska (1999) and Websdale (2001)? How would the micro-linguistic details of moral, social, institutional identity management manifest and negotiate themselves in the sequential structure of their talk?

The principle of equality assumed in recent shifts in the policing paradigm, however, encounters an inconsistency given the coercive capacity of the police. Thus, as much as the rhetoric of community policing tinctures the organizational mission and prevailing ideology of the police, the fundamentally paradoxical capacity of the police to "hurt and kill" the purveyors of their authority and clients of their service gives flesh and bone to their occupational identities (Terrill and Masfrosfki, 2004; Terill et al., 2003). If, however, the authority and legitimacy of the police is politically derived and sociologically enacted, its sustenance during perceived threats and affronts to officers' authority is not: one either obeys the directives of physical control or flouts them. There is nothing abstract about being commanded to "put your hands up." The lesson is brutally simple—compliance (Klinger, 2004). Such theological assertions, however, are inconsistent with the contemporary fads in community policing because they contradict the principles of equity, egalitarianism, free speech, and movement, and only serve to dramatize the ideological and communicative asymmetry between the police and the public. As I have conjectured here, however, as much as citizens are conceptualized as partners in the fight against crime and disorder, communication first has to conform to the interactional order of the police, thus giving a driver's license or ID when requested or commanded, answering questions when asked etc. That is to say that in order to arrive at a democratic—natural—state of talk, one must conform to the institutional—coercive—authority of the police.

Although the talk between the police and the public is institutional rather than natural, using language as a metaphor for abstract notions such as democracy is conceptually viable since talk is the primordial site of sociality (Schegloff, 1999a); in a way, the empirical manifestation of egalitarianism: conversations over coffee or cold beer are managed by the participants themselves in a grassroots sort of way; consequently the burden of deciding who gets to talk, what gets talked about, and how much one gets to talk is not imposed exogenously but shouldered by the encumbered actors themselves (Sacks et al., 1974); and it is in such banal moments that people's identities, realities, and the social structure of everyday life is produced and reified (Sacks, 1992; Schegloff, 1991; see also Maynard, 2003). In that sense, talk is the micro-embodiment of democracy-in-action—talk that is not concocted as a result of metaphysical assumptions presupposed into the outline of a political theory (e.g., Rawls, 1971, 1993) or talk that is idealized as a basis for democratic and ethical systems in unrealizable conversational settings (e.g., Habermas, 1996). Institutional interactions fundamentally differ from social ones in that regard—because bureaucratic institutions possess the capacity to wield power in the grammatical, syntactical, and sequential aspects of talk (Atkinson and Drew, 1979; Drew and Heritage, 1992; Matoesian, 1993; Molotch and Boden, 1985); aside from brute coercion, it is along such lines that the police also differ from the public. Thus, the true litmus test of community policing surfaces when the aims of the community and police encounter differences and disagreements. Will the police flex their ideological and coercive muscle and simply do as they please (i.e., command), or will they really enact the role of an equal partner and agree about their capacity to disagree? One way of answering such macro-questions is to examine the conversational—micro—exchanges between them.

Limitations of *Language and Demeanor in Police-Citizen Encounters*

There are two sets of questions that I have not rigorously pursued in this study; that is because, to an extent, I have assumed them in my set of presuppositions about data analysis. However, that I have merely assumed such things does not mean that they are unimportant. For instance, readers will have noticed that I have not examined the way physical behaviors such as gestures, facial expressions, body postures, and gazes have been implicative in talk. And my Sacksian response to that legitimate question would be "it would be great to study them" (Sacks, 1992 in Silverman, 1998: 72). It's just that I haven't done them, for to do so would have taken this study in too many directions. To use gestures, gazes, and postures as units of analysis would inevitably bring in factors such as camera angles, camera placement, and lighting, and a host of other technical details which would not have been fruitful for this study (McConville, 1992; Silverman, 1998).

In this book I have blatantly assumed the implicativeness of some physical behaviors. For example, when citizens and suspects reach into their pockets with their hands during a field interview, keep their hands from plain view, or reach into the glove compartment during a traffic stop, the next turn response from an officer is a stern command not to do such things (e.g., LET ME SEE YOUR HANDS; KEEP YOUR HANDS WHERE I CAN SEE EM'). If they continue to persist, the consequences can be fatal. It is those types of gestures and physical behaviors that are of interest to scholars who examine how "social actions and activities are accomplished in and through interaction, and the ways in which talk, visual and material conduct feature in the practical accomplishment of routine events" (Heath and Luff, 2000: 26). As I have stated, I have taken some gestures for granted; hence, I have not conducted a thorough analysis of them. Someone else could do that. Such technicalities and level of detail I think are best left to scholars in other disciplines. As Silverman (1998) notes, there is no such thing as complete data any more than there can be a complete transcript. "Rather, as always in science, everything will depend on what you are trying to do and where it seems that you may be able to make progress" (Silverman, 1998: 72). If I were writing for an audience of language scholars (in a linguistics department), then my transcriptions—even some of the analytical terms—would be more detailed and filled with argot. In this study, I am concerned with and interested in verbal behavior, language use, not gestures.

A second question that can be justifiably raised is related to the notion of "context." For instance, if police officers pull over a car in what could ostensibly be called a "bad neighborhood," after a highly-publicized shooting of an unarmed minority citizen, or in a city and a police department well known for its discourteous police, wouldn't those factors affect how the police and citizens interact? The answer could be yes or no. I am not sure. I haven't looked at data from such places so I cannot say. What I can say is that even in those types of settings, in police departments whose historical and organizational patterns of citizen mistreatment are well known, the business of opening, conducting, and closing P-C encounters still has to be negotiated using language. Perhaps the way Midwest City and Southern City patrol officers and Los Angeles Police Department officers deal with citizens may be qualitatively different. Again, those types of comparative studies are open to other scholars who are interested in such issues. However, I have again taken for granted certain contextual details: the setting of the call (city, neighborhood), the identities of the participants (police, citizens), and the occasion for talk (P-C encounter). It's not that those things are not important, but in this study, I have been concerned with explicating how talk discursively constructs those labels in the first place.

The context question is related to an issue that is analytically pertinent in another way. As I have shown, some of the things that police officers and citizens say to each other do not "look like" the things that police officers and citizens would say in the context of official business. For example, there is nothing bureaucratic and business-like about asking a citizen if he is a ninja, or talking about going to a lingerie store during a P-C encounter. In fact, had the identities of the speakers in those excerpts not been identified as police officers and citizens, it would be hard to determine not only the identities of the participants, but the occasion for such talk. That gets to the problem of assigning determinative sense and meaning to the character of talk at hand. Those who might justifiably raise the context issue could say that even talk about ninja and lingerie during P-C encounters needs to be understood within the whole context of the communication. And we would be right back where we started: what is context and how does it work in communication? Is it the city in which the encounter is taking place? The neighborhood? Particular block? Intersection? Officers' personality traits? Whether they just got chewed out by their bosses and are taking it out on the citizens? Particular group and class of people? Or is context the occasion for the talk itself, as a traffic stop, suspicious person stop, or a call of a domestic dispute? In that case, how do we determine if other contexts (variables), such as personality characteristics, race, class, and gender, are not at work in the talk? Simply put, what gives the talk between the police and citizens its structure and appearance?

Sociologists and linguists who have studied talk in institutional settings—courts, emergency dispatch centers—note that talk in those settings are structurally and sequentially different from ordinary conversations (see Drew and Heritage, 1992). That is, turn taking and turn order are not natural, but imposed. By virtue of their uniform, badge, gun, nightstick, and the cruiser with flashing lights, police officers differ from ordinary citizens, and their institutional identities already convey a message—semiotically—before any substantive communication take place with the public. To understand the institutional character of talk in P-C encounters, two analytical choices are available.

In the first, a "quantitative" stance can be taken: all of the questions posed in this camp would be categorical. It would presuppose an understanding of the phenomena that the questions seek to answer and would place a constraint, a priori, in the field of analytical possibilities. Hence, a uniformed officer who pulls over a motorist, makes a request to see official identification can be categorized as a police officer, and the work that he/he does as police work. Similarly, in a *COPS* episode, we can look at a video tape of a police officer pulling someone over in a certain city, and formulate a master context (P-C encounter) for understanding what the participants are doing by offering descriptions about categories of related context (city, recent history, neighborhood, race of the citizen, etc.) prior to examination of actual sequences of talk. In this view, context is exogenous. The context and categories are imposed by the analyst and what actually goes on in the encounter is interpreted within the confines of those assumed contexts. In this view, variables such as race, class, and gender etc. are static; they are static because the mechanism which drives the social encounter is always left in the backseat: language is used as a vehicle for describing those preformulated categories. The mechanism itself remains as a resource but never a warrantable topic in its own right.

The second option is to view the notion of context and other structural variables generatively, "that is to show how the context or the setting (the local social structure), in that aspect, is procedurally consequential to the talk" (Schegloff, 1992b: 111). In other words, concepts such as roles, status, and class do not determine the character of talk a priori but in a constitutive manner—those variables are enacted, demonstrated, performed, and contextually used as a resource in the production of further communication, as a topic in their own right. In this option, the goal is to discover contexts, "and to discover new sorts of such things...in the members' worlds, if they are there" (Schegloff, 1992b: 128). Let me offer a concrete example from one of the chapters.

In chapter 5, I discussed in detail the social organization of a domestic dispute. It is entirely possible to view that call as a context in itself, or divide it into a beginning, middle, and an end stage, as prior police researchers have done (Bayley and Bittner, 1984; Bayley and Garofalo, 1989). However, as I have shown, there are other contexts that arise in the opening moments of the call: (1) the officer asks yes/no questions to both participants to create an identity establishing context. (2) The female disputant repeatedly accuses the male disputant of a crime, and she attempts to tell a story; she treats the opening interrogatives series as a story telling context. (3) The male disputant remains silent until the woman accuses him of possessing drugs; as a result, he places his denials adjacent to hers, and creates an argument context. (4) The officer berates both disputants for straying from the interactional order of P-C encounters: he chastises and physically separates them, thus creating a parental mediation context. Is it possible to isolate any one of these "contexts" as overriding another?

This shows that the notion of context can be intra-contextual, embedded within another context (see Garfinkel, 1967; Schegloff, 1997, 1992b, 1991, 1987). That is, in the context of a domestic disturbance call, the participants have displayed four other contexts of talk. And in order to assign a determinative sense to the operative context, the participants have to mutually orient to these contexts as the talk unfolds. Of course, in the "Jimmy Dean" excerpt, the officer uses his coercive and contextual power to define the interactional footing that is consistent with his "definition of the situation," and overrides other competing contexts. Contexts, their place, and meaning in a conversation are interactionally managed, locally produced moment to moment, in real time production of talk. Context is topically produced at the same time it is used as a resource (Goodwin and Duranti, 1992). If there is a "master context" that overrides all others during routine calls for service, it is one that the police define. Police power means having the ability to define the footing of the situation.

If context is endogenous, embedded within the mechanism itself, always in flux and changing, then how do we narrow down which context is operating in talk? Two analytical choices are possible: the analyst can assume the privileged position and define the context a priori, or that privilege could be granted to the actual participants in the conversation and the structures within. What are the subjects of transcripts trying to do in and through their talk, and how can their understanding be shown in the analysis? In this book, I have tried to faithfully capture the essence of what the police and citizens are trying to do—word by word.

For future research it might be worthwhile to gather a collection of domestic disputes, traffic stops, suspicious person stops, and systematically examine them. Is there a pattern in the way disputants attribute blame and deflect responsibility in "domestics"? Is there a pattern in the way police officers make "requests" and in the way citizens give excuses? Another warrantable topic of study could involve the editing process. How do editors go about selecting shots and frames? What gets included and what gets left out? How is the editing process, as a conversational phenomenon organized? As I have already suggested, examining the way physical behaviors influence talk in P-C encounters could be an invaluable research topic. In this study, I have provided a broad look at actual and mass-mediated P-C encounters. There are many more things to be discovered in the data; whether other researchers choose to examine them is entirely up to them.

REFERENCES

Adams, S. 1996. "Statement Analysis: What Do Suspects' Words Really Reveal?" *FBI Law Enforcement Bulletin* 65:12-20.

Angronsino, M., and De Perez, K.M.A. 2000. "Rethinking Observation." Pp. 673-702 in *Handbook of Qualitative Research.* (2nd ed.). Edited by N. K. Denzin and Y. S. Lincoln. Thousand Oaks, CA: Sage.

Allen, R. C.1987. "More Talk About TV." Pp. 1-65 in *Channels of Discourse.* Edited by R. Allen. Chapel Hill: University of North Carolina.

Althusser, L. 1971. *Lenin and Philosophy.* New York: Monthly Review Press.

Anderson, E. 1999. *Code of the Street: Decency, Violence, and the Moral Life of the Inner City.* New York: W.W. Norton.

Antaki, C. 1994. *Explaining and Arguing: The Social Organization of Accounts.* Thousand Oaks, CA: Sage.

Atkinson J. M., and Drew, P. 1979. *Order in Court: The Organization of Verbal Interaction in Judicial Settings.* London: Macmillian.

Atkinson, J. M., and Heritage, J. 1984. "Preference Organization." Pp. 53-56 in *Structures of Social Action: Studies in Conversation Analysis.* Edited by J.M. Atkinson and J. Heritage. Cambridge: Cambridge University Press.

Austin, J. 1962. *How to do Things with Words.* Oxford: Oxford University Press.

Bailey, B. 1997. "Communication of Respect in Inter-ethnic Service Encounters." *Language in Society* 26(3): 327-356.

Baker, M. 1985. *COPS: Their Lives in Their Own Words.* New York: Pocket Books.

Bahktin, M. 1981. *The Dialogic Imagination.* Austin, TX: University of Texas Press.

Baldwin, J. 1993. "Police Interview Techniques: Establishing Truth or Proof?" *The British Journal of Criminology* 33(3): 325-352.

Banton, M. 1964. *The Policeman in the Community.* New York: Basic Books.

Baudrillard, J. (1988). "Simulacra and Simulations." Pp. 166-184 in *Jean Baudrillard: Selected Writings.* Edited by M. Poster. Stanford, CA: Stanford University Press.

Bauman, R. 1986. *Story, Performance, and Event: Contextual Studies of Oral Narrative.* New York: Cambridge University Press.

Bauman, R., and Briggs, C. 1990. "Poetics and Performance as Critical Perspectives on Language and Social life." *Annual Review of Anthropology* 19: 59-88.

Bayley, D. H. 1974. *Forces of Order.* New York: University of California Press.

———. 1986. "The Tactical Choices of Police Patrol Officers." *Journal of Criminal Justice* 14: 329-348.

———. 1994. *Police For the Future.* New York: Oxford University Press.

Bayley, D. H., and Bittner, E. 1984. "Learning the Skills of Policing." *Law and Contemporary Problems* 47: 35-39.

Bayley, D. H., and Garofalo, J. 1989. "The Management of Violence by Police Patrol Officers." *Criminology* 27(1): 1-25.

Beach, W. 1990. "Language as and in Technology: Facilitating Topic Organization in a Videotaped Focus Group Meeting." Pp. 197-218 in *Communication and the Culture of Technology.* Edited by M.J. Medhurst, A. Gonzalez, and T.R. Peterson. Pullman, WA: Washington State University Press.

Benson, D. 1992. "The Police and Information Technology." Pp. 81-98 in *Technology in Working Order: Studies of Work, Interaction and Technology.* Edited by G. Button. London: Routledge.

Berk, R. 1993. "What the Scientific Evidence Shows: On the Average, We Can Do No Better Than Arrest." Pp. 323-336 in *Current Controversies on Family Violence.* Edited by R.J. Gelles and D. R. Loseke. Newbury Park, CA: Sage.

Berk, R., Campbell, A., Klap, R., and B. Western. 1992. "The Deterrent Effect of Arrest in Incidents of Domestic Violence: A Bayesian Analysis of Four Field Experiments." *American Sociological Review* 57: 698-708.

Besnier, N. 1990. "Language and Affect." *Annual Review of Anthropology* 19: 419-451.

———. 1992. "Reported Speech and Affect on Nukulaeale Atoll." Pp. 161-173 in *Responsibility and Evidence in Oral Discourse.* Edited by J. Hill and J. Irvine. New York: Cambridge.

Billig, M. 1999a. "Whose Terms? Whose Ordinariness? Rhetoric and Ideology in Conversation Analysis." *Discourse and Society* 10(4): 543-558.

———. 1999b. "CA and the Claims of Naivety." *Discourse and Society* 10(4): 572-577.

Bimstein, D. 1973. "Sensitivity Training and the Police." Pp. 165-177 in *Police-Community Relations.* Edited by P. Cromwell Jr., and G. Keefer. St. Paul, MN: West Publishing Co.

Bittner, E. 1967a. "The Policeman on Skid-Row: A Study in Peacekeeping." *American Sociological Review* 32: 699-715.

———. 1967b. "Police Discretion in Emergency Apprehension of Mentally Ill Persons." *Social Problems* 14: 278-292.

———.1978. "The Functions of the Police in Modern Society." Pp. 32-50 in *Policing: A View from the Street.* Edited by J. Van Maanen and P. K. Manning. Santa Monica, CA: Goodyear Publishing.

Black, D. 1971. "The Social Organization of Arrest." *Stanford Law Review* 23: 1087-1111.

————. 1980. *The Manners and Customs of the Police.* New York: Academic Press.

Black, D., and Reiss, A. Jr.1970. "Police Control of Juveniles." *American Sociological Review* 35: 63-77.

Blum-Kulka, S., Danet, B., and R. Gerson. 1985. "The Language of Requesting in Israeli Society." Pp 113-139 in *Language in Social Situations.* Edited by J. Forgas. Berlin: Springer.

Boggs, S. 1978. "The Development of Verbal Disputing in Part-Hawaiian Children." *Language in Society* 7: 325-344.

Boggs, S., and Lein, L. 1978. "Sequencing in Children's Discourse: Introduction." *Language in Society* 7: 293-297.

Bogomolny, R. L. 1976. "Street Patrol: The Decision to Stop a Citizen." *Criminal Law Bulletin*: 544-582.

Bowker, L. H. 1993 . "A Battered Woman's Problems are Social, Not Psychological." Pp. 154-165 in *Current Controversies on Family Violence.* Edited by R.J. Gelles and D. R. Loseke. Newbury Park, CA: Sage.

Bracher, M. 1993. *Lacan, Discourse, and Social Change: A Psychoanalytic Cultural Criticism* Ithaca: Cornell University Press.

Brennis, D. 1988. "Language and Disputing." *Annual Review of Anthropology* 17: 221-237.

Brennis, D. 1996. "Telling Troubles: Narrative, Conflict, and Experience." Pp. 41-52 in *Disorderly Discourse: Narrative, Conflict, and Inequality.* Edited by C. Briggs. New York: Oxford University Press.

Brennis, D., and Lein, L. 1977. "You Fruithead: A Sociolinguistic Approach to Children's Dispute Settlement." Pp. 49-65 in *Child Discourse.* Edited by S. Ervin-Tripp and C. Mitchell-Kernan. New York: Academic press.

Briggs, C. 1992a. "Since I am a Woman I will Chastise my Relatives: Gender, Reported Speech, and the Reproduction of Social Relations in Warao Ritual Wailing." *American Ethnologist* 19: 337-361.

————. 1992b. "Linguistic Ideologies and the Naturalization of Power in Warao Discourse." *Pragmatics* 2: 387-404.

————. 1993. "Metadiscursive Practices and Scholarly Authority in Folkloristics." *Journal of American Folklore* 106: 387-434.

————.1996a. "Introduction." Pp. 3-40 in *Disorderly Discourse*, edited by C. Briggs. New York: Oxford University Press.

————. 1996b. "Conflict, Language Ideologies, and Privileged Arenas of Discursive Authority in Waro Dispute Mediation." Pp. 204-242 in *Disorderly Discourse*. Edited by C. Briggs. New York: Oxford University Press.

Briggs, C., and Bauman, R. 1992. "Genre, Intertextuality, and Social Power." *Journal of Linguistic Anthropology* 2: 131-172.

Brougham, C. G. 1992. "Nonverbal Communication: Can What They Don't Say Give Them Away?" *FBI Law Enforcement Bulletin* 61:15-18.

Browne, A. 1987. *When Battered Women Kill.* New York: Free Press.

Brown, P., and Levinson, S. 1987. *Politeness: Some Universals in Language Usage.* Cambridge, UK: Cambridge University Press.

Butler, Judith.1997. *Excitable Speech: A Politics of the Performative.* New York: Routledge.

————. 1993. *Bodies that Matter.* New York: Routledge.

Button, G. 1987. "Answers as Interactional Products: Two Sequential Practices Used in Interviews." *Social Psychology Quarterly* 50(2): 160-171.

Button, G. and Lee, J.R.E. 1987. *Talk and Social Organization.* Edited by G. Button and J.R.E. Lee. Philadelphia: Multilungual Matters.

Buzawa, E.S., and Buzawa, C.G. 1993. "The Scientific Evidence is Not Conclusive: Arrest is No Panacea." Pp. 336-356 in *Current Controversies on Family Violence.* Edited by R.J. Gelles and D. R. Loseke. Newbury Park, CA: Sage.

Chafe, W. 1992. "Seneca Speaking Styles and the Location of Authority." Pp. 72-87 in *Responsibility and Oral Discourse.* Edited by J. Hill and J. Irvine. New York: Cambridge University Press.

Chevigny, P. 1969. *Police Power: Police Abuses in New York City.* New York: Vintage Books.

Clare, I.C.H., and Gudjonsson, G.H. 1993. "Interrogative Suggestibility, Confabulation, and Acquiesence in People with Mild Learning Disabilities (Mental Handicap): Implications for Reliability During Police Interrogations." *British Journal of Clinical Psychology* 32: 295-301.

Clayman, S. 1989. "The Production of Punctuality: Social Interaction, Temporal Organization, and Social Structure." *American Journal of Sociology* 95 (3): 659-691.

————. 1992. "Footing in the Achievement of Neutrality: The Case of News-Interview Discourse." Pp. 163-198 in *Talk at Work: Interaction in Institutional Settings.* Edited by P Drew and J. Heritage. Cambridge: Cambridge University Press.

Collins, J.1987. "Television and Postmodernism." Pp. 327-353 in *Channels of Discourse*. Edited by R. Allen. Chapel Hill: University of North Carolina.

Conley, J. M. and O'Barr, W. 1990. *Rules versus Relationships: the Ethnography of Legal Discourse*. Chicago: University of Chicago Press.

———. 1998. *Just Words: Law, Language, and Power*. Chicago: University of Chicago Press.

Corsaro, W. 1977. "The Clarification Request as a Feature of Adult Interactive Styles with Young Children." *Language in Society* 6: 183-207.

———. 1979. "Young Children's Conception of Status and Role." *Sociology of Education* 52: 46-59.

Corsaro, W., and Rizzo, T. 1990. "Disputes and Conflict Resolution Among Nursery School Children in the U.S. and Italy." Pp. 21-66 in *Conflict Talk*. Edited by A. Grimshaw. Cambridge, Cambridge University Press.

Cummings, E., Cummings, I., and L. Edell. 1965. "The Policeman as Philosopher, Guide, and Friend." *Social Problems* 12(3): 276-286.

Dersley, I., and Wootton, A. 2000. "Complaint Sequences within Antagonistic Argument." *Research on language and Social Interaction* 33(4): 375-406.

———. 2001. "In the Heat of the Sequence: Interactional Features Preceding Walkouts from Argumentative Talk." *Language in Society* 30: 611-638.

Dobash, R., and Dobash, R. 1979. *Violence Against Wives: A Case Against Patriarchy*. NY: Free Press.

Dobash, R. E., Schlesinger, P., Dobash, R., and C. K. Weaver. 1998. "'Crimewatch UK': Women's Interpretations of Televised Violence." Pp. 37-58 in *Entertaining Crime: Television Reality Programs*. Edited by M. Fishman and G. Cavender. New York: Aldine de Gruyter.

Dore, J. 1977. "On Them Sheriff: A Pragmatic Analysis of Children's Responses to Questions." Pp. 139-163 in *Child Discourse*. Edited by S. Ervin-Tripp and C. Mitchell-Kernan. New York: Academic Press.

———. 1978. "Requestive Systems in Nursery School Conversations: Analysis of Talk in its Social Context." Pp. 271-292 in *Recent Advances in the Psychology of Language*. Edited by E. Campbell and P. Smith. New York: Plenum.

Doyle, A. 1998. "'Cops': Television Policing as Policing Reality." Pp. 95-116 in *Entertaining Crime: Television Reality Programs*. Edited by M. Fishman and G. Cavender. New York: Aldine de Gruyter.

Drew, P. 1997. "'Open' Class Repair Initiators in Response to Sequential Sources of Troubles in Conversation." *Journal of Pragmatics* 28: 69-101.

Drew, P., and Heritage, J. 1992. "Introduction." Pp. 3-65 in *Talk at Work: Interaction in Institutional Settings*. Edited by P Drew and J. Heritage. Cambridge: Cambridge University Press.

Drew, P., and Holt, E. 1988. "Complainable Matters: The Use of Idiomatic Expressions in Making Complaints." *Social Problems* 35(4): 398-417.

———. 1998. "Figures of Speech: Figurative Expressions and the Management of Topic Transition in Conversation." *Language in Society* 27: 495-522.

Dunham, R., and Alpert, G. 2001. *Critical Issues in Policing: Contemporary Readings*, edited by R. Dunham and G. Alpert. Prospect Heights, IL: Waveland Press.

Duranti, A. 1997. *Linguistic Anthropology*. Cambridge, UK: Cambridge University Press.

Edwards, D. 2000. "Extreme Case Formulations: Softeners, Investment, and Doing Nonliteral." *Research on Language and Social Interaction* 33(4): 347-373.

Eisenberg, A., and Garvey, C.1981. "Children's use of Verbal Strategies in Resolving Conflicts." *Discourse Processes* 4: 149-170.

Emerson, R.M. 1969. *Judging Delinquents: Context and Process in Juvenile Court*. New York: Aldine.

Ervin-Trip, S. 1976. "Is Sybil There?: The Structures of Some American English Directives." *Language in Society* 5: 25-67.

———. 1978. "Some Features of Early Child-Adult Dialogues." *Language in Society* 7: 357-373.

———. 1982. "Structures of Control." Pp. 27-47 in *Communicating in the Classroom*, edited by L.C. Wilkinson. NY: Academic Press.

Ervin-Tripp, S., Strage, A., Lampert, M., and N. Bell. 1987. "Understanding Requests." *Linguistics* 25: 107-143.

Fish, S. 1967. *Surprised by Sin*. Cambridge: Harvard University Press.

———.1980. *Is There a text in This Class?* Cambridge, MA: Harvard University Press.

———. 1989. *Doing What Comes Naturally: Change, Rhetoric, and the Practice of Theory in Literary and Legal Studies*. Durham, NC: Duke University Press.

Fisher, R. P., Geiselman, E. R., and D. Raymond. 1987. "Critical Analysis of Police Interview Techniques." *Journal of Police Science and Administration* 15(3) 177-185.

Fiske, J. 1996. "Postmodernism and Television." Pp. 53-65 in *Mass Media and Society*. Edited by J. Curran and M. Gurevitch. London: Arnold Publishing.

Fletcher, C. 1990. *What Cops Know*. New York: Pocket Books.

Foucault, M. 1979. *The History of Sexuality: Vol 2. The Use of Pleasure*. London: Penguin.

———. 1977. *Discipline and Punish: The Birth of the Prison*. New York: Vintage Books.

Freud, S. 1914. *Totem and Taboo: Resemblances between the Psychic Lives of Savages and Neurotics*. Amherst, NY: Prometheus Books.

———. 1945. "Dostoyevsky and Parricide: Addiction and Guilt." Pp. 60-73 in *The Dynamics and Treatment of Alcoholism: Essential Papers*. Northvale, NJ: Jason Aronson Inc.

Fyfe, J. J. 1996. "Methodology, Substance, and Demeanor in Police Observational Research: A Response to Lundman and Others." *Journal of Research in Crime and Delinquency* 33(3): 337-348.

Galliher, J. 1971. "Explanations of Police Behavior: A Critical Review and Analysis." *The Sociological Quarterly* 12: 308-318.

Garcia, A. 1991. "Dispute Resolution Without Disputing: How the Interactional Organization of Mediation Hearings Minimizes Argumentative Talk." *American Sociological Review* 56: 818-835.

Garfinkel, H. 1967 *Studies in Ethnomethodology*. Englewood Cliffs, NJ: Prentice Hall.

Garvey, C. 1975. "Requests and Responses in Children's Speech." *Journal of Child Language* 2: 41-63.

Gelles, R.J. 1993. "Through a Sociological Lens: Social Structure and Family Violence." Pp. 31-46 in *Current Controversies on Family Violence*. Edited by R.J. Gelles and D. R. Loseke. Newbury Park, CA: Sage.

Gerbner, G., Gross, L., Morgan, M., and N. Signorielli. 1980. "The Mainstreaming of America: Violence Profile No. 11." *Journal of Communication* 30: 10-29.

Goffman, E. 1959. *Presentation of Self in Everyday Life*. New York: Doubleday.

———. 1967. *Interaction Ritual: Essays on Face to Face Behavior*. Garden City, NJ: Doubleday.

———. 1974. *Frame Analysis: An Essay on the Social Organization of Experience*. Boston: Northeastern University Press.

———. 1981. *Forms of Talk*. Oxford: Blackwell Publishers.

Goldstein, H. 1990. *Problem-Oriented Policing*. New York: McGraw-Hill Publishing.

Goodwin, C. 1986. "Audience Diversity, Participation and Interpretation." *Text* 6(3): 283-316.

Goodwin, C., and Goodwin, M. H. 1990. "Interstitial Argument." Pp. 85-117 in *Conflict Talk*. Edited by A. Grimshaw. Cambridge: Cambridge University Press.

Goodwin, M.H. 1982. "Processes of Dispute Management Among urban Black Children." *American Ethnologist* 9: 76-96.

———. 1983. "Aggravated Correction and Disagreement in Children's Conversations." *Journal of Pragmatics* 7: 657-677.
———.1990. *He Said She Said: Talk as Social organization Among Black Children*. Bloomington, IN: Indiana University Press.

Goodwin, C., and Duranti, A. 1992. "Rethinking Context: An Introduction." Pp. 1-42 in *Rethinking Context: Language as an Interactive Phenomenon*. Edited by C. Goodwin and A. Duranti. New York: Cambridge University Press.

Greatbatch, D. 1992. "On the Management of Disagreement Between News Interviewees." Pp. 268-301 in *Talk at Work*. Edited by P. Drew and J. Heritage. Cambridge: Cambridge University Press.

Greatbatch, D., and Dingwall, R. 1997. "Argumentative Talk in Divorce Mediation Sessions." *American Sociological Review* 62: 151-170.

Green, G. M. 1996. *Pragmatics and Natural Language Understanding*. Mahwah, NJ: Lawrence Erlbaum Associates, Inc.

Greenberg, M. 2005. *Citizens Defending America: From Colonial Times to the Age of Terrorism*. Pittsburg, PA: University of Pittsburg Press.

Grimshaw, A. 1990. *Conflict Talk: Sociolinguistic Investigation of Arguments in Conversations*. Cambridge: Cambridge University Press.

Gruber, H. 1998. "Disagreeing: Sequential Placement and Internal Structure in Conflict Episodes." *Text* 18(4): 467-503.

Gubrium, J., and Holstein, J. A. 1997. *The New Language of Qualitative Method*. New York: Oxford University Press.

Gudjonsson, G. 1992. *The Psychology of Interrogations, Confessions, and Testimony* Chichester, UK: John Wiley & Sons.

Gulich, E., and Quasthoff, U.M. 1985. "Narrative Analysis." Pp. 169-197 in *Handbook of discourse analysis, vol 2. Dimensions of Discourse*. Edited by T. Van Dijk. London: Academic Press.

Gumperz, J. 1982. *Discourse Strategies*. New York: Cambridge University Press.

Greatbatch, D., C. Heath, P. Luff, and P. Campion. 1995. "Conversation Analysis: Human-Computer Interaction and the General Practice Consultation." Pp. 199-222 in *Perspectives on HCI: Diverse Approaches*. Edited by A. Monk and N. Gilbert. New York: Academic Press.

Habermas, J. 1996. *Between Facts and Norms: Contributions to a Discourse Theory of Law and Democracy.* Cambridge: MIT Press.

Hagan, F. 1997. *Research Methods in Criminal Justice and Criminology.* Needham Heights, MA: Allyn and Bacon.

Hamilton, H. 1996. "Intratextuality, Intertextuality, and the Construction of Identity as Patient in Alzheimer's Disease." *Text* 16: 61-90.

Heath, C., and Luff, P. 1996. "Convergent activities: Line control and passenger information on the London Underground." Pp. 96-129 in *Cognition and Communication* at Work. Edited by Y. Engestrom and D. Middleton. Cambridge: Cambridge University Press.

————.2000. *Technology in Action.* Cambridge: Cambridge University press.

Heath, C., and Watson, D. R. 1989. "Some Preobservations on a Case of Human-Computer Interaction." *Language et Travail* 1989: 290-298.

Henry, S., and Milovanovic, D. 1991. "Constitutive Criminology: The Maturation of Critical Theory." *Criminology* 29 (2): 293-316.

————.1996. *Constitutive Criminology: Beyond Postmodernism.* London: Sage.

————.1999. *Constitutive Criminology at Work: Applications to Crime and Justice.* Albany, NY: SUNY Press.

Herbert, S.   1996a. *Policing Space: Territoriality and the LAPD.*   Minneapolis: University of Minnesota Press.

————. 1996b. "The Geopolitics of the Police: Foucault, Disciplinary Power and the Tactics of the Los Angeles Police Department." *Political Geography* 15: 47-57.

Heritage, J. 1984a. *Garfinkel and Ethnomethodology.* Cambridge: Polity Press.

————. 1984b. "A Change-of-Token and Aspects of Its Sequential Placement." Pp. 299-345 in *Structures of Social Action: Studies in Conversation Analysis.* Edited by J.M. Atkinson and J. Heritage. Cambridge: Cambridge University Press.

————. 1998a.   "Conversational Analysis and Institutional Talk: Analyzing Data." Pp. 161-182 in *Qualitative Research: Theory, Method, and Practice.* Edited by D. Silverman. Thousand Oaks, CA: Sage Publications.

————. 1998b. "Oh-Prefaced Responses to Inquiry." *Language in Society* 27:291-334.

Heritage, J., and Atkinson, J. M., 1984. "Introduction." Pp. 1-27 in *Structures of Social Action: Studies in Conversation Analysis.* Edited by J.M. Atkinson and J. Heritage. Cambridge, Cambridge University Press.

Heritage, J., and Watson, D.R. 1980. "Aspects of the Properties of Formulations in Natural Conversations: Some Instances Analyzed." *Semiotica.* 30(3/4):245-262.

Hickmann, M. 1992. "The boundaries of Reported Speech in Narrative Discourse: Some Developmental Aspects." Pp. 63-90 in *Reflexive Language*. Edited by J. Lucy. Cambridge: Cambridge University Press.

Hill, J., and Irvine, J. 1992. *Responsibility and Evidence in Oral Discourse*. Edited by J. Hill and J. Irvine. Cambridge: Cambridge University Press.

Hilton, D. J. 1995. "The Social Context of Reasoning: Conversational Inference and Rational Judgement." *Psychological Bulletin* 118(2): 248-271.

Hirsch, S. 1998. *Pronouncing and Persevering: Gender and the Discourse of Disputing in an African Islamic Court*. Chicago: University of Chicago Press.

Hutchby, I. 1996. *Confrontation Talk: Arguments, Asymmetries, and Power on Talk Radio*. Mahwah, NJ: Lawrence Erlbaum Associates.

———. 1998. "Rhetorical Strategies in Audience Participation Debates on Radio and TV." *Research on Language and Social Interaction* 32(3): 243-267.

Inbau, F.E., Reid, J.E., and J. P. Buckley. 1986. *Criminal Investigation and Confessions*. (3rd ed.) Baltimore, MD: Williams & Wilkins.

Irvine J. 1992. "Insult and Responsibility: Verbal Abuse in a Wolof Village." Pp. 105-135 in *Responsibility and Oral Discourse*. Edited by J. Hill and J. Irvine. New York: Cambridge University Press.

Jacobs, R.A. 1995. *English Syntax*. New York: Oxford University Press.

Jakobson, R. 1960. "Linguistics and Poetics." Pp. 54-62 in *The Discourse Reader*. Edited by A. Jaworski and N. Coupland. New York: Routledge.

Jaworski, A., and Coupland, N. 1999. "Introduction: Perspectives on Discourse Analysis." Pp. 1-44 in *The Discourse Reader*. Edited by A. Jaworski and N. Coupland. New York: Routledge.

Jayyusi, L. 1984. *Categorization and the Moral Order*. Boston, MA: Routledge & Kegan Paul.

Jefferson, G. 1978. "Sequential Aspects of Storytelling in Conversation." Pp. 219-248 in *Studies in the Organization of Conversational Interactiion*. Edited by J. Schenkein. New York: Academic Press.

———. 1972. "Side Sequences." Pp. 294-338 in *Studies in Social Interaction*. Edited by D. Sundow. New York: Free Press.

———.1980. "On 'Trouble Premonitory' Response to Inquiry." *Sociological Inquiry* 50: 153-185.

———.1984. "On the Organization of Laughter in Talks about Trouble." Pp. 346-369 in *Structures of Social Action*. Edited by J. M. Atkinson and J. Heritage. Cambridge: Cambridge University Press.

Kappeler, V. E., and Kraska, P. B. 1999. "Policing Modernity: Scientific and Community Based Violence on Symbolic Playing Fields." Pp. 175-203 in *Constitutive Criminology at Work*. Edited by S. Henry and D. Milovanovic. Albany, NY: SUNY Press.

Kassin, S. M. 1997. "The Psychology of Confession Evidence." *American Psychologist* 52(3): 221-233.

Kassin, S. M., and McNall, K. 1991. "Police Interrogations and Confessions: Communicating Promises and Threats by Pragmatic Implication." *Law and Human Behavior* 15(3): 233-251.

Kennedy, R. 2002. *Nigger: The Strange Career of a Troublesome Word*. New York: Pantheon.

Klinger, D. 2004. *Into the Kill Zone: A Cop's Eye View of Deadly Force*. San Francisco, CA: Jossey-Bass.

———.1994. "Demeanor or Crime? Why 'Hostile' Citizens are More Likely to be Arrested." *Criminology* 32(3): 475-493.

———.1996a. "More on Demeanor and Arrest in Dade County." *Criminology* 34(1): 61-82.

———. 1996b. "Bringing Crime Back in: Toward a Better Understanding of Police Arrest Decisions." *Journal of Research in Crime and Delinquency* 33(3): 333-336.

Komter, M. 1994. "Accusations and Defenses in Courtroom Interaction." *Discourse and Society*. 5: 165-187.

Kooistra, P. G., Mahoney, J.S., and S. D. Westervelt. 1998. "The World of Crime According to 'Cops'." Pp. 141-158 in *Entertaining Crime: Television Reality Programs*. Edited by M. Fishman and G. Cavender. New York: Aldine de Gruyter.

Kozloff, S. 1987. "Narrative Theory and Television." In *Channels of Discourse*. Edited by R. Allen. Chapel Hill: University of North Carolina.

Lacan, J. 1973. *The Four Fundamental Concepts of Psychoanalysis*. Edited by J. Miller, translated by A.Sheridan. New York: W.W. Norton & Company.

———. 1977. *Ecrits: A Selection*. Translated by Alan Sheridan. New York: W.W. Norton & Company.

Lakoff, R. 1973a. "Questionable Answers and Answerable Questions." In *Issues in Linguistics: Papers in Honor of Henry and Renee Kahane*. Edited by B. Kachru and R.B. Lees, Y. Malkiel, A. Pietrangeli, and S. Soporta. Urbana, IL: University of Illinois Press.

———. 1973b. "The Logic of Politeness: or Minding Your P's and Q's." *In Papers from the Ninth Regional Meeting of the Chicago Linguistic Society*. Edited by C. Corum, T.C. Smith-Stark, and A. Weiser. Chicago: Chicago Linguistic Society.

Labov, W., and Fanshel, D. 1977. *Therapeutic Discourse: Psychotherapy as Conversation*. New York: Academic Press.

Labov, W., and Waletzky, J. 1967. "Narrative Analysis." Pp. 12-44 in *Essays on the Verbal and Visual Arts*. Edited by J. Helm. Seattle: University of Washington Press.

Lee, J. 1990. *Jacques Lacan*. Amherst, NY: University of Massachusetts Press.

Lein, L., and Brennis, D. 1978. "Children's Disputes in Three Speech Communities." *Language in Society* 7: 299-323.

Leo, R.A. 1996a. "Inside the Interrogation Room." *The Journal of Criminology & Criminal Law*. 86(2): 266-303.

———. 1996b. "Miranda's Revenge: Police Interrogation as a Confidence Game." *Law and Society Review* 30(2): 259-288.

Levinson, S. 1980. "Speech Act Theory: The State of the Art." *Language Teaching and Linguistics Abstracts*. 14: 5-24.

———. 1981a. "The Essential Inadequacies of Speech Act Models of Dialogue." Pp. 473-492 in *Possibilities and Limitations of Pragmatics: Proceedings of the Conference on Pragmatics*. Edited by H. Parret, M. Sbisa, and J. Verschueren. Amsterdam: John Benjamins.

———. 1981b. "Some Pre-Observations on the Modeling of Dialogue." *Discourse Processes* 4:93-110.

———. 1983. *Pragmatics*. Cambridge, England: Cambridge University Press.

Lewis, C.S. 1948. *Abolition of Man*. New York: Macmillan Publishing.

Lucy, J. 1993. *Reflexive Language*. (ed.). New York: Cambridge University Press.

———. 1993. "Reflexive Language and the Human Disciplines." Pp. 9-32 in *Reflexive Language*. edited by J. Lucy. New York: Cambridge University Press.

Lundman, R. J. 1974. "Routine Police Arrest Practices: A Commonweal Perspective." *Social Problems* 22: 127-141.

———. 1979. "Organizational Norms and Police Discretion: An Observational Study of Police Work with Traffic Law Violators." *Criminology* 17: 159-171.

———.1994. "Demeanor or Crime? The Midwest City Police-Citizen Encounters Study." *Criminology* 32(4): 631-656.

———.1996b. Extralegal Variables and Arrest." *Journal of Research in Crime and Delinquency* 33(3): 349-353.

———.1996a. "Demeanor and Arrest: Additional Evidence from Previously Unpublished Data." *Journal of Research in Crime and Delinquency* 33(3): 306-323.

Lundman, R. J., Sykes, R., and J. Clark. 1978. "Police Control of Juveniles: A Replication." *Journal of Research in Crime and Delinquency* 15: 74-91.

Lundman, R. J., and Kaufman, R. L. 2003. "Driving While Black: Effects of Race, Ethnicity, and Gender on Citizen Self-Reports of Traffic Stops and Police actions." *Criminology* 41(1): 195-220.

Manning, P. K. 1978. "The Police: Mandate, Strategies, and Appearances." Pp. 7-31 in *Policing: A View From the Street.* Edited by J. Van Maanen and P. K. Manning. Santa Monica, CA: Goodyear Publishing.

———. 1982. "Organizational Work: Structuration of Environments." *British Journal of Sociology* 33(1): 118-132.

———. 1988. *Symbolic Communication: Signifying Calls and the Police Response.* Cambridge, MA: MIT Press.

———. 1997. *Police Work.* Cambridge, MA: MIT Press.

Mastrofski, S.D., and Parks, R. 1990. "Improving Observational Studies of Police." *Criminology* 28(3): 475-496.

Mastrofski, S. D., Snipes, J.B., Parks, R.B., and C. D. Maxwell. 2000. "The Helping Hand of the Law: Police Control of Citizens on Request." *Criminology* 38(2): 307-342.

Mastrofski, S. D., Snipes, J.B., and A. E. Supina. 1996. "Compliance on Demand: The Public's Response to Specific Requests." *Journal of Research in Crime and Delinquency* 33(3): 269-305.

Mastrofski, S. D., Worden, R. E., and J.B. Snipes. 1995. " Law Enforcement in a Time of Community Policing." *Criminology* 33:539-563.

Matoesian, G. M. 1993. *Reproducing Rape: Domination Through Talk in the Courtroom.* Chicago: University of Chicago Press.

———. 1997. "You Were Interested in Him as a Person?: Rhythms of Domination in the Kennedy-Smith Trial." *Law and Social Inquiry.* 22: 55-93.

———. 1999b. "Intertextuality, Affect, and Ideology in Legal Discourse." *Text* 19(1): 73-109.

———. 1999a. "Grammaticalization of Participant Roles." *Language in Society.*

———. 2001. *Law and the Language of Identity: Discourse in the William Kennedy Smith Rape Trial.* New York: Oxford University Press.

Maynard, D. W. 1985a. "How Children Start Arguments." *Language in Society* 14: 1-29.

———. 1985b. "On the Functions of Social Conflict among Children." *American Sociological Review* 50: 207-223.

———. 1988. "Language, Interaction, and Social Problems." *Social Problems* 35(4): 311-334.

———. 1989. "On the Ethnography and Analysis of Discourse in Institutional Settings." *Perspectives on Social Problems* 1: 127-146.

———. 1991. "Interaction and Asymmetry in Clinical Discourse." *American Journal of Sociology* 97: 448-495.

———. 1992. "On Clinicians Co-implicating Recipients' Perspectives in the Delivery of News." Pp. 331-358 in *Talk at Work: Interaction in Institutional Settings*. Edited by P. Drew and J. Heritage. Cambridge, UK: Cambridge University Press.

———.1996. "On 'Realization' in Everyday Life: The Forecasting of Bad News as a Social Relation." *American Sociological Review* 61: 109-131.

———. 2003. *Bad News, Good News: Conversational Order in Everyday Talk and Clinical Settings*. Chicago: University of Chicago Press.

Maynard D. W., and Clayman, S. E. 1991. "The Diversity of Ethnomethodology." *Annual Review of Sociology*: 385-418.

Maynard, D. W., and Manzo, J. F. 1993. "On the Sociology of Justice: Theoretical Notes From an Actual Jury Deliberation." *Sociological Theory* 11(2): 171-193.

Maynard, D. W., and Schaeffer, N.C.2000. "Toward a Social Scientific Knowledge: Survey Research and Ethnomethodology's Asymmetric Alternates." *Social Studies of Science* 30(3): 323-370.

McConville, M. 1992. "Videotaping Interrogations: Police Behaviour On and Off Camera." *Criminal Law Review*. 532-548.

McConville, M., and Baldwin, J. 1982. "The Role of Interrogation in Crime Discovery and Conviction." *British Journal of Criminology* 22: 165-175.

McDowell, J. H. 1985. "Verbal dueling." Pp. 203-211 in *Handbook of Discourse Analysis, Vol 3. Discourse and Dialogue*. Edited by T. van Dijk. Orlando, FL: Academic Press.

McIlwaine, B. D. 1994. "Interrogating Child Molesters." *FBI Law Enforcement Bulletin*. 63(6): 1-4.

McNulty, E. W. 1994. "Generating Common Sense Knowledge among Police Officers." *Symbolic Interaction* 17: 281-294.

Meares, T. L., and Kahan, D. M. 1999. *Urgent Times: Policing and Rights in Inner-City Communities*. Boston, MA: Beacon Press.

Mehan, H. 1990. "Oracular reasoning in a Psychiatric Exam: The Resolution of Conflict in Language." Pp. 160-177 in *Conflict Talk*. Edited by A. Grimshaw. Cambridge: Cambridge University Press.

Meehan, A.J. 1992. "I Don't Prevent Crime, I Prevent Calls": Policing as a Negotiated Order." *Symbolic Interaction* 15(4): 455-480.

Merleau-Ponty. 1962. "The Spatiality of One's own Body and Motility." In *Phenomenology of Perception*. London: Routledge and Kegan Paul.

Middleton, M. L. 2000. *Cop: A True Story*. Lincolnwood, IL: Contemporary Books.

Molotch, H. L., and Boden, D. 1985. "Talking Social Structure: Discourse, Domination and the Watergate Hearings." *American Sociological Review* 50: 273-288.

Moerman, M. 1988. *Talking Culture*. Philadelphia: University of Pennsylvania Press.

Moston, S., Stephenson, G.M., and T. M. Williams. 1992. "The Effects of Case Characteristics on Suspect Behavior During Police Questioning." *British Journal of Criminology* 32: 23-40.

Muir, W. K. 1977. *Police: Street Corner Politicians*. Chicago: University of Chicago Press.

Napier, M. R., and Adams, S. H. 1998. "Magic Words to Obtain Confessions." *FBI Law Enforcement Bulletin*. 67: 11-15.

Niederhoffer, A. 1967. *Behind the Shield: The Police in Urban Society*. Garden City, NY: Anchor Books.

O'Leary, K. D. 1993. "Through a Psychological Lens: Personality Traits, Personality Disorders, and Levels of Violence." Pp. 7-30 in *Current Controversies on Family Violence*. Edited by R.J. Gelles and D. R. Loseke. Newbury Park, CA: Sage.

Oliver, M. B. 1994. "Portrayals of Crime, Race, and Aggression in Reality Based Police Shows: A Content Analysis." *Journal of Broadcasting and Electronic Media* 38: 179-192.

———. 1996. "Influences of Authoritarianism and Portrayals of Race on Caucasian Viewers Responses to Reality Based Crime Dramas." *Communication Reports* 9: 141-150.

Oliver, M. B., and Armstrong, G.B., 1995. "Predictors of Viewing and Enjoyment of Reality Based and Fictional Crime Shows." *Journalism and Mass Communication Quarterly* 72: 559-570.

Pastor, P. A. 1978. "Mobilization in Public Drunkenness Control: A Comparison of Legal and Medical Approaches." *Social Problems* 25: 373-384.

Pate, A., and Hamilton, E. 1992. "Formal and Informal Deterrent to Domestic Violence: The Dade County Spouse Assault Experiment." *American Sociological Review* 57: 691-697.

Piliavin, I., and Briar, S. 1964. "Police Encounters with Juveniles." *American Journal of Sociology* 70: 206-214.

Pinizzotto, A.J., and G. D. Deshazor. 1997. "Interviewing Erratic subjects." *FBI Law Enforcement Bulletin* 66(11): 1-5.

Polyani, L. 1979. "So What's the Point?" *Semiotica*. 25 3/4: 207-238.

———. 1985. "Conversational Storytelling." Pp. 183-201 in *Handbook of Discourse Analysis, vol 3, Discourse and Dialogue*, edited by T. van Dijk. London: Academic Press.

Pomerantz, A. 1978. "Attributions of Responsibility: Blamings." *Sociology*.

———.1984. "Agreeing and Disagreeing with Assessments: Some Features of Preferred/Dispreferred Turn Shapes." Pp. 57-101 in *Structures of Social Action: Studies in Conversation Analysis*. Edited by J. M. Atkinson and P. Drew. Cambridge: Cambridge University Press.

———. 1986. "Extreme Case Formulations: A Way of Legitimizing Claims." *Human Studies* 9: 219-229.

Psathas, G. 1995. *Conversation Analysis: The Study of Talk-in-interaction*. Thousand Oaks, CA: Sage Publications.

Putnam, R. 2000. *Bowling Alone: The Collapse and Revival of American Community*. New York : Simon & Schuster.

Rabon, D. 1996. *Investigative Discourse Analysis*. Durham, NC: Carolina Academic Press.

Radelet, L. A. 1977. *The Police and the Community*. Encino, CA: Glencoe Press.

Rawls, J. 1971. *A Theory of Justice*. Cambridge, MA: Harvard University Press.

———. 1993. *Political Liberalism*. New York: Columbia University Press.

Raymond, G. 2000. The Structure of Responding: Type-conforming and Nonconforming Responses to Yes/No Type Interrogatives. Ph.D. dissertation, U.C.L.A. (Sociology).

Reiss, A. 1971. *The Police and the Public*. New Haven, CT: Yale University Press.

Reiman. J. 1995. *The Rich Get Richer and the Poor Get Prison*. New York: Allyn and Bacon.

Riksheim, E., and Chermak, S. 1993. "Causes of Police Behavior Revisited." *Journal of Criminal Justice* 21: 353-382.

Roth, J. A., Roehl, J., and Johnson, C. C. 2004. "Trends in the Adoption of Community Policing." Pp. 30-53 in *Community Policing: Can It Work?* Edited by Wesley G. Skogan. Belmont, CA: Wadsworth Publishing.

Royal, R.F., and Schutt., S. R. 1976. *Gentle Art of Interviewing and Interrogation* Englewood Cliffs, NJ: Prentice Hall.

Rubinstein, J. 1973. *City Police.* New York: Doubleday.

Sacks, H. 1975. "Everyone Has to Lie." Pp. 57-80 in *Sociocultural Dimensions of Language Use.* Edited by M. Sanchez and B. Blount. New York: Academic Press.

———. 1978. "Notes on Police Assessment of Moral Character" pp. 187-202 in *Policing: A View From the Street.* Edited by J. Van Maanen and P. K. Manning. Santa Monica, CA: Goodyear Publishing.

———.1984. "On Doing Being Ordinary." Pp. 413-429 in *Structures of Social Action.* Edited by J. Atkinson and J. Heritage. New York: Cambridge University Press.

———. 1992. *Lectures on Conversation.* Vol 1. Cambridge, MA: Blackwell Publishers.

Sacks, H., Schegloff, E.A., and G. Jefferson. 1974. "A Simplest Systematics for the Organization of Turn Taking for Conversation." *Language* 50(4): 696-735.

Salecl, R. 1994. *The Spoils of Freedom: Psychoanalysis and Feminism After the Fall of Socialism.* NY: Routledge.

Saville-Troike, M. 1985. "The Place of Silence in an Integrated Theory of Communication." Pp. 3-18 in *Perspectives on Silence.* Edited by D. Tannen and M. Saville-Troike. Norwood, NJ: Ablex.

Schegloff, E. A. 1968. "Sequencing in Conversational Openings." *American Anthropologist* 70: 1075-1095.

———. 1980. "Preliminaries to Preliminaries: 'Can I Ask You a Question?'" *Sociological Inquiry* 50(3/4): 104-152.

———. 1984a. "On Some Questions and Ambiguities in Conversation." Pp. 28-56 in *Structures of Social Action.* Edited by J.M. Atkinson and J. Heritage. Cambridge: Cambridge University Press.

———. 1984b. "On Some Gestures' Relation to Talk." Pp. 266-296 in *Structures of Social Action.* Edited by J.M. Atkinson and J. Heritage. Cambridge: Cambridge University Press.

———. 1986. "The Routine as Achievement." *Human Studies* 9:111-151.

———. 1987. "Analyzing Single Episodes of Interaction: An Exercise in Conversation Analysis." *Social Psychology Quarterly.* 50(2): 101-114.

———. 1988a. "On an Actual Virtual Servo-Mechanism for Guessing Bad News: A Single Case Conjecture." *Social Problems* 35(4): 442-4257.

———. 1988b. "Presequences and Indirection: Applying Speech Act Theory to Ordinary Conversation." *Journal of Pragmatics* 12:55-62.

———. 1989. "Harvey Sacks—Lectures 1964-1965: An Introduction/Memoir. *Human Studies* 12: 185-209.

———. 1991. "Reflections on Talk and Social Structure." Pp. 44-70 in *Talk and Social Structure*. Edited by D. Boden and D. Zimmerman. Cambridge: Polity Press.

———. 1992a. ""Repair After Next Turn: The Last Structurally Provided Defense of Intersubjectivity in Conversation." *American Journal of Sociology* 97(5): 1295-1345.

———. 1992b. "On Talk and its Institutional Occasions." Pp. 101-134 in *Talk at Work*. Edited by P. Drew and J. Heritage. New York: Cambridge University Press.

———. 1996. "Confirming Allusions: Toward an Empirical Account of Action." *American Journal of Sociology* 102(1): 161-216.

———. 1997. "Whose Text? Whose Context?" *Discourse and Society* 8(2): 165-187.

———. 1999a. "What Next? Language and Social Interaction Study at the Century's Turn." *Research on Language and Social Interaction* 32 (1&2): 141-148.

———. 1999b. "Schegloff's Text as Billig's Data: A Critical Reply." *Discourse and Society* 10(4): 558-572.

———. 1999c. "Naiveté vs. Sophistication or Discipline vs. Self Indulgence: A Rejoinder to Billig." *Discourse and Society* 10(4): 577-582.

Schegloff, E.A., Jefferson, G., and H. Sacks. 1977. "The Preference for Self Correction in the Organization of Repair in Conversation." *Language* (53): 361-382.

Schegloff, E.A., and Sacks, H. 1973. "Opening Up Closings." *Semiotica* 8:289-327.

Schiffrin, D. 1987. *Discourse Markers*. Cambridge: Cambridge University Press.

———. 1994. *Approaches to Discourse*. Oxford, UK: Blackwell.

Schutz, A. 1962. "Common-sense and Scientific Interpretation of Human Action." In *The Collected Papers of Alfred Schutz*, Vol 1. The Hague: Nijhoff.

Schwandt, T. 2000. "Three Epistemological Stances for Qualitative Inquiry." Pp. 189-214 in *Handbook of Qualitative Research*. (2nd ed.). Edited by N. K. Denzin and Y. S. Lincoln. Thousand Oaks, CA: Sage.

Schwartz, M.D., and Friderichs, D.O., 1994. "Postmodern Thought and Criminological Discontent" New Metaphors for Understanding Violence." *Criminology* 32(4): 221-246.

Scollon, R., and Scollon, S.W. 1995. *Intercultural Communication*. Cambridge, MA: Blackwell Publishers.

Seagal, D. 1993. "Tales From the Cutting Room Floor: The Reality of Reality Based Television." *Harper's Magazine* Nov. p 50.

Searle, J. 1969. *Speech Acts: An Essay in the Philosophy of Language*. New York: Cambridge University Press.

Sharrock, W., and Turner, R. 1978. "A Conversational Environment for Equivocality." Pp. 173-197 in *Studies in the Organization of Conversational Interaction*. Edited by J. Schenkein. NY: Academic Press.

Sherman, L. W. 1980. "Causes of Police Behavior: The Current State of Quantitative Research." *Journal of Research in Crime and Delinquency* 17: 69-100.

Sherman, L., and Berk, R. 1984. "The Specific Deterrent Effects of Arrest for Domestic Assault." *American Sociological Review* 49: 261-272.

Sherman, L., Smith, D., Schmidt, J., and D. Rogan. 1992. "Crime, Punishment, and Stake in Conformity: Legal and Informal Control of Domestic Violence." *American Sociological Review* 57: 680-690.

Shon, P.C.H. 1998. "'Now You Got a Dead Baby on Your Hands': Discursive Tyranny in 'Cop Talk'." *International Journal for the Semiotics of Law* XI(33): 275-301.

———. (2003). "Bringing the Spoken Words Back in: Conversationalizing (Postmodernizing) Police-Citizen Encounter Research." *Critical Criminology: An International Journal* 11 (2): 151-172.

Shuman, A. 1992. "'Get outa My Face': Entitlement and Authoritative Discourse." Pp. 135-159 in *Responsibility and Oral Discourse*. Edited by J. Hill and J. Irvine. New York: Cambridge University Press.

Signorielli, N. 1990. "Television's Mean and Dangerous World: A Continuation of the Cultural Indicators Perspective." Pp. 85-106 in *Cultivation Analysis: New Directions in Media Effects Research*. Edited by N. Signorielli and M. Morgan. Newbury Park: Sage.

Signorielli, N., and Morgan, M., 1996. "Cultivation Analysis: Research and Practice." Pp. 111-126 in *An Integrated Approach to Communication Theory and Research*. Edited by M. B. Salwen and S. Stacks. Hillsdale, NJ: Lawrence Erlbaum Associates.

Silverman, D. 1998. *Harvey Sacks: Social Science and Conversation Analysis*. New York: Oxford University Press.

Skogan, W. G., 2004. "Representing the Community in Community Policing." Pp. 57-75 in *Community Policing: Can It Work?* Edited by W. G. Skogan. Belmont, CA: Wadsworth Publishing.

Skogan, W. G., and Roth, J. A. 2004. "Introduction." Pp. xvii-xxxiv in *Community Policing: Can It Work?* Edited by W. G. Skogan. Belmont, CA: Wadsworth Publishing.

Skolnick, J. 1973. "The Police and the Urban Ghetto." Pp. 180-210 in *Police-Community Relations*. Edited by P. Cromwell Jr., and G. Keefer. St. Paul, MN: West Publishing Co.

Skolnick, J. H., and Fyfe, J. J. 1993. *Above the Law: Police and the Excessive Use of Force*. New York: The Free Press.

Smith, J.K., and Deemer, D.K. 2000. "The Problem of Criteria in the Age of Relativism."
Pp. 876-896 in *Handbook of Qualitative Research*. (2nd ed.). Edited by N. K. Denzin
and Y. S. Lincoln. Thousand Oaks, CA: Sage.

Smith, D. A., and Klein, J.R. 1984. "Police Control of Interpersonal Disputes." *Social
Problems* 29: 167-177.

Smith, D. A. and Visher, C.A. 1981. "Street-level Justice: Situational Determinants of
Police Arrest Decisions." *Social Problems* 29(2): 167-177.

Spencer, W. J. 1987. "Self-work in Social Interaction: Negotiating Role-Identities."
Social Psychology Quarterly 50(2): 131-142.

Spitzer, E. 1999. *The New York City Police Department's "Stop & Frisk" Practices: A
Report to the People of the State of New York from the Office of the Attorney
General*. New York: New York State Attorney General.

Strauss, M.A. 1993. "Physical Assault by Wives: A Major Social problem." Pp. 67-87 in
Current Controversies on Family Violence, edited by R.J. Gelles and D. R. Loseke.
Newbury Park, CA: Sage.

Sykes, R. E. and Clark, J.P. 1975. "A Theory of Deference Exchange in Police Civilian
Encounters." *American Journal of Sociology* 81: 584-600.

Tannen, D. 1985. "Silence: Anything but." In *Perspectives on Silence*. Edited by D.
Tannen and M. Saville-Troike. Norwood, NJ: Ablex.

―――. 1987a. "Repetition in Conversation: Towards a Poetics of Talk." *Language* 63:
574-605.

―――. 1987b. "Repetition in Conversation as Spontaneous Formulaicity." *Text* 7(3):
215-243.

―――. 1993. *Framing in Discourse*. (ed.). New York: Oxford University Press.

Taylor, C. 1984. "Foucault on Freedom and Truth." *Political Theory* 12(2): 152-246.

Tedlock, B. 2000. "Ethnography and Ethnographic Representation." Pp. 455-475 in
Handbook of Qualitative Research. (2nd ed.). Edited by N. K. Denzin and Y. S.
Lincoln. Thousand Oaks, CA: Sage.

Terrill, W., and Mastrofski, S. D. 2004. "Working the Street: Does Community Policing
Matter?" Pp. 109-135 in *Community Policing: Can It Work?* Edited by W. G.
Skogan. Belmont, CA: Wadsworth Publishing.

Terrill, W., Paoline III, E. A., and Manning, P. K. 2003. "Police Culture and Coercion."
Criminology 41(4): 1003-1034.

Tiersma, P. 1999. *Legal Language*. Chicago: University of Chicago Press.

Trojanowicz, R. 1994. *Community Policing: A Survey of Police Departments in the United States.* National Center for Community Policing, Michigan State University. Department of Justice.

Van Maanen, J. 1978a. "The Asshole." Pp. 221-238 in *Policing: A View From the Street.* Edited by J. V. Maanen and P. K. Manning. Santa Monica, CA: Goodyear Publishing.

Van Maanen, John. 1978b. "Epilogue: On Watching the Watchers." Pp. 310-349 in *Policing: A View From the Street.* Edited by J. Van Maanen and P. K. Manning. Santa Monica, CA: Goodyear Publishing.

Van Dijk, T. 1999. "Critical Discourse Analysis and Conversation Analysis." *Discourse and Society* 10(4): 459-460.

Vessel, D. 1998. "Conducting Successful Interrogations." *FBI Law Enforcement Bulletin.* 67(10): 1-6.

Vuchinich, S. 1984. "Sequencing and Social Structure in Family Conflict." *Social Psychology Quarterly* 47: 217-234.

———. 1990. "The Sequential Organization of Closing in Verbal Family Conflict." Pp. 118-138 in *Conflict Talk.* Edited by A. Grimshaw. Cambridge: Cambridge University Press.

Walker, A. 1985. "The Two Faces of Silence: The Effect of Witness Hesitancy on Lawyers' Impression." Pp. 55-75 in *Perspectives on Silence.* Edited by D. Tannen and M. Saville-Troike. Norwood, NJ: Ablex.

Walker, L. 1979. *The Battered Woman.* New York: Harper & Row.

———. 1993. "The Battered Woman's Syndrome is a Psychological Consequence of Abuse." Pp. 133-153 in *Current Controversies on Family Violence.* Edited by R.J. Gelles and D. R. Loseke. Newbury Park, CA: Sage.

———. 2000. *The Battered Woman Syndrome.* NY: Springer.

Walker, S. 2001. *Police Accountability: The Role of Citizen Oversight.* Belmont, CA: Wadsworth Publishing.

Waltman, J. L. 1983. "Nonverbal Communication in Interrogation: Some Applications." *Journal of Police Science and Administration* 11(2): 166-169.

Walzer, M. 1988. *Spheres of Justice: A Defense of Pluralism and Equality.* New York: Basic Books.

Wambaugh, J. 1987. *The New Centurions.* New York: Dell Publishing Company.

Waugh, L. 1995. "Reported Speech in Journalistic Discourse: the Relation of Function and Text." *Text* 15: 129-173.

Wardaugh, R. 1984. *Introduction to Sociolinguistics.* Cambridge, MA: Blackwell Publishers.

Watson, D. R. 1998 "Presentation of Victim and Motive in Discourse: The Case of Police Interrogations and Interviews." Pp. 77-97 in *Law in Action: Ethnomethodlogical and Conversational Analytic Approaches to Law.* Edited by M. Travers and J. Manzo. Brookfield, VT: Ashgate Publishing .

Weber, M. 1978. *Selections in Translation.* Edited by W.G. Runciman, translated by E. Matthews. Cambridge: Cambridge University Press.

Websdale, Neil. 2001. *Policing the Poor.* Boston: Northeastern University Press.

Westley, W. 1953. "Violence and the Police." *American Journal of Sociology* 49(1): 34-41.

Whalen, J. 1995. "A Technology of Order Production: Computer-Aided Dispatch in Public Safety Communication." Pp. 187-230 in *Situated Order: Studies in the Social Organization of Talk and Embodied Activities.* Edited by P. ten Have and G. Psathas. Washington, D.C.: University of America Press.

Whalen, M.R., and Zimmerman, D. H. 1987. "Sequential and Institutional Contexts in Calls for Help." *Social Psychology Quarterly* 50: 172-185.

———. 1990. "Describing Trouble: Practical Epistemology in Citizen Calls to the Police." *Language in Society* 19: 465-492.

Whalen, J., Zimmerman, D. H., and M. R. Whalen. 1988. "When Words Fail: A Single Case Analysis." *Social Problems* 35: 335-360.

Williams, J. W. 1999. "Taking It to the Streets: Policing and the Practice of Constitutive Criminology." Pp. 149-173 in *Constitutive Criminology at Work.* Edited by S. Henry and D. Milovanovic. Albany, NY: SUNY Press.

White, M.1987. " Ideological Analysis and Television." Pp. 161-203 in *Channels of Discourse.* Edited by R. Allen. Chapel Hill: University of North Carolina.

Whitaker, G. 1982. "What is Patrol Work?" *Police Studies* 4: 13-22.

Wilson, J. Q. 1968. *Varieties of Police Behavior: The Management of Law and Order in Eight Communities.* Cambridge, MA: Harvard University Press.

Wolfson, N. 1978. "A Feature of Performed Narrative: The Conversational Historical Present." *Language in Society* 7: 215-237.

Worden, R. E. 1989. "Situational and Attitudinal Explanations of Police Behavior: A Theoretical Reappraisal and Empirical Assessment." *Law and Society Review* 23(4): 667-711.

Worden, R. E., and A. A. Pollitz. 1984. "Police Arrests in Domestic Disturbances: A Further Look." *Law and Society Review* 18: 105-119.

Worden, R. E., and R. L. Shepard. 1996. "Demeanor, Crime, and Police Behavior: A Reexamination of the Police Services Study Data." *Criminology* 34 (1): 83-105.

Worden, R. E., Shepard, R. L., and S. Mastrofski. 1996. "On the Meaning and Measurement of Suspects' Demeanor toward the Police: A Comment on "demeanor and Arrest."" *Journal of Research in Crime and Delinquency* 33(3): 324-353.

Yllo, K.A. 1993. "Through a Feminist Lens: Gender, Power, and Violence." Pp. 47-62 in *Current Controversies on Family Violence*. Edited by R.J. Gelles and D. R. Loseke. Newbury Park, CA: Sage.

Zimmerman, D. H. 1992. "The Interactional Organization of Calls for Emergency Assistance." Pp. 418-469 in *Talk at Work: Interaction in Institutional Settings*. Edited by P. Drew and J. Heritage. Cambridge, UK: Cambridge University Press.

Zizek, S. 1992. *Enjoy Your Symptom!: Lacan in Hollywood and Out*. New York: Routledge.